GOSSIP KILLS

(The 9th/8th ? Commandment)

"You shall not bear dishonest witness against
your neighbor."   --Deuteronomy 5:20

Carole Anne Fielder

In memory of Lawrence Jackson Fielder

"You have not chosen me; I have chosen you.
Go and bear fruit that will last, alleluia."
                                    --John 15:16

Bible quotations are from the St. Joseph Edition of *The New American Bible*, translations copyrighted 1970 Old Testament, 1986 New Testament, and 1991 Psalms, by the Confraternity of Christian Doctrine (CCD), Washington, D.C. Catholic Book Publishing Co., New York.

Appendix C is reprinted by permission of the author, Pam Woodside. *The San Francisco Magazine* in which it was originally published is defunct and not to be confused with the magazine of the same name currently extant.

Almost all names used herein are real. Only a few have been changed to protect innocent parties. The author has researched all sources to ensure the accuracy of the information contained in this book. Conversations derive from the memories of the author and/or those parties with whom the conversations originally transpired, telephone answer machine recordings, legal documents, police reports, e-mails and letters, taped television appearances of the author at city council meetings. They are not intended as verbatim transcripts. Although the story is nonfiction, the speculations are strictly the author's and not presented as or intended to be used as legal evidence.

ISBN: 978-1492834779

Library of Congress Cataloging in Publication Data

Fielder, Carole Anne.
Gossip Kills (The 9th/8th ? Commandment).

Fielder, Carole Anne,
    Gossip kills: (the 9th/8th ? commandment) "You shall not bear dishonest witness against your neighbor."--Deuteronomy 5:20/ Carole Anne Fielder.
        p.cm.
"In memory of Lawrence Jackson Fielder"
ISBN: 1-932560-06-8
1. Fielder, Carole Anne. 2. Computer crimes--United states. 3. False personation--United States--Information resources. 4. Suicide--United States--Case Studies. 1. Title
HV6773.2.F54 2003
364.16'3--dc22

ACKNOWLEDGMENTS

Thanks to the friends who supported me in this effort, especially the many times I wanted to quit and hide, to Carol, Catherine, Carl, Beth. Thanks to Opal, without whose special guidance this book would not exist. To my friends in Virginia, who inspired me to begin work on this book because they, too, comprehend the chasm between bickering Christian religions, thanks. To friends in California, New York, Ohio, Indiana, Massachusetts, thanks for your encouragement that this story needs to be told. And to a Nigerian Roman Catholic priest who understands about all kinds of religious antagonisms in many different worlds, thanks for being you.

I am especially grateful to my Good Samaritan neighbor, without whom my entire community might still be terrorized without a clue as to why. Applause also goes to two courageous public servants as well: Pompano City Commissioner Lamar Fisher and United States Congressman E. Clay Shaw.

FOREWORD

Have you ever been terrorized? Affected by extreme fear or co-erced by intimidation? Most of the world was affected by the events of "9-11." Everyone knows that September 11, 2001, America's symbols of strength and leadership, the World Trade Towers, were turned to rubble after two jetliners crashed into them. It was the first time terror-ism struck home on such a grand scale. Many Americans responded in fear.

I was an exception. I had a preview.

I was terrorized eight months before that attack, in my home, doing one day what I had done many days before—nothing big, nothing glamorous. What would you do if suddenly you hear a knock at the door of your middle-class home, you open the door, and two local po-licemen accuse you of capital crimes? Accuse you of being a leader of a secret organization that is murdering people on a national scale? And you haven't left your home in years? And you don't belong to any or-ganization except your local church?

What if the accusations against you are not only absurd, but evi-dence exists easy to prove the truth, and the police continue to harass you? At the same time, you, your property and your neighbors are sud-denly besieged by assorted trespassers, vandals and burglars? As a law-abiding, tax-paying citizen, would you call the police to get help?

I did, and the terror got worse. What if you learn that someone is impersonating you on the internet and inviting strangers to come to your home? That the strangers coming to your home think that you are going to pay them to have sex parties on your yachts? But you don't own any yachts? You're too old and physically sick to think about sex parties? How will you stop them? Will you call the police for help?

I did, but the police had no idea how to stop an internet crime in progress. Do your local police know what to do? You don't have to own a computer or "be online" to be the victim of internet impersona-tion or stolen identity. You already may have experienced the hassles that result from a stolen wallet, especially if thieves ran up bills using your name and credit cards. You already may have regretted entering into one chat room too many, if some unsavory character online har-assed you.

But in those two instances, you participated: you lost your wallet, or you used a computer in a chat room online. In my instances of lost identity and terrorism, I did nothing. No lost wallet, no participation online. You don't have to own a credit card or a computer for this to happen to you. All you need is someone somewhere with a grudge against you who knows how to use (abuse) the internet.

What makes my personal terror a warning to every American is that it is more than personal: the United States military employees are using their computers at work to terrorize people living many States away from their bases. And they are getting by with it and will do it again and again, unless some authority in our country determines to stop them. There is a Congressional inquiry as this goes to press; but the military brass want to cover it up and brush it off.

What will you do if you are the next victim? Can you get your community prepared to combat the new millennium of terrorism, not only from international threats, but also from "anonymous" internet harassment and impersonation that leads to street crime? Are your local police ready? Does your local government care? Do you?

TABLE OF CONTENTS

APPENDICES

Chapter 1

"O God, whom I praise, do not be silent,
for wicked and treacherous mouths attack me.
They speak against me with lying tongues;
with hateful words they surround me,
attacking me without cause."   --Psalms 109, 1-3

Friday, February 9, 2001

The brilliant sunshine of a South Florida winter morning brightened the living room where I worked at my laptop. It almost broke the gloom of my heavy heart.

I had again awakened, crying, grieving the loss of my father in Lynchburg, Virginia, and my brother in Portland, Oregon, both gone the previous month within two weeks of each other. I had surrounded myself with pictures of them, which I looked at daily, asking the same questions, "Why?" and "How could you leave me like that?" I knew the answers, however, only too well.

A knock at the door broke my reverie. I turned and saw the outline of a man on my front porch shading his eyes and peering into the windows. I went to the door and opened it without first calling out to ask who was there.

Two young men quickly identified themselves as detectives and flashed badges too fast for me to see. They were not wearing uniforms, so I uneasily looked toward the driveway to see what kind of car they had driven. It was a Broward County sheriff's car, so I felt relieved. I looked around expecting to see some obvious auto accident or vandalism prompting the visit. I saw nothing.

"Would you mind if we asked you some questions about your brother?" The older one started the conversation.

I stiffened. These men must have come to tell me that Larry's body had been found. Only yesterday I had talked with Roger Mussler, the detective in Oregon who had been unfailingly kind and helpful since my brother's suicide note was discovered. It would be like Roger to send someone to gently break the news when Larry's body was recovered.

"Did they find him?" I asked.

The detectives looked blank. "Do you know where he is?" the younger one asked.

I stared at him. "Where he is?"

1

"Yes, do you know your brother's whereabouts?"

Given the circumstances, this was a weird question. "He's, uh, dead. What did Detective Mussler tell you?"

"Who?" they asked together.

"Detective Mussler."

"We don't know who you're talking about. When is the last time you saw your brother?"

I wondered what in the world was going on, but I answered readily, "October, 1998 when he came to visit me here." I had just looked at the pictures of that visit in my photo album, which still lay open on a nearby chair. "Why are you asking?"

"We received a letter about your brother. It indicates he could be here. When did you last visit your brother in Oregon?"

I looked at them in amazement. "I visited Larry in Oregon, let's see, uh, the last time I was able to travel. I went from my home in California in the summer of 1995."

I felt confused. "I just spoke with Detective Mussler yesterday. He didn't indicate anything new. I thought maybe he sent you. What letter?"

"We have a letter from your sister in Virginia."

"Which sister?"

"The one in Virginia"

"That gives me three choices. Which sister?" I persisted. I had sisters living in Salem, Richmond, and Hayes, Virginia.

"The one in government."

"Ok, that gives me three choices. Which sister? The one in Richmond is a Republican politician's aide. Another works for the Army in Fort Eustis. The husband of a third one is a county manager."

"Well, we can't give you any name, Ma'am, because we have an investigation to conduct."

"About what?"

"The disappearance of your brother, among other things. Do you know where he is?"

How idiotic these men sounded. Evidently they knew nothing of my brother's suicide note, or of Detective Roger Mussler, the homicide specialist who'd investigated the case in Oregon. What sister had sent them a letter about Larry? "Have you spoken with the authorities in Oregon?"

"No, we don't know anything about anybody in Oregon. We believe your brother came here to see you. The letter indicates that you lured him here to be a satanic sacrifice. Are you sure he's not here?"

My mouth dropped open. I could not believe my ears. Was this a sick joke? Were these guys really cops? Curiosity and dread gnawed at a knot developing in my gut as I wondered who the originator of such an accusation could be. After a long silence, I asked weakly, "If you have not spoken with Detective Mussler, would you like me to give you his telephone number?"

"Yes, yes, that would be nice. Could we come in?"

I backed away from the door, still mystified and tremendously disappointed that they had no news about Larry. Obviously, they needed to do their homework. What more could possibly be said about my brother's untimely death and suicide note?

The two detectives lost no time in filling the space I left at the open door. They brushed by me and walked past the foyer into the living room, obviously gathering in details as they surveyed the room. I went to the computer on my desk and retrieved Detective Roger Mussler's phone number from my AOL address book. As I did that, one detective walked down the hall peering into each room. The other one studied the photographs of my father and brother, which I had laid out on the coffee table and surrounded with a large wooden rosary.

Sympathy cards were set up nearby. On a table a large edition of the Jerusalem Bible had been opened with the memory cards of both my deceased parents lying in the centerfold. On a shelf above the computer sat two photographs of Pope John Paul II with me sitting in a wheelchair. In one I kissed the papal ring. In the other I talked with the Pope and shook his hand.

I read off the telephone number from the computer screen. "Give Roger, uh, Detective Mussler a call. Even though he's off for the next four days, I'm sure someone in that office can give you the whole report of my brother's suicide note and of the search for his body. The missing person information was entered online in the National Crime Information Center January 6th. Roger said he entered the dental records yesterday."

As I stood up to see the two men to the door, I felt more amused than troubled. They seemed foolish, but I realized they were just doing their jobs. I still wanted to know which sister wrote them such a bizarre letter. Why would she think Larry was physically able or willing to come to Florida?

As they left I said, "Please get back to me later today after you speak with the folks in Oregon. One of my sisters could be in danger."

They promised to get back to me. They left, pausing and walking around the front yard where loose dirt was scattered in piles. I had been filling in sinkholes with a truckload of dirt ordered for that purpose. A pile of dirt still stood in the driveway. The detectives picked up a stick and probed into the pile on the driveway before they got into their car and drove away.

What confused cops! Maybe they'd call in a few hours with an apology and tell me which sister sent the letter. I didn't know whether to laugh or cry.

∾⸢⸣

What was going on in Virginia? What was happening to the Fielder family?

My parents could never have envisioned their life's work tumbling into such darkness when they married in 1938, during the Great Depression. My father's high school teaching job was secure. My mother wanted to duplicate her family of origin with six children of her own. They had high hopes.

There were five children, four girls and one boy. I was number two. Their first child, Betty, was born a month before the attack on Pearl Harbor. On my last trip to Virginia in 1995, I had secured video copies of home movies filmed by an uncle. An early one showed Mother's obvious delight and pride in her first baby. How surprising it was to see Daddy smiling as he held Betty in his arms. Daddy actually picked up a kid? She must have been the only one.

I destroyed Betty's only-child status in 1944. Years later I learned from family and friends that Betty never recovered from the trauma of my birth. In those days parents had not been taught to prepare the first child for the coming of the second. I had always shrugged it off, as she seemed so much older, prettier, more advanced, and so much bigger than I ever was. I couldn't imagine being of any significance to her.

When we were children, Betty used to pick and jab at me with her long arms and fingers. Frustrated by my short ones useless for self-defense, I would finally shriek "Stop it!" in a high pitched, ear-splitting soprano. In the car, Daddy would usually reach a big arm over the front bench seat and slap me in the face, while Betty, sitting directly behind him, covered her nose and mouth with her hands and snickered quietly.

"Jack, you hit the wrong one! Didn't you see what Betty was doing?" Mother would protest.

"I did not! That noise huhts my eahs." Daddy's explanation always delighted Betty.

As she approached adolescence, the gap between us grew even wider. She was one of the taller girls in the eighth grade, and always seemed older than her classmates. I always looked two or three years younger than the next smallest person in my class. As a young child, I'd follow Daddy around in his carpentry workshop playing with scraps of wood, beating and hammering, sawing and sanding. Daddy nicknamed me "Butch," while the feminine Betty was dubbed "Toots."

Betty became interested in clothes and magazines, while I was still hanging by my knees from apple trees in my grandmother's yard. Betty was always the queen, the beauty, stately and commanding and aloof. She started using peroxide to bleach her hair. I always sported bruises, skinned knees, and dirty fingernails, and my hair turned dark after it was cut for the first time in the fourth grade.

Kay was born in January when I was four and a half years old. Mother had shared the entire pregnancy with me, from heartbeat to kicking. I was thrilled when "my baby" was born. Poor Kay, who weighed nine pounds at birth, got dragged around everywhere I went. She was already almost my size, so I'd use both arms squeezed around her middle to lift her. When her head touched my chin and her feet touched the ground between mine, I would waddle along with her.

I was "Mommy's little helper" as long as it was fun. The age difference soon separated us, and Kay became just another object in my way or wallpaper in the background to my own world. She grew up with television. Betty and I did not, and we worried about her rocking on her hobbyhorse in front of the television all day long. Daddy teased her when she had to temporarily wear corrective glasses at a young age. She always seemed to be in her own world too, filled with dozens of named stick horses, horse books, and secret journals. Daddy nicknamed her "Hoss."

Larry was born in December 1950. Kay was two, and "playing children" was losing interest to me. I was still a tomboy. I liked anything mechanical that would run if wound up. I liked it even more if it made noise, too.

Larry was a baby who cried, in pain from stomach cramps, almost every moment he was awake. His three older sisters considered him a noisy pest. Mother doted on having a son at last, but she did not discover his allergy to cow's milk until he was two years old, and she inadvertently left his favorite, chewed-up, skuzzy nipple at a relative's house in the country.

"Oh, Jack, I'm sorry but we'll have to go back. He'll only take his milk with that one nipple," Mother explained.

"If he cain't use another one, that's just too bad. We just spent thutty minutes bouncin' the springs of this old Chevy over this duht road's humps and we have a long drive ahead," Daddy pronounced and drove on.

Larry refused his milk, cried himself to sleep in the car, and for the first time was without pain; he slept blissfully all through the night. We older girls grew up believing all his later problems and his small size resulted from those unfortunate first two years. The sleep-walking which developed later, could be scary at times. Daddy ignored it.

ᑲᘇᕬ

Daddy was a tall, fair-skinned man, with blonde hair and ice blue, penetrating eyes. He was the firstborn in his family of origin, and as such was expected to take care of his four younger brothers and later to work in his father's grocery store, situated across from the white public high school. He had no use for laziness or excuses.

In the tradition of the South, he was supposed to become a doctor. He wanted to become an airplane pilot, but in 1929 his father forbade such "foolish nonsense." Although his parents pushed him to enter medical school after college, he dropped out to pursue his preferred interests. He was a self-directed man, a perfectionist workaholic. His chosen profession as public high school chemistry and physics teacher occupied only part of his workday. After school, his routine consisted of working in his father's store, or taking care of some rental properties, visiting a stock broker's office, buying food for the family, then returning home.

His physical workday began after that: working in his large garden in which he raised the family's fresh produce, or creating impressive antique reproductions in his carpentry workshop in the basement. His workday began at 7:00 in the morning and continued until 11:00 at night. His only recreation seemed to be flying small planes with the Civil Air Patrol.

All of us children seemed to be background noise to my father's life. And noise was something our mother forbade us to make around him. He was a figure to be respected quietly whenever we saw him.

I grew up thinking that all men knew how to take care of every-thing around a house, knew how to grow food, take care of cars, lawn mowers, broken window panes. Daddy's Sunday morning routine be-fore church included ironing all his starched white shirts for the following school week. What a shock it was to me to learn as an adult that some men were not born knowing all those things--in fact some had no interest in learning them!

Daddy was known in the South as "a gentleman's gentleman." He, like most Virginia men in his acquaintance, preferred the company of other men, and had clear lines of distinction between how he communi-cated to women and children and how he spoke to his peers--strictly other white men of his social class. His Virginia drawl was authorita-tive, a carryover from his classroom lecturer's style. If Daddy spoke, everyone listened. We children were no exception.

꿍◦ᕉ

Anyone who saw the early childhood pictures of the first four Fielder children could not tell one from another. By age two we were all dark blondes with curly hair and brown eyes. When Laura was born in 1958, however, she was Daddy's dream come true: the ultimate blonde, blue-eyed princess with milky white skin, "spittin'image" of Daddy and all his four brothers as children, but pretty, dainty, and feminine in appearance from the start.

By 1958, Betty was a sultry teenager, seventeen going on thirty-five. I was a selfish fourteen-year-old, mostly interested in animals and study, with sporadic crushes on boys. Kay and I shared a room. Larry and Betty had separate bedrooms. The one-bathroom house was crowded, but none of us really interacted with each other. We ignored Mother and Laura who often slept downstairs in the dining room, out of Daddy's way.

Betty left for college in 1960 and married the following year. I de-veloped from girl child to normal teenager during my sophomore year in high school. Always the student, I was driven to high grades and ex-tra-curricular activities when I learned about the stiff competition to gain acceptance to the college of my choice. In 1962 I entered the Col-lege of William and Mary in Williamsburg, Virginia.

I had completed my Freshman year and was home for summer vacation when my devastating illness began.

Chapter 2

"Is not man's life on earth a drudgery?
So I have been assigned months of misery,
...my skin cracks and festers;
my days are swifter than a weaver's shuttle;
they come to an end without hope.
...I should prefer choking and death
rather than my pains.
I waste away; I cannot live forever;"
                                        --Job 7:1a,3a,5b,6,15-16a

The illness that changed my life at age eighteen came suddenly, unexpectedly. We were visiting my mother's brother in Arlington Virginia when what seemed to be a terrible flu struck me overnight.

It wasn't flu. It was diagnosed as the newly discovered virus, Coxsackie, which had recently killed a well-known college football coach in North Carolina. My prognosis was bleak. The disease had infected my brain tissue, affecting my sense of balance, vision, memory, and mental comprehension. There was no known treatment.

I survived after an interminably long six weeks of total bed rest. During that period of motionlessness and inactivity, I began to show symptoms of skin and joint disease. When I began to resume exercises I had learned in my college modern dance classes, the expected muscle soreness never went away. Key tendons in my feet, and my left knee became intensely inflamed and swollen.

Six months of missed diagnoses and wrong treatments left me completely crippled, and practically skinless. The searing pain was brutalizing and consuming. Finally the United States Medical Research Center at the National Institutes of Health in Bethesda, Maryland made a "human guinea pig" of me, and things got worse, then better. After four months in the research hospital, my life was salvaged, but with a still bleak prognosis, and an expensive, grueling weekly medical routine. The doctors told me and my parents that I'd probably never walk unaided again, and could not expect to finish college or ever be self-supporting. My life expectancy was less than five years.

My parents were overwhelmed that my successful college career was cut short and I was back in that small house. Because I had turned nineteen after I got sick and was first hospitalized, and didn't return to

William and Mary in September, neither the family medical insurance policy nor my annual school year policy covered the horrific expenses. I now shudder to think about the period in my life before I left home. I spent most of my time in bed, or taking medicinal baths, followed by application of creams, and sometimes "plastic-wrapped for the night."

Going up and down the staircase was a challenging event for me, and I needed at least one other person to help. If I could get downstairs at all, I played the piano for as long as I could sit up. Then I needed help to climb back upstairs to bed. Weekly intramuscular injections of methatrexate, a chemotherapy formerly used only for leukemia, had horrible side effects: vomiting after every meal for years, losing my hair periodically, and enduring all the constant, assorted infections and liver problems that went with the treatment. Many times I could not talk or eat because of the horrendous sores in my mouth.

My life of excruciating physical pain was degraded further by public humiliation from the hideous manifestations of the skin and joint disease. Many children ran to their mothers exclaiming, "Mommy can I catch it?" Adults tended to avert their eyes. My depression was so deep that I entertained thoughts of suicide the first years of the illness. To the amazement of my doctors, I not only survived, but also gradually became able to walk unaided, or with crutches, a few feet. My hair started growing back, and I felt strong enough to take one class at a time at Lynchburg College. I immediately met a young man who was taking required French classes during the summer as a condition of his graduation. He had already accepted a job as a high school football coach, contingent upon his graduation. He asked me to help him with his French, which I was more than happy to do. He was a gorgeous hunk of a guy, the picture of health, and our relationship became a focus for me during the following eight years. I ignored a neighbor's admonition that he was too much like my father, only more comfortable, like an old shoe.

Who in my family could forget the years from 1964 through 1967 in that crowded little house, with me monopolizing the bathroom for the five-time-daily tub soaks and treatments of my raw, bloody skin? The awful smell of tar that permeated the air? The times Betty and her husband, King, came to visit with her small white poodle, "Swank," who insisted on munching the piles of skin flakes and chips that fell from my body onto the floor, all while Betty shrieked and tried to make him stop?

With so many problems of my own, I never really tuned into the lives of my brother and two sisters living under the same roof. I concentrated on study and frequent escapes from home with my boyfriend.

Larry, fourteen, became co-conspirator in following my doctor's order that I absolutely must gain a few pounds. Nothing stayed down long enough. The doctor suggested I try to drink a beer and eat salted nuts before dinner as a fast caloric boost. My teetotaler parents would not have agreed to the beer, so my boyfriend supplied me with both items, which I hid in my room.

"Larry, are you ready?" I'd call to him across the hallway.

"Yeah, Sis, ready to run. Pass it over," he'd answer, holding his hands ready to catch the can of Budweiser I tossed to him, football style. His brown eyes sparkled mischievously as he put the warm beer in the bottom of his trashcan, ran down the staircase, out the front door, around back to the basement entrance, and pretended to empty the trash. He'd stick the beer in the quick-freeze compartment of the freezer for me, then retrieve it thirty minutes later, and sneak it back upstairs to me. "Mission accomplished," he'd smile happily, breathlessly.

"A girl who would take a sip of beer would do anything," was a local saying that probably contributed to Larry's glee over our devious success. He always seemed happy to help me and was fascinated by my football coach boyfriend.

In those days I had no way of knowing that Larry, like me, had inherited a defective immune system. Later in life he would be plagued with many problems, both emotional and physical that exacerbated his depression, which ultimately led to his suicide: chronic arthritis, frequent kidney stones, a spinal condition requiring a steel plate in his neck, overwhelming sleep apnea, an early heart attack, lithium treatments that affected his cognitive skills, steroid treatments that caused him to gain weight to obesity, onset of blindness, among other things.

Inability to stay awake caused him to lose job after job. In time his wife and son left him. He wrote to all in the family a gut-wrenching letter ten years before his death. He laid out for us his recent history, extreme depression and thoughts of suicide. (See **Appendix B**.) He lived in terrible pain and without hope of recovery the last year. He had often spoken of suicide, and once told me that he had "made arrangements to take care of it," implying that he would only have to make a phone call to end his life by a pre-chosen assassin. I hoped that was his mental illness speaking and not real.

Even when his talk of "ending it" faded, as a Catholic I worried about Oregon's law that permitted assisted suicide. His doctors gave up on him and put him on morphine. I tried to persuade him how much I needed him to stay around for me. The final rejection that he suffered from the family when he visited my father in Virginia last year seemed to be the last straw that broke him completely. I had tried to warn him how hateful his sisters could act, and to save his efforts and his strength. But he had to go back to Lynchburg, as sick as he was.

Now he had settled his affairs and left a note that the Oregon detective classified "a classic suicide note." Even though his body had not been found, I was sure that Larry had taken his own life. How could anyone who knew him doubt it? And now one of the same sisters that treated him so badly had concocted this horrible accusation against me. I needed to find out about that letter the police received.

Chapter 3

"He who is a friend is always a friend,
and a brother is born for the time of stress."
--Proverbs 17:17

Friday, February 9, 2001 10:15 A.M.

This whole thing had to be some kind of perverted joke, didn't it? I decided to call Barbra Milhaus, Larry's friend in Portland Oregon and share the experience with her. She would find the cops' visit and insinuations ludicrous, maybe comic relief to our many sad and tearful conversations over the past five weeks.

Barbra and her family had been Larry's closest friends, perhaps his only ones at the end. They had met Larry when he was assistant scoutmaster for his son George's scout pack, and Barbra was a den mother. After Larry's divorce, he and the Milhaus family grew closer. (See **Appendix B,** Larry's 1990 letter.) Barbra was especially supportive of him. I had met her once five years earlier, when I traveled to Oregon and stayed with Larry's son George, and his mother. Larry asked me to meet him at Barbra's, and I didn't recognize him when he arrived there until I heard his voice. I was startled that his voice came out of that man. He was so bloated and heavy and wore the dissipated look of years of sickness and medication. Seeing him in 1995 blasted my memory of him from eleven years before, when he could pass as a Chevy Chase look-alike.

Barbra was cordial to me at our meeting. I was the only family member of Larry's that she had ever met. Due to our common concern for Larry, we had exchanged some phone calls last year, especially when I was unable to reach him by telephone for many days on end.

It was Barbra who found the suicide note, and, though still in shock herself, called to give me the news and asked me to pass it on to the rest of our family. We had exchanged frequent phone calls since that terrible morning, January 3rd, when she found Larry's note, his keys, his credit cards and driver's license, the title to his car transferred to her, and all his medications and his breathing machine essential to his survival. All left behind. But Larry and his gun were missing.

When I heard her voice that day, I had responded, "Tell me quick, Barbra, I already know," as my heart pounded into my throat at anticipation of news I didn't want. Larry and I talked for two hours Christmas Day night. I'd sent him a special birthday present, asked him to call me collect when it arrived, and told him to be sure to open it *before* his 50th birthday New Year's Eve, which he planned to celebrate at the Milhaus'.

My eagerness for his call turned into dread as the days passed, and he did not answer his phone. I had called and sung Happy Birthday into his answer machine December 31st, but in my heart I knew he was gone. He would have called. I could feel the emptiness in my bones when his phone just rang and rang. My father seemed to share this intuitive knowing, because when I called him January 4th to tell him of Larry's note, he immediately responded, "He killed himself, didn't he?"

Now I felt eager to tell Barbra about this latest development. Aware of the difference in time zones, I waited until I was sure she'd be awake. She answered on the first ring. "Good morning from sunny Florida!"

"Oh Carole. How are you?"

"I'm surviving, but only just. I wake up mornings feeling sad, angry, betrayed. I cry awhile and get over it. How are you doing?"

Barbra sighed. "Oh, not too bad, today, although I had another dream about Larry last night. He came walking in just like usual, and I scolded him for pulling such a stunt to worry me so much. Then I hugged him and welcomed him back, so happy that he was home."

"Gosh, that's a great dream!" I wished it were real. We both knew that Larry couldn't survive without his breathing machine. At first we had spent hours on the phone imagining wishful scenarios in which he was still alive.

"I'm grateful to Larry for making sure I would not be the one to find his body, but if I had, it might be easier to realize he's really dead."

"Barbra, you won't believe what happened to me this morning." I told her about the visit from the Pompano police, a division of the Broward Sheriff's Office (BSO).

"That's awful! Something strange happened here last night just before Bob and I went out to dinner. A Portland city police officer called and asked us all sorts of questions about Larry and if I knew you. He said he had received a letter from one of Larry's sisters. I called Detective Mussler, since he's in charge at the Washington County Sheriff's Office and ought to know, but he's off until next week. What's going on, Carole?"

"I wish I knew. I suppose the Pompano BSO cops were just doing their job. I gave them Roger's number so they can straighten it out and tell me who wrote that letter. This letter has got to be a doozie. I'm supposed to be some sort of cult leader, too. Seems like half the Pompano police force goes to my Catholic church. They must see me up front every weekend, either lectoring or distributing Communion, even if they don't know my name. I'm sure they'll get back to me this afternoon with some answers."

"Well, I should hope so."

"Can you do me a favor and call the Portland cop and ask for a copy of that letter? I wonder if it's the same thing."

"Sure. I already knew your family is strange, but this takes the prize for bizarre. Keep me informed if anything else unusual happens."

Barbra told me that she couldn't yet face sorting through Larry's belongings which she had put into storage. She had cleaned out his apartment according to his written instructions, but she still picked up his mail there, mostly bills that his note instructed her to ignore. His attorney told her, however, that in her capacity as his permanent power of attorney until his body was found, she was obligated to keep track of everything.

"I think I've finally cancelled all the automatic payments from his checking account. Now I just have to worry about all those Social Security checks piling up that sooner or later the government will want back. Why did your brother have to dump this on me?" Barbra laughed.

"He was fortunate to have you and your family as his friends."

We said good-bye, and I tried to go on with my day. About five o'clock I checked for messages and found one from Detective Blankenship, one of the policemen who had visited during the morning. I called him back expecting a laugh, an apology and an answer to who had written the letter.

He was already gone for the day, so I asked for his supervisor, Sergeant Montgomery. The sergeant acted first as though he didn't know what I was calling about. I explained in detail the visit I'd had in the morning, and my need to know who wrote the letter.

"I can't tell you that," he responded curtly.

"Oh, you are not aware of this matter?"

"I'm fully aware that there is an ongoing investigation and you are a suspect, and I will not give you any information," he snarled.

Utterly amazed, I asked, "Have you been in touch with the detectives in Oregon today?"

"No."

"Well, if I am a suspect, of what?"

He refused to answer, and then announced he had to hang up.

I felt both puzzled and angry. How could they show up on my doorstep with a frivolous inquiry about my brother when I was in the depths of grieving, then accuse me of something unspecified, and then leave me hanging overnight? It was cruel, but more importantly, what if one of my sisters had completely flipped out because of Larry's and Daddy's deaths two weeks apart? Could this insane letter about me be just a symptom that one of those Virginia sisters might accuse or endanger the others as well?

None of us could have reasonably expected Daddy to die so suddenly. He fell out of bed. He twisted his leg under his own weight and lay there for hours before he got help. People don't generally die from falling out of bed. The hospital staff was discussing his discharge with Kay and Charlie just three days before his death. Heart failure? I had questions, and maybe the sisters in Virginia did also. Which sister was possibly "pushed over the edge" by these back-to-back unexpected deaths?

It would be a long night if I couldn't get to the bottom of this business about the letter.

ഗ∻ഏ

"Life isn't easy," I said to the cats as I gave them their dinner.

But then for me it never had been. Living at home, always sick, I struggled through school a few classes at a time. Dates with my boyfriend on weekends comprised my only social life. Nevertheless, I graduated from Lynchburg College *magna cum laude* and class valedictorian.

The day of my graduation my father asked, "Carole Anne, jes' when are you plannin' on movin' out?"

"I was hoping I could stay until my internship in Washington, D.C. for Congressman Poff is over, uh, July sometime. Is that ok?"

"Well, you jes' be sure you pick up that stack of unpaid medical bills on your way out the doah," he replied.

After the internship in Washington, I carefully planned the long drive to Baton Rouge, Louisiana, between injections of methatrexate. My boyfriend helped with the move and the driving.

For a few months I attended graduate school at Louisiana State University on a teaching assistantship in accounting that also paid all my medical expenses. When a doctor there introduced me to taking methatrexate orally, a whole new world opened up. I had more time for other things if I didn't have to plan my life around a day at the doctor's office to receive those awful injections in the buttocks.

Corporate interviewers were a constant on the LSU campus in 1967. Before long I landed a job as a handicapped employee with IBM, a major corporation with a small division in the aerospace industry at Huntsville, Alabama. IBM was gathering top students that year, but the report from my doctor about the seriousness of my disease and treatment almost stopped them from hiring me. My college record offset their concerns, especially when I explained what a difference taking methatrexate orally had made in my lifestyle. I had stopped vomiting after every meal!

For two years I didn't miss a day of work, helping to put a man on the moon before the Russians did. I loved being part of "America's finest hour," a part of the coordinated industrial efforts that were positive for all mankind. My starting salary, as a financial analyst, was higher than my father's public teaching position after his thirty-plus years' experience.

I married my boyfriend, convincing him that my salary was worth his relocating away from his home. We kept in touch with our relatives, traveling frequently to Virginia. Betty and family, Kay and boyfriend came separately to visit me, as did Mother, Daddy and Laura. I was thrilled with being in the real world, although I still juggled my life according to weekly chemotherapy and side effects.

The third winter in Alabama, the respiratory infections became serious. I usually kept the arthritis and skin lesions under control by taking methatrexate pills three days per week. If I stopped taking methatrexate to take antibiotics, the arthritis flared, and it was hard to recover the balance of enough methatrexate to control the disease without the side effect of more infections. It was a downward spiral. I began missing work more and more over the next two years. Local doctors told me that I was too sick to work, and the fear of not being self-supporting, as I had promised my husband, hung over my head. I insisted on dragging myself to work on crutches whenever possible, even if it meant wearing sandals on my swollen feet during the wintertime, not a fashion statement with my tailored suits. The company doctor finally insisted that I transfer to Florida.

My husband, who had never really wanted to leave Virginia, and felt he had sacrificed his career dreams in exhange for mine, decided to leave me and return home before my illness and loss of career could drag him down further. The transfer with IBM was slow coming through. I flew to Florida on a househunting trip, but when I arrived, I was so ill with respiratory infection and liver disease, that I entered Boca Raton Community Hospital on my second day in the State. Six months later both my boss and the head of personnel visited and pronounced me "totally and permanently disabled" from psoriatic arthritis and the treatment for it.

I never returned to Alabama. The company packed my things and sold my house.

Betty and Kay ceased to contact me. When I begged my parents to come help me in Florida, my father asked, "Carole Anne, do you know jes' how fahr it is to Floriduh?"

Florida was in a period of rampant development, and demand for housing was pushing prices up on a weekly basis. I asked my father for a temporary loan to put down on a house, promising to pay it back with interest within two years.

"Naw, now I cain't do that. I just gave Betty ten thousand dollahs to buy their second house in Richmond. The first one they decided to rent out, 'cause they found a bigguh one they liked bettuh."

Betty and husband King had two children by then, a girl, Karen, and a boy, Marc, born within fourteen months of each other.

I felt as though I had lost everything: my health, my job, my big colonial home in Alabama, my husband.

The following summer, my parents and fifteen-year-old Laura paid a brief, polite, superficial social call. One night I saw Laura taking a pill at bedtime and asked, "What is that?"

"Oh, it's just half a valium. Mother gives it to me to help me sleep."

After that visit, I did not see my youngest sister again for twenty-one years.

It was a harsh four years alone in Florida. Whenever I was physically well enough, I tried to make the best of it, which caught the attention of the director of the State's Arthritis Foundation. He asked me to testify before a special Congressional Commission in 1975 in answer to the question, "How has having arthritis affected you emotionally and in relationship to others?" (See **Appendix A** for full testimony.)

It was a logistics challenge to safely transport me to Tampa. It was the first time I'd traveled anywhere since my disastrous arrival in Florida three years before. The Arthritis Foundation supplied me with a wheelchair and someone to push it. I wore a kerchief over my nose and mouth in the crowds at airports.

More important than the testimony, my ability to travel there attracted the attention of the man who would become my husband two years later, after a sporadic "long-distance courtship," and a marriage proposal conditional upon my ability to live in California. I met my husband-to-be in Florida shortly before he moved to California. He despised living in Florida and was not seriously interested in me unless I could live in California. We married in 1977 and I moved to northern California. My health was always a challenge in that climate, but sailing had become my passion while in Florida, and pursuit of it on San Francisco Bay kept me going in spite of the many physical setbacks. (See **Appendix C** for reprinted 1990 feature from *San Francisco* magazine about me as a handicapped sailor.) I lived in California until my deteriorating health forced me back to Florida in 1995. I returned sick without a husband, once again.

Now in 2001, I was divorced, living alone again in Florida, had been too sick to travel anywhere for more than five years, had lost my mother, father, and brother in a short fifteen months. And on top of the losses, this letter. From a sister in Virginia.

ை∞ல

"Well, my darling kitty-cats," I said to the contented trio licking their paws, "since a sister wrote that letter, I have three choices: Betty, Kay or Laura. Kay seems least likely, but maybe she can tell me who the author is."

In the two weeks after I transmitted the message about Larry, Kay was the only family member, besides Daddy, who called Barbra. Barbra told me that she read Larry's suicide note to Kay. She didn't read it to Daddy. He didn't ask for it. The following week, while Daddy was in Kay's car, he had turned to her out of the blue and said, "I blame Betty for what she's done. I blame Betty and Laura for what has happened to Larry."

My clock chimed and I realized it was 10:00 P.M., so I tried Kay's number.

"Kay, please don't hang up on me when I ask you a question, but I have to ask you, anyhow. Did you write a letter to the Pompano police about Larry?"

"What? What the...why are you asking me that? Of course not. Why are you calling me?" She was complaining, because I knew Kay hated to talk on the telephone.

I explained the events of the day, and she told me emphatically, "Carole, there is no way that Laura has enough mental ability left to do anything that would fool police. You know how Betty likes to write letters. She's got the history for it. She's the one who must have done it. Why don't you get a copy from the police? Is it anonymous like all her others?"

Her question stopped me momentarily, because I had forgotten about an incident many years ago. I had received an anonymous letter in California, postmarked Virginia, that Kay felt sure was sent to me by Betty.

"No, Kay, the police know which sister in Virginia. They just wouldn't tell me which one. They didn't call the detectives in Oregon before coming to my door to accuse me of doing something to Larry-- of luring him to Florida or something. It doesn't make any sense, but I had a cop snarl at me over the telephone this afternoon that I am a suspect in a criminal investigation. He won't tell me of what, exactly. Something about a satanic sacrifice, if you can believe that."

"Oh that can't be true. What do you mean? What could you possibly have to do with what happened to Larry?"

"That's my question, Kay. But since you haven't exactly been calling me back lately, I wondered if something happened to you, knowing how much you fear Laura and Betty."

"No way Laura could have written it," Kay interrupted. "Laura is utterly nuts. She couldn't get it together enough to write a letter that anyone would take seriously, much less the police. It's Betty."

"Do you think Betty knew anything about my part in Daddy's replacing her with his friend Charlie as health care surrogate and power of attorney the Sunday before Daddy died?"

"I doubt it. She was the one who told the hospital staff that she wouldn't drive to Lynchburg, that she was too busy and might not come for a few weeks. And then Daddy died and upset her plans, so it didn't matter about the changes. Why would she care? Charlie and I have done all the work."

"Why does Betty do anything that she does?"

"I don't know. ...I don't want to know. I really don't want to know anything about her or Laura. I've had another rough week, have a sore throat, and want to go to bed. If you want to know what's going on around here, why don't you come up and see for yourself?"

"*Right*, Kay, like that's possible," my sarcasm dripped. "Why would you say a thing like that?"

"Because I'm sure if you wanted to you could get someone to put you in a wheelchair and load you into a van and drive you up here," Kay grumbled.

I was shocked. Kay was actually serious. "Kay, do you have any idea what my life is like? What it takes to keep surviving without an immune system?"

"No, but I'm sure you can do whatever you want to do."

I gave up. Kay had no comprehension of my health situation, just as Larry believed she had no idea of his, even after his last trip home. He had told me repeatedly that Kay didn't know or want to know. She wanted to live in her own world and ignore what she did not wish to see. But before the call ended, she did promise to contact the Pompano police and try to "explain Betty."

As I hung up, I thought back ten years to a day in June when I received an anonymous letter warning me that Kay's seven-year-old daughter, Kate, was desperately afraid of her father and very much in need of an aunt to intervene in what was happening to her. At that time I was living in California and had little contact with Kay. When Kay refused to return my calls, I confided in my father, and contacted the Virginia State child welfare services to investigate. There was no follow up.

In September that year, I flew to northern Virginia, alone and with wheelchair as usual, for a family gathering of my mother's relatives. I found little Kate apparently happy and healthy. She seemed to have a good relationship with her father, from what I could see over the weekend. As Daddy and I watched Kate playing ball happily in the yard with her father, we discussed our mutual distress over the implications of the anonymous letter. Daddy believed that there was nothing wrong between Kate and her father. He didn't speculate on who had written that letter to me in California, postmarked in Virginia.

When I showed the letter to Kay for the first time that afternoon, she said, "Looks like another one of Betty's crazy letters to make trouble. Throw it away." She implied that she had seen others, but she never told me any particulars.

Now ten years later, was Betty still writing crazy letters to make trouble?

Earlier in the day I had e-mailed Betty's grown daughter Karen, married and living in Atlanta, an account of the police coming to accuse me of murder. I asked her to call me. To my surprise, I found an answer in my e-mail.

"Carole," I read, "Sorry you're caught in the middle of something so heinous. But you should have absolutely no doubt about who would fabricate such a story. Your sister Laura is completely and utterly mentally disturbed to the point of being a danger to herself and to others. And yes, she would make up a story, and she'll think and believe …that it's true. That's how sick she is. Whether she compiled it all on her own or she had a bug planted in her ear (by Betty) is hard to say.... I would suggest to any police or court of law that Laura be completely investigated. Perhaps this will get her the help she desperately needs."

I e-mailed her back with the telephone numbers for the BSO and asked her to please call them.

So Kay thought it was Betty and Karen thought it was Laura, and I didn't know what to think. I needed to see that letter.

༄ৡ

The next morning after that shocking visit by the detectives, I called the Pompano police records department to get the case number of their visit. They had no record of any detectives coming to my house. Had the whole thing been a hoax? I suppressed a feeling of panic and eventually got Sgt. Montgomery on the phone only to be met with accusation and hostility.

"Well, if there *is* an ongoing investigation, what is the crime and what is the case number?" I asked.

"I'm not telling you that, but it's based on the letter we received from your sister!" He hung up.

I walked outside to browse among my tropical plants and think. A white car slowly drove by with two women inside. I couldn't see their faces, but I felt uneasy. If Betty and Laura, my oldest and my youngest sisters, had made up something that the police were taking seriously, what if they were actually, physically coming after me? I went inside and called 911.

Within minutes, four Broward Sheriff patrol cars had arrived. I don't think they took me seriously, but they promised to keep extra patrol cars in the area. Deputy Carl Spear later filed a report that omitted the details of the intense telephone conversation I had in his presence with Sgt. Montgomery. He did write, "She was irate because she believes that she is being investigated and she demanded to know why."

Fear and uncertainty were wearing me down. Before Deputy Spear departed, I found myself shouting at Sgt. Montgomery, who finally and reluctantly asked if I'd feel more comfortable if I had a copy of the letter.

"Yes, sir, that's what I've been asking for since yesterday. Can you send it out to me or do you want me to come get it?"

Sgt. Montgomery complained that he wasn't even supposed to be working that day, and didn't know who could make a copy of the letter and deliver it to me. Since I was scheduled as a lector at St. Coleman's Catholic Church for the four-thirty mass, I suggested he send it by one of the many policemen who attended that service regularly and give it to Father Foudy, the pastor. I was sure Father Foudy would help end the confusion immediately.

"No, no, no, I'll get it to your house," Sgt. Montgomery interjected. "I can't tell you exactly what time, but I'll get it there."

"Thank you. Thank you very much." I hung up, escorted Deputy Spear to the door, and said, "It takes what it takes."

After the mass, I waited until confessions were finished to speak to the pastor.

Father Thomas Foudy was a genial Irishman with slight brogue, a consummate politician who never forgot a name with a face. He was a tall, large-boned, handsome man in his mid-fifties, with a full head of salt-and-pepper hair, and an easy smile to match his "Hi how are ya?" followed by the name of the parishioner he was greeting. Although he did not know me personally, I was a visible "fixture" in the parish because of my volunteer ministries in the liturgy, the formal services of the church. I also was active in the process through which adults could become Catholic, as I had done decades before, called the Rite of Christian Initiation of Adults (RCIA).

The first year I was active in St. Coleman's RCIA, I became well acquainted with the woman who later became a party to a scandal that rocked Father Foudy's world. That scandal wreaked havoc in the parish and community, received widespread press that could still be found easily online. I had been fully supportive of him during his slanderous ordeal, offering to testify on his behalf. "Turnabout is fair play," so I assumed he'd be very supportive of me in putting a quick end to this letter to the police.

I confided in him the bizarre events of the previous twenty-four hours.

He reddened, laughed, and said, "Carole, don't you know those cops are at a local pub tonight talking about the crazy woman in north Pompano, elbowing each other in the ribs and rolling their eyes? They're just following a routine and will get it straightened out. Don't take it too personally." He agreed with me that they were not the classiest of guys, but I should let them bumble through their job.

"Well, Father, I am assigned as a eucharistic minister at tomorrow's nine o-clock mass. I'll let you know then what happens."

I arrived home to find, at last, three pages, rolled loosely together and stuck between the doorknob and doorjamb. I rushed to read them.

Chapter 4

"Courage under Persecution
There is nothing concealed
that will not be revealed,
nor secret that will not be known.
Therefore whatever you have said in the darkness
will be heard in the light,
and what you whispered behind closed doors
will be proclaimed on the housetops." --Luke 12: 2-3

Cold chills ran over me as I read the letter again and again. (See **Appendix H.**) I needed to talk to someone to put this insanity into perspective. How could the police have taken this seriously? And how many years of hatred had nourished this rotten growth? I decided to call my Aunt Madeline, the widow of my father's youngest brother, living in Lynchburg. I had telephoned her during the night as soon as I learned of my father's death. I had always felt close to her, perhaps because she was Catholic.

In her generation, the animosity between Catholics and Protestants was extreme. Even as I grew up in Lynchburg, I was forbidden to socialize with anyone Catholic. Catholicism was considered a minor cult, sometimes called the "whore of Babylon." I didn't know what that meant, but I believed, along with the others in our majority Protestant community, that Catholics worshipped statues and Mary, a dead Jewess. I heard that the Pope was the Anti-Christ and that Catholics were somehow cannibals.

Indeed, the "whites" did not consider Catholics white. They were expected to sit in the back of the bus with the "coloreds."

My uncle Bill Fielder had violated the social norms to marry the love of his life. His parents welcomed her, however, as he and Madeline seemed always to be a couple newly in love, despite the ups and downs of raising four children. Then, tragically, Madeline was widowed in 1975 when Bill suddenly died of a heart attack. No illness, no suffering, just gone in a moment of sleep after an evening out at dinner with her.

"Madeline, I know it's hard to believe, but the police here received a letter from Laura accusing me of all sorts of things including murdering Larry."

"Police? What in the world is goin' on?" Madeline half laughed in her disbelief at what I'd said.

"May I read this letter to you?" I explained that the heading bore the name of Laura's pony farm in Hayes, Virginia, and that it was addressed to the Pompano Beach Police Department. "'Chief Wright: I am contacting you reference a possible cult disappearance/suicide.'"

"Oh my gosh, Carole. What is wrong with Laura?"

"I told you, it's unbelievable. Listen carefully. 'I have a 50-year-old disabled brother in very poor physical and mental condition, living in Portland, Oregon, who is currently missing. I think he has been missing for a couple of months. I have a sister in Pompano Beach, Florida who has her own cult of which my brother is a member.'"

"Carole, a cult! I cain't believe she talks that way. And I didn't know you'd seen Larry recently." Madeline added, "She sent this to the police? How'd you get this?"

"It wasn't easy. At first the police refused to give me the letter. There are enclosures that I still don't have. Based on the whole letter, the police are accusing me of being a criminal. Let me read on."

I continued. "'I do not know how many persons my sister has under her mind control. Carole is fifteen years older than me and left home and moved out of state when I was only four years old, so I have few memories of her. I have met her only a few times and have observed her mainly from an 'outside' perspective. I recognized the 'cult' aspect of her activities and control about ten years ago.'"

"Was she just four when you left? That doesn't seem right."

I thought a moment, "Let's see, uh, 1967 is when I left Virginia to go to Louisiana State University in Baton Rouge. Laura was born in 1958. So she was nine years old when I left."

"That makes more sense, cause I know she's close to the same age as my daughter. She should have memories of you if you were there when she was nine. Does she have you confused with Betty, maybe?"

"Who knows, Madeline, who knows?"

"Wait a minute, Carole. Laura has few memories, hasn't seen you since she was four, or nine, but has been observin' you for the past ten years. Hmmm. When did you last see her?"

"Not counting the few seconds I saw her at her house in 1995, the last time I visited with her in person was twenty-seven years ago. She was fifteen, and Mother and Daddy brought her to Florida for a visit during the summer of 1974. You know, I had recently become Catholic then, but I don't remember her paying any attention to it. I do remember on one of my earlier visits to Virginia that she thought all Catholics were cultists. But I never thought much about it."

Madeline whistled softly. "This is total nonsense. If she hasn't seen you in twenty-seven years how could she possibly know what she seems to think she knows?"

"Madeline, I think it's something else in her mind. Let me continue. 'I recognized the "cult" aspect of her activities and control about 10 years ago. Other people are now recognizing it as well. She is aware that I recognize what she is and what she is doing. She (and her followers) are extremely afraid of me and literally physically run from my presence. This is not just a matter of family arguments. There is a very intense satanic aspect to this situation.'"

"Carole, she's out of her head. You have followers? Who is she talkin' about? If she hasn't seen you and has few memories of you, how can she know? And what followers, where, are runnin' away from her? Who could possibly take that seriously?"

"The Broward Sheriff's department," I answered.

"But worse, what does she know about a 'satanic aspect?'"

"I know she used to play with all sorts of odd creatures like snakes and lizards and rats and, ugh, crawly things that make me shiver, but lots of youngsters get into that, don't they?"

"I just remember her likin' guinea pigs."

"I do remember in 1995 that the license plate on her white pickup truck said 'REPTILE'. But I don't see the necessary connection between strange pets and satanism."

"I really don't know Laura," Madeline continued, "but there was something very wrong with her at your uncle Jimmy's funeral, and she wasn't too friendly at your Dad's, either."

"Several people mentioned that they overheard Laura talking at Jimmy's funeral and saying that she was sorry she didn't kill her sister the last time she saw her, but she'd be sure and do it the next time. There was some confusion about which sister she meant. Kay's daughter overheard it and thought she was talking about Kay and got scared."

"My daughter heard her and got away from her in a hurry."

"Madeline, we're getting off track. Let me keep reading this," I tried again.

"You mean there's more?" Madeline gasped.

"Oh, yes. Lots. Paragraph number two: 'I am a civilian Military Police Dispatcher at Fort Eustis, Virginia, and I assure you that this is not a joke. I have openly told my co-workers that if another "Heaven's Gate" suicide/murder/whatever incident happens, don't be surprised if my sister is involved....but she would never be included as one of the victims. I also have reason to believe that she may be preparing to fake her death.'" I paused.

"Oh my gosh," Madeline sucked in her breath. "She is talking to her co-workers like this about you? That sounds crazy. How can she keep a job?"

I pushed on: "'At age 42, I am the youngest of five children. Only my oldest sister now communicates with me; as of this past summer, my elderly father was "not allowed" to communicate with me anymore, but my oldest sister was able to forward occasional news.'"

Madeline interrupted, "That's ridiculous. Nobody ever told your father what he could or couldn't do. And I happen to know that Laura visited him two days in a row last Christmas. What does Betty have to do with this?"

"Good question, but there's more. Listen. 'I shall include here some discussion we have had via e-mails within the past few weeks. My father died a couple of weeks ago and my Florida sister, who claims she is on her deathbed, faxed an essay which she ordered to be handed out and read at the funeral. It was not read, but I got a copy of it. In it she states four times that the brother is dead--not just missing. In my opinion this essay is rather incriminating. I am including it here-with.'" I paused, waiting for Madeline to absorb the paragraph.

Madeline said slowly, "So she thinks the eulogy you wrote for your father is proof of your criminality? Why does she say you ordered it to be read?"

"Who knows? Maybe Betty told her that the funeral director suggested I write something to hand out and she just made up the rest. Remember how I gave the eulogy for Mother over speakerphone from Florida?" (Transcription in **Appendix F.**)

"Yeah, Carole, that was nice."

"It wasn't practical for Daddy's graveside service. But, Madeline, I've searched through that written eulogy for Daddy for anything that made Laura believe I murdered Larry. I did mention Larry's death and its effect on Daddy four separate times." (See **Appendix G** for eulogy.)

"Carole, I want to ask you this. Without Larry's body bein' found, how can anybody be sure that he's dead?"

"How can anybody doubt it? His suicide note. The investigation. Larry's health. His threats to kill himself. His fiftieth birthday."

"What if he's just in hidin' somewhere?"

"How I wish that were true. But lots of things he did were his way of saying good-bye to us. He planned his suicide for years, and if he didn't want his body to be found, I bet it will never be found."

"There's no way to hide a dead body. It'll show up."

"Madeline, have you ever been to Oregon, or out West? Do you know how rugged the mountains are, and how wild?"

"No. But bodies are found up in the Blue Ridge Mountains."

"The West Coast is different. Larry could have stepped outside his door, taken a bus to the downtown Portland terminal, paid a taxi driver for a thirty-minute drive up to Mt. Hood, given him an extra tip to drop him off on the side of a mountain road. No trace. Armed with morphine, whiskey and his gun, he could have found a ravine down which his body could tumble when he shot himself. By the time the snow thawed, the animals would have finished everything."

"How can you talk like that?" Madeline's voice shook.

"It's an idea the detective in Oregon and I discussed. He said they do solve most missing persons cases, but it might take ten years or more. If a hiker finds remains in the wild, the teeth are usually missing, scattered by animals. A jawbone is most commonly left uneaten and, if a relative can be found for a DNA test, sometimes an identification can be made

"Oh, oh, I don't wanna think about that, Carole. So, back to the letter, do the police agree with Laura that the eulogy you wrote is incriminatin'?"

"Who knows, Madeline? They didn't include it with these three pages."

I continued reading. "'My sister is extremely intelligent, vicious and cunning, and has amassed considerable wealth through her decades of deceit and manipulation of other people. She currently has a home and yacht in Florida; I am not sure of the status of her home and yacht in California, or of her home in France. I know that she has convinced...'"

"Carole," Madeline began chuckling, "why didn' you tell me about all this wealth you've got? And three homes? I thought your ex-husband made sure you had nothin' left, didn' he?"

"You thought right. And the so-called house in France, never more than a tiny apartment, was sold fourteen years ago. Let me read on. 'I know that she has convinced a lot of people that she has been on chemotherapy for 38 years and is near death and cannot travel. I also know that that is a medical impossibility and that in fact she does indeed do quite a bit of traveling. I think she may have traveled to Portland and brought the brother to Florida so there would be no body to discover in Portland.'"

I paused, then added, "You know, Madeline, she's got the part about chemotherapy almost right. I was on methatrexate from 1964 till last year. It's true that most doctors think it is medically impossible for someone to survive so long like that. That's why it's been hard for me to find a doctor willing to treat me. They can't believe I could still be alive after all that. They don't want to deal with the complications created by the side effects."

"So you cain't come to Virginia?"

"I haven't spent a single night out of my own bed in this house since I came here in October 1995. My whole life revolves around getting my infusion of gamma globulin in order to live another two weeks. Of course I can't travel."

"Why does Laura think that Larry could have traveled? I thought he was so sick after his trip here last year. Your father said he seldom got out of bed."

"That's true. Now we come to the funniest part of the letter. Only I'm not laughing. 'Do not underestimate the evil viciousness of this woman, and do not be deceived by her soft, "weak" voice and gentle persuasion. She has...'"

"Good grief, Carole, she certainly doesn't know you at all, does she?"

"Obviously." I continued reading. "'She has the charisma that has described Jim Jones, David Koresh and Marshall Applewhite. Via telephone, she has convinced...'"

"*You*?" Madeline interrupted, "like those people? What on earth is she.... Jim Jones was the San Francisco preacher that took all those people to Guyana, in South America, and had them all drink poison Kool-aid, back in the '70's sometime."

"I remember that happened shortly after I moved to California."

"Oh yes. And a Congressman was there, or got killed or somethin'."

"I think so. I had to ask somebody about the other two names-- David Koresh was the Waco, Texas whacko, where the government burned out those people."

"Oh Waco, oh yes, I know about that one."

"The Marshall Appleseed, or whoever, was that bald guy in California in the ritzy house where those people killed themselves in order to get on the comet or something from outer space, I think."

"Yeah, that's the one. Boy, she sure is up on all that stuff."

"Well, here's the part for you, Madeline. 'Via telephone, she has convinced a cemetery in Virginia to dig a hole on top of a relative and prepare a footstone for her. There is no death date in the stone yet,'-- gee, I wonder why not?" I chuckled, then continued, "'There is no death date in the stone yet, but it is in place, and the hole is ready to receive her cremains. Imagine the shock of my aunt when she discovered a hole dug on top of her late husband's grave. A few subsequent three-hour phone conversations had the aunt relieved and proud to share the grave with her.'" I stopped, and waited for Madeline's response.

"Well, I, I uh, how in the world did she come up with that? I never talked to her about the mistake at the cemetery, and I cain't imagine your father...although, he was right upset about that mess over there at Spring Hill, 'cause when I saw it, I was upset."

I interrupted, "Yeah, I know about that only because Daddy told me months after the incident at Spring Hill Cemetery. He was really upset that you even considered moving Bill's body from the family plot. You know how important family graveyards are to him. My gosh, Betty and her husband King ingratiated themselves to him above all else when they went up to the old Saunders family graveyard in Franklin County and cleaned it up with him. He sent me more than a dozen photos of that event."

"But Carole, I told your father I changed my mind. He did take Betty over to Spring Hill Cemetery to show that hole they dug in the wrong place to her, though. He told me about takin' her over there. I had gone over there on Veterans Day, you know, I always do then and on Billy's birthday and our anniversary, and I saw that hole they dug to put in the concrete for your footstone. It was smack dab next to Billy's grave, which is where your grandfather, and your father, told me I was s'pose to end up. I thought, well, if there's not gonna be room for me there, then I'll go to the Catholic cemetery with my family, and move Billy over there. So I told Jack. I didn' know he was so upset about it."

"Madeline, you, of all people, know that Daddy never got over Billy's death. He and his brother Jimmy were the most important relationships in his life. Ever since Uncle Jimmy died a couple years ago Daddy's priority topics of conversation have been his own impending funeral and graveyards. With all his plans, you can imagine that he couldn't accept any change in them. Did you ever know Daddy to accept any change, ever?"

Madeline laughed, "I don't think any of those Fielders were too happy about changin' anything. I just didn't know he was so sensitive about that. But he did tell me that he took Betty over there to explain it all to her. I thought that was kinda strange, even when he said it. What could she do about their mistake?"

"My father is the only one on the title now. He would have to approve any changes. My grandfather bought that plot when his son Tom died so young from that automobile accident. He was just five, I think."

"And I still remember when Frank Fielder died of cancer at age twenty-five. Billy and I were still dating. Gosh, when I think back now, it seemed so tragic that he, the athlete and picture of health died so young. But Billy, dead at age fifty-three, that seemed pretty young, too."

I broke in to Madeline's memories, "So it looks like Betty must have told Laura something about the cemetery error in placement of my pre-ordered footstone. Their error upset you and Daddy, and he had to make them fix it. He told Betty about it, who must have told Laura something about it, and Laura made up the rest? Wow. All because I tried to please my father with his wish that I'd plan to be buried in the family plot. Good grief. I wish he'd never asked me. Did you ever talk to Laura or Betty?"

"No, I haven't seen Laura in years, except at Jimmy's funeral, and at Jack's. And I told you about that. I reckon I haven't seen Betty, either, except for those two times. As far as I know, she didn't come to see your father but a couple or three times a year. Kay was always comin' up heah to take care of your parents."

"Really? That surprises me. The way Daddy talked, I thought Betty was there quite often. So Kay was the only one of those Virginia girls taking care of Daddy, yet, in his eyes, she was always wrong and Betty was always right. Until that last two weeks..."

"Carole, why would Betty make up such a story to tell Laura?" Madeline half asked, half mused. "Do you think she made up the rest of the stuff and Laura believes it?"

"I'm not so sure that Betty didn't write this whole letter and sign

Laura's name to it, Madeline. It's certainly in keeping with her past character and behavior. But sending such craziness to a police department? I just can't imagine Betty jeopardizing her job that way. But wait, there's more." I began reading again: "'I think she could very well send some cremains from Florida to fill the hole, but they will not be hers. She has too much to profit from other people's deaths for her to die anytime soon. She is enraged that she cannot control my mind; she has tried various attacks against me since 1974, but has had success only in the past few years, by commanding her followers to break off any relationship with me. She is desperately afraid of me and cannot afford to have her followers interact with me.'"

"It gets worse and worse, Carole, doesn't it? That sounds really mean and nutty. She sure gives you lots of credit for controllin' minds and givin' commands. Where could she get an idea like that about you when she hasn't seen you in so many years?"

"You know the answer to that, Madeline. One person. Betty."

"How could Betty persuade her that you have attacked her, when neither one of them has seen you or knows you?"

"Beats me, Madeline. How did Betty persuade Daddy that everyone she doesn't speak to wronged her, and that she is still the perfect Queen Bee? And who are my followers that Laura once had a relationship with, but no longer does? Do you suppose Betty got mad at Laura sometime, and now Laura has me confused with Betty?"

"Carole, I don't know what to say. I've never in my life heard of anything like this."

"Nor have I, Madeline. The worst part is that the Broward Sheriff's office is taking it seriously. Even when Laura states that *I* am desperately afraid of *her*, not the other way around, the police here came after me."

"Don'tcha think they called her before comin' to your house?"

"Who knows? They didn't mention it. The letter itself is absurd and full of so many contradictions, none of the detectives must have even read it. Their boss probably just sent them out here and they came. And the sergeant acting hostile to me over the phone, well, I guess he's just overworked and underpaid and the public is always the enemy."

"Gosh, I don't think our police act like that. At least they sent you out that letter, but what about those enclosures? What cousins on your Mother's side could Laura or Betty be talkin' about?"

" I don't know. I'm hoping Charlie and Mr. Lowry will come up with some answers tomorrow."

"They know about this, Carole?"

"Yes, because Charlie was Daddy's friend, and is in charge of the estate, I turned to him just as I would have turned to Daddy to ask what to do. He told me to immediately fax a copy of Laura's letter to the lawyer, Mr. Lowry, because they're meeting tomorrow morning and will take care of it. I sure hope they talk to Betty and Laura and get to the bottom of it. But, Madeline, there's more to this letter."

"Oh my. Go on and read it."

"'I expect the death of my brother is very highly probable, and I have no doubt that if she commanded him to go out and kill himself, he would readily do it *for her*.'"

"Carole! That's ridiculous. I thought Laura and Larry were close. How could she say something like that about him?"

I ignored her and continued reading: "'At this point, the question of my brother's whereabouts and status is going to need to be resolved, as he stands to inherit 1/5 of my father's estate. My oldest sister....'"

"Is that because you four girls will get Larry's share if he's dead?"

"No, not possible. If Larry's body is found, and it can be proven that he died before my father did, then Larry's inheritance goes to his son, George. I already talked to Mr. Lowry about this. If his body is not found, then it's up to the courts to work out, I suppose. That's why my brother's legal representative, Barbra Milhaus, needs to talk to Charlie and Mr. Lowry. Larry is legally considered alive for the next seven years, unless his body is found and identified. She is his power of attorney, which, in the State of Oregon, means she is responsible for keeping all Larry's finances."

"Are you sayin' she'll get Larry's inheritance?"

"No. He left everything to her and her family in his suicide note, though."

"Carole, why, if she's got a husband an' family, did that woman get so involved with Larry? I don' understaind it. Did she expect to get money when he died?"

I gasped. "No! Certainly Larry had a copy of Daddy's trust and assets, but he did not expect Daddy to die anytime soon. Are you saying that his friend would go with Larry to all the doctor's visits and hospitalizations based on a secret hope there might be money at the end of years of drudgery?"

"Well, I was just curious. Jack mentioned some woman taking care of Larry, and I wondered what was goin' on," Madeline chuckled.

"Yeah. Larry sent Daddy and all of us a letter in 1990 that explained how much the Milhaus family helped him." (See **Appendix B**.) I only met the Milhaus once, but they seemed to be salt-of-the-earth type people. Barbra is a caretaker type, like Kay. She's always taking care of people who need it, and has taken in a nephew to raise, too."

"Oh. Well, Kay sure came up heah to Lynchburg a lot to take care of your parents."

"Back to the letter: 'My oldest sister does not want to get involved with any law enforcement aspect, and my husband wants me to not be involved in family matters of this type AT ALL. However, I cannot ignore what I strongly suspect may have happened. I truly think the situation has gone from "freedom of religion" to the criminal.'" I stopped and waited.

"So there it is again," Madeline sighed, "you must be a criminal since you chose to become a Catholic. It is really, really warped thinkin'."

I pushed on reading: "'I certainly hope you will take me seriously on this. On the other hand, it would be a satisfaction, albeit perverse, for me to be able to say *I told you so* when some sort of bizarre incident hits the media. I am including below the addresses of me (Laura), my missing brother (Larry), my Florida sister (Carole), and my oldest sister (Betty). I am also including the e-mail conversations I have previously mentioned. My brother and my Florida sister do not know my e-mail address and I absolutely want to keep it that way. I have also sent an e-mail to Portland police (police@teleport.com), but have not heard back from them yet. Thank you. Feel free to contact me, preferably via e-mail but by voice if necessary. I will do whatever I can to help you investigate this matter. Respectfully,' and it's signed Laura F. Crews," I finished.

"What e-mail conversations?" Madeline broke the silence.

"Between her and Betty, evidently. She lists the names and addresses of Larry, me, and Betty, and then handwrote at the end that there are three enclosures: 'Carole's essay, summary e-mail I sent to my 2 cousins, and extended e-mail log with my sister Betty and me.' That is what I haven't seen.

"Carole, didn't you like to die when you first read that thing? I mean it is really hard to believe. Why doesn't her husband do something about her?"

"Why didn't Daddy do something? Why didn't Daddy talk to her about what we all know was bothering her, about the circumstances of her birth and all? Larry wrote to her about it, in 1999. He wrote to all of us trying to get to the bottom of the Laura/Betty hatreds. Larry, Kay, and I asked Daddy to talk to Laura about it. He didn't. You and Aunt Virginia are now the only ones left that can tell her the truth. Are you going to talk to her?"

"I'm not planning to talk to her, no. I don't imagine I'll ever see Laura again. But you say Larry knew about Laura? And Betty?"

I explained to Madeline Larry's valiant efforts to bring his sisters together. (See letters in **Appendix E**.)

"Considering how Laura acted when Larry was there last March, her husband, who works for the Navy, is not going to do or say anything. He was there when she was chasing Kay's daughter Kate around the house threatening to rape her. Betty's daughter Karen was there visiting from Atlanta. Both Larry and Karen believed that no matter what Laura does, her husband just goes along with her."

"My gosh, Carole. What a mess. What was on those enclosures Laura sent?"

"I don't know, but I need to track them down."

Chapter 5

"I hear the whisperings of many:
'Terror on every side! Denounce!
Let us denounce him!'
All those who were my friends
are on the watch for any misstep of mine.
'Perhaps he will be trapped; then we can prevail,
and take our vengeance on him.'"   --Jeremiah 20:10

Monday, February 12, 2001

I awoke full of hope that the day would resolve the questions, silliness, and frustrations surrounding the letter. (Reprint in **Appendix H**.) I needed to talk to Larry or to Daddy about it. The thud of realization that Larry and Daddy were gone forever hit me. For the first time, I felt too numb to cry. I slowly reviewed in my mind all the contacts I'd made over the weekend, and the expected responses.

There were none.

Neither Charlie Loving, nor his attorney Mr.Lowry called back with how they proposed to "take care of it," as Charlie had promised me when I first read the letter to him over the phone Saturday night, and he told me to fax it to Mr. Lowry immediately.

Father Foudy didn't call as promised. Before the children's mass on Sunday, I had given him an envelope containing the memorial card of my father, a picture of me with Pope John Paul II in 1982, and a snapshot of the last visit I had from Laura and my parents in 1974. I had included Larry's suicide note, and contrasting snapshots of him healthy with me in California in 1978, and terribly ill in Virginia last March, 2000. I also gave him my niece Karen's long e-mail from that same visit in Virginia about Laura chasing Kay's daughter and threatening to rape her. Given that documentary evidence of my family, my few contacts with them, and Laura's apparent insane behavior, Father Foudy was armed to call the Pompano police and put in a good word for my character in contrast to the absurd accusations in Laura's letter. I expected him to call the police and then call me. He didn't.

When I could not reach Betty, Kay, nor Laura by telephone on Sunday after I received the letter, I called the police in each of their localities to ask for urgent hand-delivery of it to them, because one of them might be endangered by the other. Neither Kay nor Laura nor their local police called back. Only one policeman I contacted, Sgt. Marion from Chesterfield County, called me to report Betty's strange reaction to his arrival at her door with the letter. She turned her face away as soon as he showed it to her. His conclusion seemed to be that Betty already knew all about the letter. He asked her to give him a copy of the e-mails between her and Laura, indicated as an enclosure at the bottom of the letter, but she refused.

Sgt. Marion left me a message saying, "...You may be better off dealin' with the authorities in the original jurisdiction to make this thang work."

Following his advice, I called Sgt. Montgomery in Pompano, again.

"I sent everything I had out to you," he grumbled at me. "If you think there's anything else, then call Detective Blankenship."

I called and left an urgent message for Detective Blankenship.

At the end of the day, I was still hanging. I e-mailed my niece Karen to ask if she'd had any luck reaching the Broward County detectives. The suspense was wearing me out. I needed someone in authority who could go head to head with the Broward Sheriff's department to make them produce the enclosures to the letter.

I turned for help to the Oregon detective on Larry's case, Roger Mussler. He should have received Barbra's message concerning the letter that prompted the Portland city police to call her. Detective Mussler knew nothing about any of the Fielders until my brother became a case number to him, a missing person that he concluded was a suicide. But Roger had seemed very kind and concerned when I talked to him about Larry before my father died. He had been so responsive and gentle since then. Barbra trusted him. Maybe he would be willing and able to help me with this mess in Florida.

I sat down at my computer to e-mail him, sorting out my own thoughts about the possibilities behind these strange events on both coasts. I began by writing to him about the weekend's events and my frustration with the Broward detectives' apparent confusion. I asked if he'd gotten the enclosures to the letter that was also sent to the Portland city police department.

I knew that Roger had spoken by telephone with Kay about Larry, so must have some sense of her personality and opinions. I e-mailed him that I found it odd in the letter allegedly signed by Laura that there was no reference to Kay, because I knew she had been the main object of Laura's hatred in recent years, and she no longer had any relationship with Betty. I wrote him that I couldn't tell which sister, Laura or Betty, had written the letter, in spite of Laura's signature affixed. I explained that Laura could not possibly know any of the events about which she wrote—except second-hand from Betty, or my father, or from Kay or Larry during the years Laura still spoke to them.

In the e-mail to Roger I wrote, "I haven't known Betty or Laura for decades, but had one brief encounter at their respective homes in 1995 at the specific request of my father. They each acted demented—screaming, red-faced, glittery-eyed, slamming doors, etc." I mentioned Betty's apparent penchant for writing anonymous letters to harm other family members, and how she verbally attacked Kay, me, Daddy, and Larry in letters or by phone after Larry's valiant and diplomatic attempt to bring the sisters together in 1999. (**Appendix E**)

"Larry confronted Betty about a flagrant lie she told against him," I continued to Roger, "on a four-way call between him, Betty, Daddy, and me, near the end of 1999. Betty then *black-listed* Larry and never spoke to him again. He had a very difficult time accepting that both Betty and Laura turned on him and stopped speaking to him. Part of his motivation to make the trip to Virginia last March was to go face-to-face and explain his situation to them, to get back his relationship with them. I had tried to prepare him for the hateful rejection that I feared he would receive; but he seemed driven to go. I think the emotional damage done on that trip, and the fact that my father never seemed to understand his health—physical or mental—nor tried to back him up against Betty, just broke what was left of him. When his estranged son verbally attacked him on July 4th and again at Thanksgiving, he was decimated."

I remembered the conversation Roger and I had about those two encounters between Larry and his son. Barbra told him first, and in his investigation he later asked me if I knew anything about it. I had felt so bad for Larry, knowing that it was a family tradition for members to decide to cut each other off and never speak again. It sounded to me like another generation repeating the pattern. My heart had sunk at Thanksgiving time when I realized that Larry might never see his son again. And he didn't, as Roger's investigation concluded.

In the same e-mail I wrote Detective Mussler a brief history of the problems in the family that I believed affected Larry's ultimate tragic decision. "My father and I, as well as Larry and I, recently discussed many of the family problems to which my father remained oblivious for so many years. Daddy ignored my mother's 30-year-long drug addiction (valium); he ignored my sister Laura's being given valium from infancy (till age 15 that I know of); he denied knowing anything about why my mother told me of my sister Betty's abortion at age 19, or the effect it must have had on my mother or my sister. I believed that was probably the last straw that broke my mother.

"She only told me of the event," I continued to Roger, "because she feared that I would get into the same trouble, and probably because she had to tell someone, not my father. She told me that she was forced into delivering her first-born grandson of 6-months-term, after my sister's back-alley coat-hanger procedure. She said she stuffed the child into the family furnace. When she told me, I was too young to care or comprehend. As my mother's mind deteriorated, she insisted that she had six children, I believe because she cradled six new-borns in her arms. She had had a nervous breakdown after Laura's birth in 1958. The abortion was supposedly in 1960, and she was never quite right ever again."

"Larry figured these things out on his own," I continued in my e-mail to the detective, "after I mentioned to him that the book *Prince of Tides* could be the biography of our family. It took him a little while to figure out the murder cover-up part, but he did ultimately guess. I tried to console him that he was in good company by being maligned and avoided by Betty. She and her husband conveniently got rid of an unwanted child, according to our mother, ceased speaking to me decades ago; wrote Kay off years ago; no longer spoke to their own daughter. Larry had learned too late that Betty's lies about me had poisoned him against me for most of our lives. But it was seeing her do to him what she had done to me while he just went along with it that terrified him. Daddy and Laura were going along with it as Betty character-assassinated him and cut him off, too. Larry felt like he was a total failure in the family if he couldn't pull the girls together for Daddy's sake."

"My father was intentionally and stubbornly blind to all of Betty's manipulations until the week before he died," I continued writing to Roger. "It took Larry's suicide to move Daddy. Kay told me—as well as Barbra—that Daddy confided in her that he blamed Betty for all that she did, and Betty and Laura for Larry's death. I believe Kay was telling the truth based on my last telephone conversations with Daddy before he died. That was a first in sixty years! But that's second-hand to me; you can verify it by talking directly to Kay."

"Firsthand to me, however, is the desperation I felt when I and a nurse-witness at the hospital heard my father's plea to change his trust documents to replace Betty with his friend Charlie. He needed a *Do Not Resuscitate* order signed, but Betty told the hospital staff, according to the nurse, that she was too busy to be bothered to drive to Lynchburg—to do nothing until she could get there. They were horrified, and so was I. I managed, by telephone, to locate my father's trust attorney in Lynchburg, Mr. Lowry, and convey my father's wishes. Mr. Lowry complied with them on the Sunday before my father died. None of us expected my father to die, however, and Kay and Charlie discussed Daddy's discharge from the hospital on Monday. They decided which nursing home he'd go to at the end of the week. Daddy was lucid; I spoke twice daily with him."

I paused in my typing to think back to my conclusion about Daddy's unexpected death. I wrote Roger, "I think Daddy finally recognized in the history of the family both Betty's part and his own neglect, and he just ran out of energy when he faced the truth."

I explained to Roger that Kay or Betty's grown daughter Karen could fill in details of Betty and Laura's ongoing terror tactics. Kay had found it necessary to have a police escort for her family to attend our father's graveside service! I wrote, "You can access Betty direct online if you go to the Virginia government pages. Simply type in her name, 'Lorraine Waddill' and she'll appear as a legislative assistant in the Virginia General Assembly for the Republican Senator Watkins."

After asking Roger to call me whenever he could, I hit the send button for my long e-mail to him. It had been a long, unproductive day, and I went to bed feeling confused and frustrated.

With both Laura and Betty employed in positions as trusted government employees, I wondered if anyone could believe their crazy behavior in family life and help put a stop to it. Would my father's trustee, Charlie Loving, be able to persuade them to get professional help as a condition to receiving their inheritance? Would he even try to be that responsible? Charlie was, like my father, a product of the culture of no-see, no-hear, no-speak evasion of responsibility in unpleasant matters. Would Charlie just compound the problems that Daddy had left behind?

I remembered the days in the Bible belt of Virginia, with its Anglo-Saxon Protestant whites-to-front, all others-to-rear mentality. "What will people say" was the primary moral value. "It's none of my business," and "I don't want to get involved," were close seconds. I found such an attitude anathema to my beliefs as a Roman Catholic, because we believed that the sins of omission were as bad as the sins of commission.

At every mass as a Catholic I prayed "I confess to almighty God and to you, my brothers and sisters, that I have sinned through my own fault in my thoughts and in my words, in what I have done and in **_what I have failed to do_**." I doubted anyone in my family ever thought they had a moral obligation to **do** anything. To be a good Christian simply meant to refrain from doing bad. I had been thinking nonstop what I had failed to do during my lifetime after my family cut me off. What could I have done when they refused to speak to me or see me? I knew now that I must **do something.** I could never again ignore them, even if I never saw them again.

҂ঌ৵৻

The next day, Roger responded to my long e-mail with a note:

Subj: RE: Sorry we've missed
Date: 02/13/2001 5:15:21 PM Eastern Standard Time

Carole, is it just me, I mean am I wrong, or are all the old family generational stories of the South so damn fascinating? If you ever write this up in book form, however fictionalized, please be sure to send me a copy. In the meantime, exercise your great sense of humor and stay healthy. Thank you for the information,

Roger Mussler, Det.
Washington Co. Sheriff's Office, Oregon

He also called to say he wanted me to fax a copy of Laura's letter, because he didn't get it from the city police of Portland. They had thrown it out.

"Well, Carole, you don't have to worry about that crazy letter to the police. I faxed my report over to Detective Blankenship Monday, after speaking with him briefly. Monday, I figured Detective Blankenship would have already seen my missing persons report online in the NCIC files, but he said he hadn't, so I faxed it to him." Roger always spoke slowly and gently, as though he were never in a hurry, even when he had an upcoming appointment on another case. If only the Pompano police had a small portion of his style!

Barbra called me from Portland later in the evening.

"I talked to Roger today, and he told me how concerned and sorry he was for you. He said he straightened out the police down there," she giggled. "You really live in a wonderful place," she added sarcastically. "What is their problem?"

"Who knows? Did you or Larry's attorney hear back from Charlie or Mr. Lowry yet?"

"No, not that I know about."

"They haven't called me, either. You'd think they'd have called me when they met Monday morning to discuss Laura's letter," I complained.

"They just probably wrote it off as a sick joke," Barbra offered an excuse.

"I still haven't heard back from Kay, or Karen, either. They both indicated they'd call the Pompano police, but...."

"Would it do any good?"

She made her point. Still later in the evening, I missed an important message from the Pompano police.

"Miss Fielder, this is Detective Blankenship. Sorry I didn't get back to you until later, but I didn't work until nighttime. As far as I know, they dropped the letter off to your residence Saturday and they left it in the door of your house. As you know, there is no case number and there is no report to give you other than that three or four page letter. If you have any other questions, please call 786-4286. I'll be working tomorrow after nine or ten o'clock."

I wondered aloud, "That's it? It's over?" I sighed in relief for an instant, but wondered how the police could have taken that letter seriously, without its clearly indicated enclosures. And what about Charlie? What must he think? I had been put through the emotional wringer over the weekend. I still had no way of knowing whether Betty or Laura was the instigator. It was Laura's signature, maybe, although it looked like Betty's handwriting. Betty's local deputy sheriff, Sgt.

Marion, had suggested that Betty knew all about it.

And were there cousins involved, really? And why was there still no call from Kay about it?

Even with all these unanswered questions, I felt too good to worry anymore. I grabbed my biggest cat, Danny, the lynx-point Siamese with white paws, gave him a hug, listened to his purr and fell asleep.

ॐ

Valentine's Day, 2001

The day was not filled with cupids and love. I still needed Laura's, (or Betty's?) enclosures to get to the bottom of the letter. I called and got nowhere with Detectives Blankenship and Montgomery.

About 2:30 p.m., I called Mr. Lowry, my father's trust attorney, twice. The first time he "wasn't in," according to his secretary, but the second time, thirty minutes later, I persisted with her when she told me he was on another line. I waited on hold for five minutes. When he finally got on the line, his attitude towards me had done a 180-degree turn from my previous conversations with him before my father died and shortly thereafter. He had been so helpful to rush to my father's bedside in the hospital at my request. He had explained to me Virginia law pertaining to a legally missing person and inheritance rights.

"There's nothing I can say to you about that letter," he responded to my question.

"Charlie said that he and you would do something about it," I protested. "Are you going to call the detective in Oregon?"

"No."

"What about Larry's legal representative, Barbra Milhaus? Have you called her?" I asked.

"No."

I asked again about Larry's status and what Barbra was supposed to do.

"The courts will take care of it," he brushed me off.

The feeling of dread crept all over me. Mr. Lowry, and evidently, Charlie, refused to talk to me. What was going on? Did they believe Laura's letter? Was that possible? What about Kay? Had she talked to Charlie about it yet?

Maybe Detective Mussler could help. I hated to bother him again, but e-mailed him that the lies seemed to be growing and spinning out of control in Virginia. I asked him if he would please simply call my father's trustee, Charlie Loving, and voice his professional opinion. I wrote, "I cannot believe that my character has been completely maligned with one insane letter, but it seems that it has happened. I would really appreciate your help." Little did I know then what an understatement that would turn out to be.

Later, I finally reached Detective Blankenship.

"Thanks for your callback, but I'm a little confused about the missing enclosures. Where are they?"

"I can't tell you that, Miss Fielder."

"What do you mean? Weren't they included with the letter, as stated in the letter?"

"All I know is that you are a suspect in an ongoing investigation, and I can't answer that."

"Didn't you talk to Roger Mussler in Oregon? I asked him to call you."

"He faxed me a report."

"Well, I was calling you for two things: one, to find out about the missing enclosures, and two, to request a written report from you that my name has been cleared, and…"

Blankenship interrupted. "I can't give you anything like that."

"But, but why?" I asked, feeling a sense of dread creep into my confusion.

"There is an ongoing criminal investigation," he repeated.

"About what crime?"

"Based on the letter we received."

"So, are you going to investigate who wrote the letter?"

"No, and that's all I can say. I have to go." Blankenship abruptly hung up.

I was shocked. The contrast of attitudes of the police on each side of the country was stark. My head was spinning. When I later checked my e-mail, the contrast was even more noticeable. Roger had already complied with my earlier e-mail request, within ten minutes of my sending it.

Subj: RE: Please help!
Date: 02/14/2001 5:27:49 PM Eastern Standard Time

Dear Carole,

I really cannot interject myself into the middle of complex family civil problems. However, I did call Mr. Charles Loving this date at approximately 1:50 PM and provided him with my name, phone number, case number of the investigation, and the fact that Larry is missing and to date no body has been found. I offered to speak with him or his attorney at any time should they have questions regarding this investigation. He wrote down the information and said he was very glad I called.

I hope this may be of some assistance.

Sincerely,
R. Mussler

It was an anomaly to use the same word, "police" to describe both Roger Mussler of Oregon and the detectives in Pompano Beach, Florida.

It was the longest, unhappiest Valentine's Day of my life.

Early the next morning, I found Barbra's e-mail to me after she'd spent a wholesome Valentine's Day having pizza with her husband and children. What a different life from mine! Tuesday I retrieved the envelope of documents I had left with Father Foudy when I asked him to help me with the Pompano police. He didn't seem the least concerned about the horror I was living in, but remarked that someone told him that Sgt. Montgomery was "very thorough." I was shell-shocked that Father Foudy accepted such a description of the unseen sergeant who had acted so hateful and, I thought, unprofessional towards me. He made me feel like a fool for asking for help.

I passed on that remark and attitude to Barbra, and we discussed by telephone what I could do to end the mystery, or what I should have done or not done to prevent the attack from Betty and Laura and the Pompano police. We had ended up laughing at the impossibility of foreseeing all eventualities when dealing with crazy people, but we both knew that it was hatred of Catholics behind the language of the letter. She had urged me to get help from my church, but Father Foudy seemed oblivious that there existed extreme anti-Catholic sentiment, or that I was in trouble.

Barbra e-mailed me, "Do not let your priest make you feel foolish. What could you have done earlier? To my knowledge this is the first time anyone has done something to defame you so blatantly. I think it's possible that you will be able to join forces with the Catholic Church, a church that is not poor, to help you sue people who call Catholics satan-worshiping pagans. Run with that, maybe your bishop, if not the parish priest, will see the need for this. You alone will not be taken nearly as serious as you and the Catholic Church together will be. Think about it."

She went on to say that she had no news from Larry's Portland attorney, Pamela Yee, nor from the Lynchburg trust attorney Mr. Lowry, but that she wanted Lowry to know "why I feel strongly that Larry would not want George to receive his father's money at this time." I knew that Barbra was still upset over Larry's distress because of his son's treatment of him. She wrote, "As the only people who talked to Larry and knew how he felt about the estrangement with George, I challenge them to say they knew him better. My devotion to my friend is coupled with my grief that so many people (George and other sisters) pushed him to feel that he had no choice but to escape the pain of their rejection and lack of support. The thing that hurts me is that you and I were not enough."

Her e-mail gave me the courage to contact both Roger and Father Foudy again. Father Foudy just told me to be patient with the police. I e-mailed Roger that Detective Blankenship considered me a suspect in an ongoing criminal investigation based on Laura's letter, and I asked him for guidance. He responded before the end of the day.

Subj: RE: Did I misunderstand you?
Date: 02/15/2001 6:19:14 PM Eastern Standard Time

Carole,

I cannot speak for Detective Blankenship and/or his Office. I can only tell you what I know, and that is as I've told you. I spoke briefly with Det. Blankenship on Monday, 02-12-01, at 9:27 AM, Pacific time, and it was my understanding from what he said that he was closing the case at their end with the receipt of my report, which I FAX'd them the same morning.

I do not believe they consider you a suspect in any murder, or of anything else, for that matter. If they did, I would expect them to have a lot

of questions for me to answer at this end – and they certainly have not communicated anything of the like to me.

Carole, I think your problems are with your sister, or sisters, not the Broward County Sheriff's Office. There is such a thing as "a no-body homicide investigation" – but they are rare and it takes a lot (and I mean a lot) of valid reasons to even attempt such a very difficult investigation –– not a letter accusing someone on the opposite side of the continent of possibly being involved in the disappearance of someone.

To my knowledge the only current investigation involving your family is a Missing Person case here in Washington County, Oregon. Should it turn in to a murder case you most assuredly will hear about it.

As far as our case file reports being released, Carole, the Sheriff's Office (as do most agencies) has a policy not to release reports while the investigation is "on-going" (as they call it) because there are, of course, a lot of unanswered questions – such as, in this case, What has happened to Larry? Know what I mean? But I've tried to keep you, your sister Kay, and Barbra up to date – since you all have stayed in touch.

As far as your father's trustee, and his attorney, believing your sister's letter, I don't know. I told you I spoke with Mr. Loving yesterday and was very impressed with his thoughtfulness – I am under the impression from what he said that he has known your family, including your sisters, for many years.

At any rate, I really must get back to work as we in this profession are usually swamped. If you don't hear from Det. Blankenship don't worry about it.

Take care,
Roger R Mussler, Det. WCSO

At 10:00 p.m., I made one last attempt to reach Charlie. He answered, and his attitude towards me was hostile and closed. He said he knew nothing about the letter, and didn't want to know.

I felt betrayed by my father's trustee; by my father's trust attorney; by the Pompano police; by the pastor of my church; by most of my family. Had Larry felt like this?

Unfortunately, my feeling of betrayal was not yet at the bottom of the pit. Before another week passed, I received two unbelievably hateful e-mails from both my niece Karen and my sister Kay. Out of nowhere, they seemed to have created a new history for Larry, and erased their memories. I had communicated with the authorities in Oregon, as had Kay and my father, regarding Larry's suicide, his health, his letters. No one, not the Oregon detective nor Barbra, nor Kay, nor Daddy, nor Charlie, nor Daddy's church pastor or his neighbors that visited him to console him on the loss of his only son, ever indicated to me that they didn't believe what had happened to Larry.

When the incredible letter to the Pompano police surfaced, Kay and Karen had seemed to be supportive of me; then a few days passed without any communication, and they now seemed to be collaborating in how to be spiteful and *un*supportive. Their e-mails were full of ominous religious connotations, and seemed to indicate that they had together decided that Larry had not, indeed, killed himself!

Had they decided that Daddy imagined it? Had Charlie Loving lied to them? What next?

Terror from every side.

Chapter 6

He proposed another parable to them.
"The kingdom of heaven is like a mustard seed
that a person took and sowed in a field.
It is the smallest of all the seeds,
yet when full-grown it is the largest of plants.
It becomes a large bush, and the 'birds of the sky
come and dwell in its branches.'"

--Matthew 13:31-32

Friday, February 23, 2001

Only one thing had sustained me during the weeks after learning of Larry's suicide: the impending visit of my friend from Lynchburg, Mrs. Helen Barrett. She did not know how instrumental she had been in my life decision to become Catholic. She called me "out of the blue" the day after Barbra found Larry's note, asking to come and visit me. I was thrilled. It was a sudden bright spot in the dark, heavy grief I felt for my brother. When my father died suddenly two weeks later, she attended his services and continued to stay in touch with me when I was feeling so terribly alone.

I talked to Barbra about the impending visit. "I want to put all this mess behind me before my friend, Mrs. Barrett, arrives here. She's a sweet and courageous woman of honor and integrity in spite of raising her children in Lynchburg."

"That's nice to know. A normal family from your home town, Carole?"

"Yes, I suppose normal. But for sure Catholic, in Lynchburg, and lived to talk about it. When people ask me why I became Catholic, I usually begin my story with her. She told me yesterday that she telephoned Charlie for me. She volunteered to bring me some special books I gave my father that Charlie planned to send back to me. She said that he was just as nice as could be and very charming."

"A Virginia gentleman," Barbra snickered. "Is he going to give her the books you wanted?"

Barbra and I had discussed my desire to get some personal mementos of my parents, including some special books I'd recently given my father that he had enjoyed. One was about trains, another about air-

51

planes. Charlie had told me that Kay helped him sort through personal items and put a box together of things for each daughter.

"He told her he wasn't sure he could find them. He previously told me, as did Kay, that they are sitting in a box in my father's living room. Maybe he's forgetful?"

"Sure he is, Carole. So what are you going to do about the enclosures to Laura's letter?"

❧

Barbra's question hung in the air as I walked outside and sat down with the cats, remembering the day after I learned of Larry's suicide. I had been immediately consoled when I heard Mrs. Barrett's voice on the phone. It was the first time she had ever called me, but I instantly recognized her voice from the depths of my shock and grief.

Her call and anticipation of her visit comforted me during the two weeks after Larry's death. Even more after Daddy's death. I had met her during high school, when her sons were on the debate team of the Catholic high school. I was on the team from the white public school. Her prayers meant a lot to me. She had lost her husband a year ago. I did not now want to burden her with the crazy nonsense of the past two weeks.

She had already been helpful by referring me to her sons to get the name of an attorney in Lynchburg, just in case I needed one. It didn't help much, but I learned a valuable and ominous piece of news: Mr. Lowry, the lawyer who lived across the street from my father and thereby became his trust attorney, was also the lead attorney for Jerry Falwell Industries. Regardless of how one viewed the President of the Moral Majority, Jerry Falwell had put Lynchburg on the map, and into world-view via his television evangelism. My father and Jerry had known each other from childhood as second generation Lynchburgers, and had always remained friendly. My father had even served on a Board of one of Falwell's projects. But did Lowry's affiliation with this fundamentalist Bible Belt leader contribute to his apparent sudden antagonism towards me as a Catholic after he got Laura's letter?

Bizarre as it seemed to me living in a more "accepting" culture of California or Florida, it was truly something I needed to consider. I had indeed, as my Aunt Madeline reminded me, been gone from Lynchburg for a long time. I had happily forgotten the extreme prejudice of my childhood.

By 2:00 P.M. I was preparing a special lamb roast dinner to welcome Mrs. Barrett to my home. I picked fresh hibiscus blossoms for arrangements around the house, and put four o'clocks and night-blooming jasmine in her room to scent the tropical evening air. I searched through old boxed files in my garage to find the little pastel blue envelope I had kept throughout the years and during many household moves. I found it. It was postmarked October 10, 1963, and had two five-cent stamps attached. Inside was the notepaper with raised white flowers and a silver "Get Well Soon" on the outer cover. In Mrs. Barrett's neat handwriting, was the message which at that time had puzzled me.

Dear Carole,

I have been thinking about you ever since your mother called.

I reached Larry [author's note: her son] **this morning. He was very concerned about the change in your condition and will be in touch with you, I'm sure.**

Carole, I am enclosing a "miraculous medal" (more than a good luck charm, really). It's an extra one of Larry's; wear it if you will.

Please do not be offended that I offered it to you and I promise not to be offended if you choose not to wear it.

God be with you, you are in our prayers.

Much love,
Mrs. Barrett

I'd tossed the note aside with a vague question mark left deep inside my head.

I kept the miraculous medal in a jewelry chest made by my father. I could still remember as though it were five minutes ago how I had pulled the silver chain out of the envelope with wonder. Why would she send me a necklace when I've been in two hospitals the past seven days? Then I stared at the bas-relief imprint of a woman in a robe, and the inscription printed around the outer edge of the oval disc, "O Mary conceived without sin pray for us who have recourse to Thee." What did that mean? On the backside was a cross on top of the letter "M," with tiny little stars at the outer perimeter, and a couple miniature Valentine hearts at the bottom. Why would anybody send such a piece of jewelry to somebody wearing a hospital gown? I had muttered to myself, "I guess it's some of that Catholic junk." That was thirty-eight years ago.

I was so excited as I left for the airport at 4:30. As I drove, I thought how "miraculous" it was that I still owned that miraculous medal, and that I now understood what it meant. I had not even thought about it or looked at it until ten years after I received it, when my intellectual curiosity led me, along the strangest and most twisted of paths, to the discovery that I believed all my life what millions of other people believed.

Most of my life I had thought I was just an "agnostic Methodist." I'd also grown up with an oversized dose of intellectual arrogance, and one of my favorite intellectual heroes was the Swedish psychologist Carl Jung. When I read his statement in *Answer to Job* that he considered the Catholic dogma of the Assumption, which I'd never heard of, "the most important religious event since the Reformation," I felt both ashamed and intellectually insulted. How could I, always a "straight-A" student, who had studied Western Civilization under the famous Dr. Henry Fowler at the College of William and Mary in 1962 not know this?

I laughed out loud in the car at the thought of my youthful arrogance. The only "assumptions" I had studied were in geometry. I needed a Catholic library to satisfy my curiosity about what Jung's "Assumption" meant. My next-door neighbors in Alabama were Catholic, so I asked them where I could go. They gave me the name of the priest at their church to ask. He invited me to come the following Wednesday to meet with a group of non-Catholics that had similar questions, as he could cover all of them at once. To be polite, I went. That first night turned out to be an "inquiry" class, which led to my choice to become a practicing Roman Catholic.

I was confirmed Catholic in Huntsville Alabama, in January 1973, two days before my business trip to Florida that ended my career. It was the beginning of a new life. I hadn't really "converted" to a different religion; I just discovered serendipitously that I was Catholic all my life in my private beliefs. I had secretly wondered why I often felt uncomfortable in some Christian churches, why I felt like a misfit with my Protestant upbringing. I believed that my new-found faith pulled me through the horrendous circumstances of my arrival in Florida three decades ago.

The experience of choosing Catholicism had been liberating for me, but through the years of comparing my beliefs with born-and-raised Catholics, I recognized great differences of understanding between pre-Vatican II old-timers, and us truly post-Vatican II newcomers. Many Catholics did things by rote without any apparent understanding why, because they'd "always done that since childhood." Always the questioner and the student, I never did anything unless I found a satisfactory answer to "Why?"

I noticed also how many Catholics seemed to put priests up on a pedestal, as though they were superhuman. My Jewish ex-husband and I never had that attitude, and we entertained many priests who seemed perfectly relaxed and at home with us. We both, however, had a memorable experience when we personally met Pope John Paul II in Rome. It electrified us both, and we had agreed that the circumstances surrounding that meeting were beyond the mundane.

We had later laughed about the "lesson" the pastor of my Sunnyvale parish gave us when we talked too much about the experience in his presence. He taught us that the Pope was no different from any other bishop, and all the Catholic Church clergy were basically equal priests serving Christ. It was a point well made to me. I remembered the Presidential election of 1962 when living at home in Lynchburg, I believed with the majority there that if John Kennedy were elected, the Pope would be giving him "orders," and the United States would be doomed to hell, like all those "mackerel-snapping Catholics."

I looked forward to sharing all this with Mrs. Barrett. She knew I'd become Catholic, but she had no idea how or why or when. I had sent her a framed photograph of Pope John Paul II and me together in 1982, and she told me she treasured it.

It was no coincidence that Mrs. Barrett telephoned me the day after I learned of my brother's suicide. I needed her support more than she could imagine. Since Barbra's awful telephone call to me fifty days ago, two major differences in core beliefs between Catholics and Protestants had slapped me in the face. The first Catholic belief was often expressed by the pastor of my Pompano church: Given the creation stories in Genesis, Catholics believe that human beings are created basically good, "very, very good." Many Protestants believe that human beings are basically bad, in need of salvation. Suicide, for some people, is one of the worst sins, and proof of a "bad person."

The second difference is that most Protestants don't pray for the dead, or to the Saints. It was unimaginable to me that Larry's family would not recognize his illness and tragic life, and pray for him now, as never before. But, no one in Virginia expressed interest in a memorial service for him. Instead, it seemed that the family was ashamed that he'd existed.

୨୦୦

The traffic at Fort Lauderdale airport interrupted my thoughts temporarily until I found Mrs. Barrett, and we began sharing all this, and caught up on the years gone by. The time flew from Friday at the airport until Saturday afternoon. We chatted, and dined, and chatted and looked at pictures, and chatted some more. I was scheduled at St. Coleman's church to be a lector at the 4:30 Saturday mass, and a eucharistic minister at the 9:00 children's Sunday mass. Mrs. Barrett loved attending both with me, and I introduced her to Father Foudy.

"What a huge church," Mrs. Barrett commented. "And I could understand your proclamation very well. You didn't seem nervous at all."

"I leave it up to the Holy Spirit, Mrs. Barrett. But the microphone system here is pretty good, too. Now you are the second person from Lynchburg to see me functioning in my little job here."

"Really, Carole? Who else has come to see you?"

"Kay was here, with her family, for thirty-six hours starting New Year's Eve in 1996. They had gotten lost getting off the interstate highway, and just stumbled onto this church, assumed it was the only Catholic church around, and so I must belong here. My brother-in-law was asking for me by name just before the mass started. It was amazing. They even sat through the service, which is probably the only time they set foot in a Catholic church. I don't think they ever realized how unlikely it was that they found me here, that there are huge Catholic churches every five miles, and thousands and thousands of parishion-ers. Few people know my name."

"Well, it is very different being in a town with just one small Catholic parish," Mrs. Barrett began. "I've learned to love our little community in Lynchburg."

We attempted to go sailing Sunday afternoon, and although she was a trooper, her seasickness overtook her best intentions before we were much past the sea buoy. We returned and she quickly got off the boat and took a nap.

Just before I finished closing the boat, I slipped on the compan-ionway steps and took a bad fall. When I got to the house, I found an e-mail message from Barbra, who wrote, "Just wanted to say good morn-ing and I hope you're having a wonderful time with your friend. I guess I am neurotic because I have transferred all my worry-for genes to you since Larry left. I like to hear from you everyday to make sure you're all right. Just an e-mail saying hi, I'm fine. How weird am I?"

I laughed, but picked up the phone and called to tell her to keep her worry genes intact. "I did a really dumb thing a little while ago," I ex-plained about the fall. "I just took a tumble on my boat and smacked my left boob so hard I thought it fell off."

"That's a good trick, Carole. What else have you and your friend been up to?"

We talked about my houseguest, how I almost didn't recognize her at the airport except for her unmistakable Connecticut accent. "She is such a treasure, and so brave to come to visit me. She has traveled be-fore, with her husband, who died exactly one year ago January 18th— the day my father was buried. She gets a little forgetful and disoriented sometimes, and moves with some effort, but she is otherwise very sharp and with it. She retrieved the books I wanted from Charlie in Lynchburg and lugged them with her on the airplane."

"Have you talked to her about our little situation?"

"Last night after the 4:30 mass, uh, excuse me, I meant to say 'cult,' you know, she asked me about the letter Laura wrote. I showed it to her. She couldn't understand it. I read some of the e-mails from Kay and Karen, but she got sleepy and confused. Thought Kay's letter was nice."

"You've got to be kidding."

"It gave me some real insight. First, I realize that Kay and Laura were still close when Kay visited me and saw me at the microphone up front in my church. If she told Laura, which she probably did in an off-hand way, that explains Laura's whole idea that I was a leader giving orders in the Catholic cult. Get it?"

"Yeah, Carole, that probably makes sense in her twisted mind, since she considers all Catholics cultists. And you at a microphone in front of hundreds of people. Sure!"

"I also understand now just how easy it is for people to get con-fused about what has happened to me. Mrs. Barrett suggested that I just let it drop. When I asked her if she meant that I should let the police continue to harass me with their suspicions that I'm a cult leader plan-ning a mass suicide, she seemed shocked and said 'Oh no!'"

"And what does she suggest you do about that, Carole?"

"Just like everybody else, Barbra, she thinks they should tell the truth. Riiiight! Why didn't we think of that? When I told her that I've tried every conceivable alternative to a civil action, but that's all that is left to do, and I need an attorney, she just said 'Oh.' She doesn't want anyone to have to spend any money."

Barbra and I laughed together, but our silence soon confirmed our bewilderment. I wanted to support Barbra in representing Larry, but I could do nothing about the way Charlie and my family were treating her. I told her I planned to call the auction company in Lynchburg to check on the date and set up a method so I could bid by telephone for my father's hand-made furniture, and that perhaps Mrs. Barrett would go there for me. "Charlie called the auction owner a 'lyin'bitch.' She's probably a very nice person."

"Probably, Carole, but I think the Virginia group is pretty well set to do whatever they want. And they don't want outsiders interfering. You or me."

Barbra was right, more than I could know at the time. I foolishly thought that sooner or later the Virginia gang would have to pay atten-tion to Detective Roger Mussler's official report and opinion, and that likewise the Pompano police would soon give up their pursuit of me.

Monday, February 26, 2001

It was Mrs. Barrett's last day in Pompano. I drove her to Boca Raton to meet Catholic friends from my first parish in the 1970's, and we lunched with other friends I'd met in my current parish in 1990. We returned from lunch and Mrs. Barrett took her afternoon nap, as I checked my messages. Barbra had left me a message that sounded ominous.

"Carole, you're not going to believe this. I just got a call from Roger, who said they got a call from a man in Virginia who said he was Larry's uncle. Wanted to check up on Larry. Didn't have a case number, but gave them my telephone number. I didn't know Larry had an uncle anymore. What do you think is going on? Call me."

The next message was even more ominous. I was accustomed to having strange voices on my recorder the past couple weeks, as I traded messages with many attorney offices. It was not surprising when I listened to another male voice.

"Monday, two o'clock," my recorder announced.

"Yeah, Carole, my name is Marvin, uh, give me a call at (954) xxx-xxxx. You had a profile on Yahoo.com that, uh, I'm not sure you're aware of that's got your name and address and everything in it. Uh, anyway, you can reach me at this number, it's local, anywhere between probably 9:00 and 4:30 P.M. Ok. Thanks. Bye."

Suddenly an eerie burning started at the base of my spine and moved upwards. I remembered that the past few weeks, among all the other phone messages and calls, I had received several calls from men using my name as though they knew me. Once I determined it was not an attorney calling back, I just hung up, or they did. A couple of them, however, had identified themselves with first and last names, and acted surprised that I didn't know who they were. This one, Marvin, only gave one name. And Yahoo? I used AOL, not Yahoo. It must be a mistake.

I went to my computer, and entered my own name under "search." The only thing that came up was the obituary for my father. I went to a Yahoo page and tried again. Nothing. It was almost 4:30, so I decided to call the number given, cautiously, just to check it out.

Marvin told me that he was a neighbor, and during lunch one day, he and his work associates were cruising the internet when my name and address popped up. He recognized that my address was close to his own home.

"No one ever uses their real name and address on the internet, Carole."

"Really? I don't know that much about it. I just use it for e-mail and financial news. But you said it was on Yahoo, and I don't subscribe to Yahoo."

"Well, it's definitely on Yahoo, and it's your name, address, and telephone number, uh, among other things," Marvin's voiced cracked slightly.

"Before I called you, I tried to find it, but nothing comes up when I search."

"Oh, uh, that's probably because, uh, you have to get into the site," Marvin explained. "You need a password."

"I enter my password at the beginning...."

"No, uh, no, not just to get on. It's uh, well, we get it at work, here, uh, I don't know how to explain..."

"Well, can you access it on any computer, for instance, mine?"

"Yeah, uh, sure. Uh, but you need to be a member of Yahoo..."

"But I'm not! I only have AOL. Are you saying you could show it to me, here?"

"Look, uh, I don't know how to say this, but uh, I can tell you my name, and describe my truck and give you the license number, too, if you'd like for me to come over and find it for you," Marvin offered, sounding both timid and nervous.

Mrs. Barrett was sleeping. With her here, what harm could there be? "Sure, that would be nice, if you think it's really my name." I still thought there must be some mistaken identity. The man sounded straightforward on the phone, and he certainly was willing to identify himself to me.

Marvin came to my door just as Mrs. Barrett was stirring in her bedroom. Before I opened the door, I told her briefly that a neighbor was coming to show me something on my computer. He introduced himself and gave me his business card. He was tall, attractive, well dressed and well spoken. I showed him to my computer in the living room and he sat down.

"It'll take just a minute for me to access the Yahoo site," he talked as he typed.

Mrs. Barrett came into the living room and I introduced her. He seemed to blush, stood up and shook hands with her, then sat down again. "Ok, ok, I think I've got it now," he sounded excited, but subdued. "Uh, uh, there are quite a few pages here, and uh, I have to scroll through them." He seemed antsy. Suddenly he stood up, looked at his watch and said, "You know, uh, I'm going to be late if I don't leave now, but you can find it, I'm sure. Just keep hitting this arrow," he pointed to the screen and moved the cursor, "until you find it. You can't miss it. It's the only page that has an address and telephone number, and I'm sure it'll jump out at you. There are some 40 pages, I think, so just keep going till you find it. Uh, and you have my number if you want to call me."

He couldn't leave fast enough. Mrs. Barrett had a puzzled look on her face as I walked him to the door and locked it behind him.

"Who did you say that is?" she asked me. "A neighbor? And he teaches computers?"

"No, no, he left a message while we were at lunch to say there is a website that belongs to me..." I sat down and stared at the screen. "But it doesn't make any sense, and I couldn't find it. He came over to show it to me, and said it must be here," I explained while scrolling through page after page of weird names that linked elsewhere. I barely read the screen, scanning quickly for my own address. Page after page, and suddenly, sure enough, Marvin said it would jump out at me, and it did, at the 18th page.

There, indeed, was my address in the lower middle of the page, sandwiched between "IHUNGWELL" and, "If it's wet, LICK IT!" I sat staring in disbelief, then my eyes focused on the statement to the right of my address, an invitation: "anyone interested in sex-partying on my yacht? E-mail me!"

What was this? I looked at the top of the page, and the heading was **SEX PARTNERS IN FLORIDA**, followed by FLORIDA RESIDENTS FIND DISCREET SEX PARTNER, followed by Yahoo! Clubs. Beneath the word Members was printed "Listing members 341-360 of 787, Page 18 of 40." The headings of the columns were on the next line: **Members--Yahoo! ID | Age | Gender | Location | Comment.** My eyes searched quickly down the columns, spotted my address, age, and gender, then rested on the one word "imasophistmaster." I was scared to double click to see where it went. Mrs. Barrett came and stood beside me at the computer, so I hurriedly clicked it to get the nastiness of the current page off the screen.

"What is it, Carole? Are you ok?" She sounded concerned.

"Uh, no, uh, I don't know. I just don't....can't....believe this."

Imasophistmaster's profile page came up on the screen, with the notation: Last Updated February 3, 2001. "Ohmigosh, it's been in here for several weeks, at least. Oh, oh, no wonder I've been getting the strange phone calls....ohmigosh, oh no, oh my...." There was my full name, telephone number, address, age, plus "Divorced," "Female," and "Occupation: Independently wealthy/retired." The lump in my throat began to choke me as I continued reading the next heading.

More About Me

Hobbies: sailing, sunbathing on my yacht; investing; collecting antiques, turning other's misfortunes into my profits

Latest News: Am about to acquire large inheritance (e-mail me privately for details)

Favorite Quote

"Your world is whatever you create it to be; you deserve the power and profit that others owe you!"

"Carole, who was that man? What did he tell you? Why are you upset?" Mrs. Barrett kept asking, sensing my awful reaction.

"It's a web page, Mrs. Barrett. And it's a hoax. Someone is trying to impersonate me, and this man is a neighbor who found it and came to warn me about it. He's doing me a favor, really, I guess."

"Well are your doors locked? Shouldn't you shut your windows?" her fear showed.

"No, no, don't you worry. Look, let's just shut this down for now. I don't want to waste our time on it. How about we drive over to the beach?"

Chapter 7

"Be gracious to me, Lord, for I am in distress;
with grief my eyes are wasted,
my soul and body spent....
To all my foes I am a thing of scorn,
to my neighbors, a dreaded sight,
a horror to my friends."   --Psalm 31: 10,12

After we returned from the beach, Mrs. Barrett went to bed, but not before admonishing me to lock all my doors and windows. It was a beautiful, warm February night in the subtropics, and a gentle breeze wafted through my open doors and windows. I worried how stressed she was by the afternoon's events and tried to downplay her fears.

She locked herself in her room, the windows closed. It must have been close to 86 degrees in there. As for me, my underlying terror was palpable.

I refused to give in to fear. I quietly used a phone far from Mrs. Barrett's hearing to call the police and report the websites. Not allowed! I explained about the previous case number and asked if I could simply add information to that. No. A uniformed officer would have to come out to my house.

"Not tonight, no, uh, no, I have a houseguest. Can I make an appointment for tomorrow morning?"

The answer was a simple no. I would have to call back whenever I could sit and wait. I complained that there had been no follow-up to my report two weeks ago, but the nameless person on the phone said, "It takes a few days to get to the detectives."

Patience. I needed patience, not fear. I checked my phone messages, which had stacked up while I was visiting with Mrs. Barrett. Five different law firms in Virginia had returned my last week's calls, in which I had briefly summarized the police accusations followed by the sudden change in attitude and behavior of my father's trustee. I had asked for help. But each simply recommended another attorney and wished me good luck. A notable exception came from a libel specialist in Charlottesville, who stated, "You have a good case, and huge. Don't give up, but beware of disreputable libel attorneys out there."

I wondered what he'd think now that the websites seemed so similar in language to the letter the Pompano police received. Those websites were posted all over the world. Is that "more huge?" I had book-marked the web page I found earlier after my neighbor's departure, so I went back to it and printed out a copy. It seemed worse than at first glance. I noticed for the first time the column of blue print with blue underscores. They were "links" to other web pages, so that a person looking at that page could just "click" on any of those lines and automatically go to another web page.

There were links all over the place, under each "Interest" category. I began reading down the list: "Lesbian, Gay and Bisexual, Furniture, New Age, Philosophy of Mind, Bisexual, Age Play." I shivered and stopped. I didn't have the courage or energy to start tracking the links. But I had to get this stuff off the internet, now!

I searched and found "Yahoo! Messenger," a link to report problems. I "clicked" on it, and an e-mail form popped up. I e-mailed Yahoo! Messenger to take down all pages that contained anything about me—that I had not done it and wanted my name and personal information removed.

Soon afterwards I found an e-mail from Barbra. She wrote that my sister Kay called her and chatted. Nothing important, just a "social call." She was surprised that Kay had carefully avoided mentioning either Charlie, Daddy's trustee, or anything related to the trust. Barbra speculated about the coincidental timing of Kay's chatty call and the "fake uncle" call to the police in Oregon. I had forgotten about that!

The horrible discovery of the website with its widespread impersonation of me made the "impersonating uncle" pale in comparison. Barbra's e-mail reminded me of Kay's (and my niece Karen's) sudden reversal of attitude towards me exhibited in their e-mails sent a week before. They had consistently refused to call me by telephone and have direct communication. Why? Charlie refused to communicate directly with Barbra. Why? There seemed to be a huge invisible triangle, more ominous than the infamous Bermuda Triangle, between Oregon, Virginia, and Florida. Facts and people seemed to drop into a swirling whirlpool and spin out in the most unpredictable directions.

I e-mailed Barbra to tell her about the websites, and commented on the similarity of language between the letter to the Pompano police and the phrases used on the web page. Did the same sister create both? I asked her to get more information about the "fake uncle" call, since impersonation seemed to be the name of the game. I hit the "Send" button and looked back at the list of incoming e-mails. There was a response from Yahoo! Messenger already. Unfortunately, it was generated automatically and did not address my problem. I wrote again:

Subj: Please answer my message---Yahoo! Messenger
Date: 02/26/2001

Dear Yahoo;

Thank you for your quick response, but it was not to my question/complaint. I DO NOT HAVE A YAHOO ACCOUNT. Someone has set up a total profile (false, about me) on one of your pornographic sites.

I need to know what police/FBI/whatever can trace the person who has done this. It includes my personal address and telephone number and I am afraid I am now being stalked as a result. This is extremely urgent.

Please call me, or e-mail me the phone number for Yahoo where my local police department can reach you about this matter.

I needed sleep. Was I getting paranoid, or was it possible that all those Virginians, Charlie included, had decided to make me a murderer rather than accept Larry's suicide? And who, besides the author or authors of the letter to the Pompano police could dream up those dreadful web pages? I fell into bed, praying the fear away.

In the morning, I went out to water the plants in my yard, but Mrs. Barrett came to the door and called to me, "Carole, don't you think you should come back in? Is it safe for you to go outdoors like that?"

I felt awful that her trip was ending on such a fearful note. We had breakfast, then drove to the Deerfield Beach Amtrak station. Neither of us mentioned the website. While we waited for the train, I took some snapshots. I hated to see her leave. I needed her strength and goodness and transparence that seemed like a life saver thrown to me as I was getting sucked down and down into a whirling dark pool. I hugged her goodbye and let go reluctantly. I kissed her and she boarded the train as I fought back the tears, grateful for the sunny day and my sunglasses.

This was reminiscent of the emotions I felt when I said good-bye to my own mother at the residence care facility in Lynchburg in 1995. Mother never did know who I was during that visit, but she was so happy to go out with me each day. She sang songs whenever I played the piano, but the night before my departure, as I played and she sang in the hallway, her fragility triggered in me a premonition that I'd never see her alive again.

And I didn't. Not because she died shortly thereafter, but because within months my health had so deteriorated that I was not able to travel to see her again. Now, Mrs. Barrett looked so small and fragile. I waved to her as the train departed, then walked as fast as I could to the car and sat and wept uncontrollably for the next ten minutes.

The bone-crushing loneliness of losing all my family, of feeling betrayed wherever I turned for help, and the latest attack by strangers using the hideous website I'd just discovered made me want to die. Did Larry feel like this?

I tried to remember my favorite Psalm 31, but my mind was blank except for "In you, Lord, I take refuge....In your justice deliver me..." I gradually got the sobbing under control and started the car. What next? As I drove home, I mentally reviewed what was happening. Clearly, I needed to stay alert. I could not wish away the letter to the police nor ignore the websites. I had no control over what was happening, and I needed help.

Who could tell me more about the websites? I had friends who seemed to know a lot about computers and the internet, so I stopped by their house and confided what had happened. I hated to show the web page to anyone else, but I had to get help.

The reaction I received sent daggers through me. My friends acted offended that I would be in such a pickle. First a letter to the police and now this? I suddenly became the object of their suspicion. I was devastated. They told me to "straighten it out" with the police. Certainly, if *I* hadn't done something wrong, the police would be able to track down the creator of those pages.

I arrived home from the train station weighed down with dread and loneliness. At 10:00 A.M. I called the Pompano police, also known as the Broward Sheriff's Office, or BSO for short. They said someone would come immediately. I checked my e-mail while I waited. Barbra had been unable to find the web pages. I found them on my computer again, and cautiously explored some of the links. It was sickening.

Thirty minutes passed before the doorbell rang, and Officer Carl Spear arrived to take my information about the websites. I showed him to my computer so that he could see for himself. He seemed more interested in looking at the website's salacious content than in listening to my fears about the consequences for me. I shuddered when I saw the key statement that I considered the main clue to the author's identity. "Latest News: Am about to acquire large inheritance (e-mail me privately for details.)" Who could have written that except for someone in my family who knew of my father's death? And really, who except the family members who had access to the trust documents could know anything about my father's estate? Only Kay, Betty, Laura, and Charlie. And I didn't believe Kay capable of doing anything like this.

As Officer Spear stared at the screen, my eyes focused on the words, "**More About Me** Hobbies: sailing, sunbathing on my yacht; investing, collecting antiques, turning other's misfortunes into my profits." Wasn't that similar to Laura's letter to the police? That I had "amassed considerable wealth through decades of deceit and manipulation of other people?" She had written in that letter about me that, "She currently has a home and yacht in Florida." Who else would call my old little sailboat a yacht?

I pointed out to Officer Spear that the web page, which I printed out for him, was posted world wide with many other possible links.

"Did you notify Yahoo about this, Miss Fielder?"

I showed him the e-mails to and from <u>Yahoo! Messenger</u>. I told him that I had received multiple strange phone calls recently. I had also ignored a large number of cars full of guys driving by, who screamed obscenities out of the windows accompanied with assorted gestures. There was lots of traffic in front of my house all the time, so I hadn't paid much attention, but I had wondered vaguely if some unknown women neighbors had moved in recently to attract such types. Now, I told him, the websites provided a possible explanation of all that activity.

He basically ignored me, but agreed that the letter and the websites were similar. He took a copy of the web page to ask his superiors whether or not it was a crime. He didn't think so, but said it was hard evidence for a civil action should I want to initiate one. He suggested I call a local criminal attorney in order to subpoena the BSO for the attachments to Laura's letter.

"How can I do that? A lawyer can't issue a subpoena without initiating a case. What is the charge? What crime? My case apparently is libel and slander created by a person or persons in Virginia. Meanwhile, I'm the one in danger in Florida because of their actions, and I need help in Florida." I wanted to cry.

He shrugged and suggested I call the FBI. He told me to call "911" every time I saw anyone in my yard I didn't know, and he recommended I hire a local civil attorney to sue Yahoo if they didn't get back to me with the information. He gave me a case number, and departed.

It was gradually dawning on me that the letter to the police was nothing compared to the internationally posted websites. It was a one-two punch. The second one was the knockout punch. Had the people in Virginia masterminded this plan to harm me? But which people, exactly? And why? Why was I so important to any of those virtual strangers that they should go to such extreme measures to get at me?

I e-mailed Yahoo again with the same message, but included the police case number. Within the hour, I got another automated response back, so I wrote them for the third time.

Subj: Re: Yahoo! Messenger
Date: 02/27/2001

To: messenger-abuse@yahoo-inc.com

PLEASE stop responding with your form letter. It is not relevant to this crime going on your site!

PLEASE track this person and get back to me immediately, as well as to the police. What is taking you so long??????

Next, I tackled the call to the FBI. Finding a local number to call was a challenge. I finally found a live person in the Miami office, but she said that the FBI could not initiate anything that the local police did not report first. If the police did not report a crime, it was a civil matter. Another circle. I needed an attorney.

I had been participating in a discussion group at my church, and my regular meeting was scheduled for the afternoon. One of the women in the group, with whom I shared what was happening to me, convinced me I should go ask Father Foudy again to intervene with the police, or ask him to recommend an attorney. I went to the rectory, told the receptionist briefly what was happening, and that I was desperate to hire an attorney to defend my participation at St. Coleman's Church against the incredible accusations that I was a cult leader. She disappeared for a moment, and came back saying Father Foudy didn't know of anything he could do.

"Doesn't he remember the name of the attorneys he used?" I stared at her. It was well known that he had high-powered attorneys to defend him in his slanderous ordeal several years before. "Thanks. Thanks for all the help." I turned and walked out, angry at myself that I had bothered to ask for help again.

In the parking lot, I was commiserating with a friend, when another acquaintance of mine from church came running towards me with a message from Father Foudy. "Carole, Father asked me to ask you to come back. He really wants you to come back to the rectory."

"Why?"

"I don't know. He said it was important and asked me to catch up with you."

I shrugged and headed back to the rectory. When I entered the office, he told me his attorney was on the phone, to follow him to a back office to speak with him.

Within sixty seconds I regretted my effort. Father Foudy disappeared. The attorney talked down to me as though I were the village idiot. He didn't offer to set an appointment. I briefly told him about the letter to the police and their continued withholding of its enclosures, and the websites containing language similar to the letter but issuing invitations to the world of internet porn to come to my house. He didn't offer any legal advice. He didn't say a word about the criminal nature of website impersonation. He just said he couldn't help me. I hung up and walked out without a word. What was the use?

When I arrived home, I received an e-mail of more bad news from the Lynchburg attorney that Mrs. Barrett had helped me find.

Subj: legal issues
Date: 02/27/2001 1:33:27 PM Eastern Standard Time

I do not recommend filing a libel lawsuit in VA since you cannot travel to VA to participate in the case. My previous e-mail was limited to the trust issues surrounding your father's estate.

If I couldn't travel, I could not even consider getting justice. No handicapped access to the courts in Virginia for me, for sure.

No help from friends, no help from the police, no help from

church, no help from lawyers. I was so discouraged when I saw an e-mail from Barbra. She had a new suggestion, and wrote, "If there is no other way, CALL THE ENQUIRER. Tell them that you cannot get a lawyer to pay attention to you. They might be interested enough to get involved."

Given the looks of disbelief and suspicion I had encountered, I suspected my story seemed too incredible even for the *National Enquirer* to believe. I e-mailed Barbra with my discouraging news and the creeping credibility problem. I asked her again to find out from Detective Mussler who had called pretending to be Larry's uncle. I wrote, "It *is* impersonation. If it's Charlie, why??… I certainly can't figure out anything from here. I've got no help, even after speaking to my pastor's attorney. He apparently didn't believe me."

While I was writing to Barbra, my neighbor Marvin called. He brought me a print-out of the scurrilous profile of me, as well as other linked pages. It looked worse and worse with every printed page. (See **Appendix I** for sample web pages.)

It turned out that "Imasophistmaster" was corresponding with porno-interested men, impersonating me, leading them on, inviting them to my house for specific *rendez-vous*, etc. Marvin had found out online in real time: the power of "instant-messaging" (IM's).

That knowledge frightened me into redoubling my efforts to hire an attorney—no matter who, no matter where. This had to stop. I followed every lead for an attorney in Virginia, from Virginia Beach to Lynchburg, to Roanoke, to Richmond. The next few days seemed to go by with me being caught in the spin-dry cycle of a clothes washer, only it was the spinning of telephone calls trying to hire an attorney, or get help from the police. It started slowly, then got faster and faster. Tha-whump, tha-whump, whirrrr. Ring, ring, ring.

৩৹৵

ASH WEDNESDAY, February 28, 2001

It was a beautiful winter morning when I awoke to the sound of the telephone ringing. Mrs. Barrett called to say she arrived safely in Daytona after the longest train ride of her life. I encouraged her to take good care of herself and get home to Lynchburg, because Barbra and I needed her to help us. She laughed good-naturedly.

I took my first cup of tea outside to survey my flowers. My heart sank when I saw that my Thunbergia vine, once healthy and climbing a palm tree, concealing the guide wires to a utility pole, had withered. I inspected the base and saw the cuts a couple feet from the ground. Someone must have come in with bolt cutters. I didn't want to think about vandalism. It was too close. Getting closer all the time. I remembered hearing voices that sounded close by last night after I went to bed, but I assumed they belonged to my neighbors.

I went inside to call the utility company. I hoped that they had done it. But when? It had been intact late yesterday afternoon with a beautiful display of cascading purple blossoms. After Florida Power and Light Company checked their records and assured me they had not cut through the thirty-five-foot-high vine, I called the BSO police, again.

While waiting and fighting back the fear, I e-mailed Barbra and wrote, "Happy Belated Mardi Gras! Hope you had a wonderful dinner last night. We *cultists* have to fast today."

Knowing that Barbra was unfamiliar with Catholicism, and Larry had passionately hated Catholics, I tried to demystify some of the practices I remembered were sore points with the Bible Belt folks. Ashes placed on Catholics' foreheads always created questions and dissension to outsiders, who would often wonder why a business associate had a "dirty face." Today was supposed to be a quiet day of reflection that we will one day be the food of worms in the ground. "Remember, man, that you are dust, and to dust you shall return." I explained to Barbra that it was not a Holy Day of Obligation, but was popular because of the powerful symbol that the ashes represent.

I had long ago concluded that doing things by rote, especially things that look like magic or secret rituals to outsiders, with no apparent logical explanation, is fundamentally what creates fear and prejudice. Any minority religious group that appears to exclude the general population is subject to the same thing. I reminded Barbra of what happened in Australia to Lindy Chamberlain, who was sent to prison for murder basically because she belonged to an unpopular religion. I tried to explain that although we Catholics are an inclusive group, it's not our habit to run up and shake hands, smile, and encourage any visitor to come back and join up, as I had experienced in many non-Catholic churches as a child. What might seem cold-shouldered at first is simply the Catholic culture of "live and let live," and no proselytizing. Quite different from my childhood experiences!

I couldn't help but wonder if the letter to the police, and the websites, were all prompted by that historic distrust between the religions. I'd been gone from Lynchburg and the Bible Belt mentality for a long time. Under the circumstances, however, maybe not long enough or far enough away. Barbra agreed.

The doorbell rang and I greeted Officer Carl Spear once again. "We've got to stop meeting this way." I wasn't sure he appreciated my humor.

"So what is it this time, Miss Fielder?"

I showed him the base of the vine, and told him of the voices I'd heard but ignored last night. I asked him about follow-up to my previous two reports, and his assessment of the danger.

"Oh, that has to be handled by the detectives. We don't get into that, Miss Fielder."

"Do you know the names of the detectives in charge? I called the FBI at your suggestion, but they said the police had to initiate a criminal action. So to whom can I speak about that?"

Spear shrugged, "I imagine they'll assign someone who will call you."

He didn't seem concerned that there might be a connection between the incidents. Were the police today so specialized and compartmentalized that there was no place for common sense? When did the detectives plan to follow up? After another vandalism? After the lowlifes responding to the websites entered my house? When? I felt like a "sitting duck" in a pond waiting for the hunters to shoot.

Better to get back into the spin-dry cycle of calling for lawyers. Thawump, whirr. I had connected with one local attorney interested in my case, but we both speculated that the websites and letter had the same author. The libel in the letter to the Pompano police required jurisdiction in Virginia, so he advised me to get a Virginia attorney. I e-mailed him as soon as Officer Spear left to ask if the now-obvious danger to me might yield a legal reason for Florida jurisdiction. I told him of my frustration at getting no real response from Yahoo, and no help from the FBI. I added that the police would not do anything until I was physically harmed. I reluctantly offered to fax him the web pages my neighbor had printed out, provided no one else would see them. I explained that my neighbor had engaged the internet impersonator in instant messaging, and I was desperate to stop the dangerous invitations online.

I went outside and wandered around my yard, thinking, weeding, praying, pruning. How could I, the ex-wife of a Silicon Valley executive, be pushed into a state of helplessness over a computer problem? The culture of the '80's in Silicon Valley, California, did not use the phrase "computer problem." There was no such thing. There were people problems, organizational glitches, programming errors, garbage in and garbage out, and occasional hardware failures. Nothing was impossible. Nothing unsolvable. Define the challenge. Meet it. Change it. Do it right. And always, always, the first step involved one word: START.

I marched inside to my computer, went to the Yahoo Financial Pages, looked up Yahoo Corporation, and wrote down the address and telephone number of the Yahoo Chief Executive Officer (CEO). If anybody could get rid of the nasty websites I wanted removed, he could. After all, without Yahoo Corporation, the pages couldn't exist. I began calling at 11:30 in the morning, and kept a log of numbers and names. It turned into another spin-dry cycle.

Calls to Yahoo! Feb. 28, 2001

1130	(408) 731-3300	Asked for CEO and was given # to call.
1133	(408) 616-3637	Cathy McGoff recording, left message to call back.
1135	(408) 731-3300	Asked for President's office. Refused. Asked for legal.
1137	(408) 328-7941	Attorney Josh Russell recording.
1141	(408) 731-3300	Asked for Tim Koogle, CEO; recording by Luna, left message.
1143	(408) 731-3300	Asked for Susan Decker, CFO; reached live Sondra, who tried to find someone. Said to call back in one hour when someone would be at work. Meanwhile gave me number of John Zent.
1150	(408) 820-0976	Left detailed message, then called pager of John Zent.
1151	(408) 328-7781	Entered my tel. # on Zent's pager.

John Zent called back shortly thereafter. Progress! He asked me to forward to him all the e-mails I had sent and received from Yahoo so far, and he'd try to get the offensive web pages down as soon as possible. The CEO's assistant, Sue Florimonte, called me too, expressing her

concern and offering me her direct phone number. She explained, however, that Yahoo could not reveal to me the name of the person who
had created the websites without a court order. I needed to sue Yahoo
in order to protect myself.

Moments later, Detective Roger Mussler called me from Oregon.
He had previously spoken with Barbra about the impersonating "uncle"
call and the pornographic websites impersonating me. A police dispatcher's note showed simply "Uncle Kingwood Ill," with Betty's
phone number attached. Barbra figured it must be King, Betty's husband, so Roger called and spoke to them, giving them the same
information he'd given us over the past six weeks. It was King who had
pretended to be an uncle to Larry! Who knew why? Simply to avoid
speaking to Barbra or to me or to Kay to get direct information? That
impersonation was resolved, but it made me wonder if Betty or King
were impersonating me online.

Roger told them that everyone was "hopeful" that Larry was still
alive and might show up someday, but that in his professional opinion,
it was unlikely.

"Gosh, Roger, if you used the word 'hope' to them, they'll twist it
backwards and forwards in their Virginia lingo to prove that I did
something wrong by passing on the news that he was gone. Please call
them and be very specific that you do *not* think Larry is alive. I hear
that Kay has misquoted both you and Barbra about the circumstances of
finding Larry's vacant apartment and suicide note."

"Oh Carole, is that possible?"

"It seems so, Roger. With the letter to the police and the website
language so similar, it must all come from the same mindset. But I am
making progress with Yahoo." I explained the legal steps required of
me, and he sympathized and offered to help. I felt better, but I still
needed an attorney.

I called the Florida attorney I had earlier e-mailed and left a message, asking, "Do you have time to file a suit against Yahoo (which is
what Yahoo instructed me to do) immediately, here in Florida? They
need the police case numbers (there are 3 now), the nature of endangerment and damages to me, and a court case number in order to
release the name of the culprit--under court order. If you can't do it,
will you recommend someone who will?"

Back into the spin-dry cycle of telephone calls, I talked to Barbra,
who gave me a great idea: go online and search for an attorney. I did,

made more calls, got more referrals, but finally, I found one in Fort Lauderdale under the category "internet crime specialist." SHE AGREED TO SEE ME AT THE END OF THE DAY!

Chapter 8

"A lawsuit devours the tillage of the poor,
but some men perish for lack of a law court."
                                    --Proverbs 13:23

I felt relieved after all the hours spinning around in marathon telephone calls, but my father's admonition still rang in my head: "If you need a lawyer, you've already lost."

Excited by the prospect that the Fort Lauderdale attorney would help me, I sat down to e-mail Barbra, and found one from her. "We had an earthquake while you and I talked on the phone yesterday. Actually, it was in Seattle, Washington. But we felt it down here in Portland. I thought that I felt something, then decided that it was quick dizzy sinus thing, so didn't mention it to you."

I wrote Barbra back immediately. "Are you still shaking? I'm rushing out the door to give an attorney $2500 to get the name of the people who put me on that vile website. She can't handle trust issues, may not be able to do all the libel involved, but thinks she can force the BSO to give me the enclosures to Laura's letter, and force Yahoo to reveal the Yahoo user who posted the sites. Says if it has to go to Federal Court, may cost me at least $10,000. (oh dear) If your computer wasn't damaged in the quake, you can still find the web page by going directly to the URL, (the Universal Resource Locator), I gave you. Just type that URL in the skinny line near the top of your computer screen," I tried to explain, "then go to page 18."

I was a novice at the internet, and so was Barbra, but I was forced to learn faster and more than I ever wanted. I never dreamed that there were lawyers who were "internet specialists."

When I walked into Leah Mayersohn's office overlooking the Bahia Mar Marina in Fort Lauderdale, the view took second place to the beautiful, young blonde attorney. She looked like a freshly scrubbed, wholesome teenager. We shook hands and I collapsed into a seat in a heap, handed her the letter from Laura and the web pages, which she immediately read.

"Oh my god! Oh, oh, this is awful!" she looked up at me over the page. "I can't believe how well you're holding up under all this." She continued reading.

I frowned in surprise at her comment. I felt like a big mess, black shadows under my eyes, disheveled hair, frumpy, wrinkled dress that showed the strains of the long day. "I didn't think I was holding up at all," I smiled weakly at her.

She quickly sized up the situation and laid out her plan for me. She picked up the phone and called Detective Roger Mussler in Oregon, spoke directly with him, and requested that he fax to her a letter about his investigation. She called my neighbor Marvin, and left him a message to please call her back, that she represented me, thanked him for helping me protect myself, for being "a Good Samaritan," and wanted to ask him a few questions.

Next, she called the State Attorney's office to inquire about any police report regarding me. They were closed. She then typed up a contract, and I paid her the $2500 with a check. She advised me to continue my search for a Virginia attorney for both the libel and the malfeasance of trusteeship issues. She would not know until later if the police letter libel issue could be moved to Florida, pending the outcome of an emergency court order she would seek in the Broward court. She hoped to get the necessary information from the BSO or State Attorney's office. She agreed that the websites appeared to have the same author as the letter signed by Laura, but we couldn't know for sure until Yahoo! Corporation notified us officially.

After our discussion, she gave me several assignments: (1) create a narrative of the chronology of events; (2) make copies of all the family correspondence, including Larry's letters; and (3) find all of the websites containing my personal information by checking out each "interest" link. As I was leaving, she reminded me to keep trying to call my "Good Samaritan" neighbor Marvin. She also listed our priorities: first, secure my safety; second, identify the perpetrators of the endangering impersonation; third, stop them. Two hours had passed quickly.

When I arrived home I found an e-mail from Yahoo's John Zent, whose attempt at humor left me flat, with his "have a great day! ☺" smiley face and his question "do you Yahoo!?" I e-mailed him that the "*Imasophistmaster*" page was accessible to anyone, and I wanted it removed immediately. I asked him to notify me and my attorney, Leah Mayersohn, as soon as it was taken down.

I left a telephone message for Marvin, then e-mailed Barbra that the situation was in hand but becoming "curiouser and curiouser." I fell into bed exhausted, but hopeful.

The next morning I found Barbra's e-mail. She was recovering from both the earthquake aftershocks and her dental problems. I laughed out loud at her conclusion, "We need to live in Shangri-la. That would buffer us from natural disasters as well as man-made disasters (unpredictable family members.) Maybe Mayberry, North Carolina would be nice. Escaping into 1960's television! What a solution."

It would be nice to escape into a saner world, for sure. I had to jump back into the spin-dry whirl of telephone calls hunting for a Virginia attorney, and calling BSO to follow up on my previous reported incidents. My personal information was still online, and I was tired from spending seventy-two very difficult hours that also included additional incoming phone calls --who usually hung up when I answered; hyper-gonadic cruisers driving by my house; and vandalism. Any escape sounded very inviting.

The only bright spot was the co-operation from my neighbor. Marvin called as soon as he got the messages from me and from Leah. He had been working all night at a power plant, but he definitely wanted to help me. If responders to the websites and instant message (IM) conversations came into the neighborhood cruising for a good time or a pay off, I was *not* the only one in danger. My neighbors, including Marvin and his family, would also be subject to the same kind of strangers. Marvin asked me what the police were doing about it. Oops.

I called the police non-emergency number to find out which detectives were assigned to my various case numbers. That began a furious spin cycle of calls to at least nine different voices. Whirrr. Whirrr. Whirrrr. Finally, I was told I'd have to get a uniformed officer to come out to answer any question I might have. Again. Another one.

Why not cut to the chase by putting the Pompano police officer in direct touch with Yahoo? It was practically miraculous that BSO's Officer Mellies was driving up at the same time the corporate attorney for Yahoo, Josh Russell, returned my call. At first Josh acted as though he knew nothing of my previous e-mails and calls, but after I repeated my story, he gave me his direct telephone number in case I needed to call him again.

"Carole, you need to get the local police to send a subpoena or search warrant, with all the particulars. It doesn't have to be formal. **We handle lots of these cases every day.** We'll get started taking down everything immediately. In fact, the police can simply write it on paper and fax it to (408) 328-7941, then follow up with a mailed hard copy." He gave me the address in Santa Clara for the Yahoo Custodian of Records.

I breathed a sigh of relief, and continued on the phone as I opened the door for Officer Mellies. It seemed so simple and quick. The police officer could use the fax machine in my kitchen immediately to send the URL of the websites and the police case number to the Yahoo office.

Josh Russell explained that a criminal subpoena was preferable to a civil one, and a much speedier process. My tax dollars should pay for this service. Why should I have to pay out big bucks to a private attorney? While we were still on the phone, Josh, from his end, had been zapping out some of the websites, and announced, "I think they're all gone now."

I thanked him and nodded to Officer Mellies as I said, "Josh, I have a policeman standing right here. I'll give him the fax number you just gave me, so you should have some of the paperwork shortly." I turned to Officer Mellies and offered him the phone. "This is the legal counsel at Yahoo Corporation in California, Officer."

He put his hands palms up and shook his head, saying, "No, no, I don't want to speak to anybody."

I thanked Josh again and hung up, expecting to follow up with Officer Mellies. He acted as though he had no idea what I was talking about, didn't know why he was sent out to my house, did not have any of the previous reports. I tried to cut through the detail, and just relay to him what the attorney at Yahoo had just told me.

"There's a fax machine in my kitchen you can use, Officer, to send the required information to Yahoo and get this process going."

"Oh no, I can't do that. I can't send anything. You'll have to call the State Attorney's office."

"I do? Why didn't they tell me that when I called the police station?"

"I don't know anything about that. We just make the reports and the detectives get assigned to the cases, Miss Fielder."

"But that's what my call was about today. Assigning a detective to my previous reports before more damage occurs." I was getting exasperated. "You know, these websites have been posted *at least* since early February; I learned about them Monday, filed the report Tuesday, had vandalism yesterday. What's the problem? This is a dangerous situation and must be remedied immediately before anything worse happens. Why didn't the police on the telephone tell me to call the State Attorney? Do you have the number?"

Officer Mellies had been sitting on the arm of my living room chair gazing with interest at some of the salacious websites. I seemed to startle him with my question. He finally looked up, groped through several pockets and came up with the number for the Broward County State Attorney, Michael Satz.

"Can't you call for me so I don't have to repeat every police report made this week?"

"No, I can't do that."

"Then why are you here? Why did I have to make another appointment to make another report about the same problem? I don't get it."

"Well, if you want to start at the beginning and tell me what happened today..."

I interrupted him. This was going nowhere. I asked him to leave. He gave me a new case number.

I immediately called the State Attorney's office, but found myself in another spin cycle of telephoning. Four or five names and voices passed me around, each one taking the same basic information from me—name, address, telephone number, why I was calling, what the case number was—on and on it went round and round. I described the internet impersonation and the danger it created until I sounded like a tape recording to my own ears.

The day's spinning of nonstop phone calls got worse as I pursued attorneys in Virginia again, spoke with the auction company in Lynchburg, discovered that four website pages of pornography were still carrying my personal information, so had to inform Yahoo that all was not well.

One very troublesome fact became apparent from the telephone attitudes of Virginia attorneys: they almost all recognized my sister Betty's name, "Lorraine Waddill" to them, as a "power" in the Republican party. They couldn't get off the phone with me fast enough. It was similar to the problem I encountered trying to hire an attorney in Lynchburg for the trustee malfeasance. Once attorneys learned that the opposition was represented by the lead attorney for Jerry Falwell Industries, they wouldn't dare represent me.

Plus, my hope for a legal solution was deflated by a conversation with a local libel attorney, who emphatically told me that even the internet libel had to go to the source/creator of it for jurisdiction—to Virginia if indeed one of my sisters did it. Would Leah really be able to do anything in a Broward County court? That telephone call prompted me to e-mail Leah with an update and ask her about the progress she was making towards getting an emergency order against Yahoo.

The evening brought worse news from the one Democrat attorney in Virginia that had seemed somewhat interested in taking my case. Jeremiah Denton decided that my case was primarily a "family dispute." He admitted it had gone way beyond the family, but he agreed that the person who posted the websites was probably the author of the letter to the police, either the signer, Laura, or another family member. He didn't recommend another lawyer.

Thomas Albro, the libel attorney in Charlottesville who had encouraged me before, was interested, but too busy to take on another case. I had run out of names and ideas. I counted my two blessings. I was grateful for finding Leah Mayersohn in Fort Lauderdale. And the attorney at Yahoo, Josh Russell, took it very seriously.

Still later in the evening, the assistant to Yahoo's CEO called me again, stating that she couldn't find anything else posted that contained my personal information, and John Zent, the "Risk Management Services" manager sent me another upbeat e-mail boldly stating, "*imasophistmaster* has been removed and hope all is well & quiet for U!"

They were both wrong. I checked and found there were still some "clubs" with my information online. The profile page that included a column of links below the title "My Interests," still sent viewers off to other pages that displayed my name and address, age, telephone number. I had tracked most of the links, but didn't get to the bottom of the list, which included <u>Hypnosis</u>, <u>Disabled</u>, <u>Philosophy</u>, <u>Teens</u>, and <u>Fisting</u>. (See **Appendix I** for some of the web pages.)

I called Leah Mayersohn to report on the frustrating day of calls and the continued existence of the websites.

Later I checked again, then e-mailed John Zent my displeasure.

Date: Thursday, March 01, 2001 9:32 PM
Subject: Fielder personal still on Yahoo sites

Dear John:

Am not happy that it has taken so long to take down the salacious web-site, and 2 of the links. Thanks to Josh Russell for eliminating the 2 Relationships categories. There are still 2 sites remaining:

Teens (1056 members) at:
http://members.yahoo.com/interests/Teens-600077343?.oc=c&.cc=18

Furniture (26 members) at:
http://members.yahoo.com/interests/Furniture-1600913268

Please remove my address from those sites and any others, and notify me when it is done. Thank you.

How long would it take Yahoo to zap everything? No sooner did I send that e-mail to Zent than Leah faxed to me a copy of the letter Detective Mussler had written to her. It gave me encouragement when I needed it. He was so helpful, and so prompt--what a contrast to the BSO and to the foot-dragging at Yahoo.

WASHINGTON COUNTY SHERIFF'S OFFICE
Jim Spinden, Sheriff
215 SW Adams Avenue, MS #32
Hillsboro, Oregon 97123-3874
*phone: (503) 846-2700 * fax: (503) 846-2719*

February 28, 2001
Law Offices of Leah H. Mayersohn
Re: Fielder, Lawrence J. DOB/12-31-50
Missing Person Investigation
Washington County Sheriff's Office Case #2001-00441

Dear Ms. Mayersohn:

In regard to our telephone conversation of this date, 02-28-01, this office is conducting an investigation into the disappearance of Mr. Larry Fielder. Because this investigation is currently "on-going" and the reasons for Mr. Fielder's disappearance are unknown, police reports generated by this investigation are not available for release at this time. However, I have no problem with answering any questions you may have as there is no indication at present of any crime being involved.

The circumstances are briefly as follows: Mr. Fielder was reported missing on 01-06-01 by a close friend, Barbra Milhaus, who since 06-02-98, has had Durable General Power of Attorney for Mr. Fielder. The Milhaus family last had telephone conversation with Larry on December 28th or 29th, 2000, wherein he gave no indication of leaving. Kay Sammons tells me she had an odd conversation with Larry on December 28th in which she noticed at the time strange pauses in his conversation, but dismissed it. Carole Fielder believes she last spoke with Larry on the 25th of December, but received a card post-marked on the 29th of December thanking her for the birthday present and informing her he would open it on his birthday at the Milhaus family residence. Carole found this to be odd, as he had never thanked her [by note card] for a birthday present before. This birthday present and other Christmas presents were later found unopened in his apartment when the Milhaus family searched the apartment on 01-08-01.

Also found by the Milhaus' at this time was a letter addressed to "Hey, Barbra", which expressed an appreciation for all that the Milhaus family has done for him and the fact that he loved them all. The second paragraph reads: "I have the opportunity to leave with 'Mac,' the Greek and the Sicilian and I am going to take them up on it. I think it will be the best thing for me to do. Who knows, I may become a great author, or even better, a great revolutionist."

The remainder of the two full pages of the letter are detailed instructions on how to settle his affairs.

There is no law in Oregon prohibiting an adult from just "up and leaving," so to speak, and Larry could have made prior arrangements for doing so in this mysterious fashion. It is primarily because of Larry's exceptional number of serious physical problems and his past problems with mental health and talk of ending his life--that leads me to believe this letter of detailed final instructions is nothing more than a suicide note.

Unfortunately, Mr. Fielder has not been found--either alive or deceased--and I have no way of knowing whether he is living out one of his fantasies (as he reportedly has in the past), or if he simply had had enough of a hard and confused life.

At any rate, there is nothing at this time to indicate anything of a criminal nature being involved and there is certainly no homicide investigation going on. And neither Carole Fielder, nor Kay Sammons, nor Barbra Milhaus, nor Betty, Laura, George or Charlie Loving are suspects of anything here in Oregon.

I do hope this helps clarify the nature of this investigation. Should circumstances change, the family certainly will learn of it quite quickly because I also investigate homicides, and I know how very concerned everyone is over Larry's strange disappearance.

Please feel free to call me if you have further questions.

Sincerely,
JIM SPINDEN, Sheriff
[signed]
Roger R. Mussler, Detective

What more could possibly be said? What was confusing? Why did I need a lawyer?

Chapter 9

"Which of you wishing to construct a tower does not first sit down and calculate the cost to see if there is enough for its completion?"

--Luke 14:28

Friday, March 2, 2001

I wished that the Pompano police were as responsive and helpful as Detective Mussler of Oregon, but all I got from the local Pompano Broward Sheriff's Office was a referral to the State Attorney, and that turned into more phone calls. I called five different numbers in the State Attorney's office before someone told me to call Chief Wright of the BSO. He was the recipient of Laura's letter! More spinning, more runaround.

My attorney Leah had better luck, and she e-mailed me, "I just talked to Ken Farnsworth this morning, from the State Attorneys office, and he doesn't have the case yet. You need to give me some time to work with the Sheriff's office to try to get everything they have. But I did talk to the prosecutor you left a message for--he's not necessarily the one who the case will be assigned to. Anyway, give me a call when you get back from the doctor's."

When we connected, Leah informed me that she had found another local (Fort Lauderdale) attorney willing to handle the filing of my case for libel, and she wanted me to call him immediately. I called Gregory S. Starr, and before the afternoon was out, he had faxed me a contract and a credit card authorization. Finally, something would start to happen.

Greg Starr became an "Attorney to represent me in a claim for damages and an injunction against any Jane or John Doe who may be liable for publishing libelous statements against me on the Yahoo web site, and for the libelous statement made to the Pompano Beach Police Department."

I faxed Greg Laura's letter to the police, plus the website pages: **Sex Partners in Florida** and **Imasophistmaster's profile. (Appendix I)** I explained the links I had found to Furniture, Relationships, Teens, and Florida, and highlighted the upper right-hand corner: **Last Updated: February 03, 2001.** I reminded Greg that the pornographic invitations with my name and address and phone number had been available to the world for one full month, at least.

Greg told me he'd try to get the suit filed in court on Monday. "The letter Detective Mussler sent confirms the facts distorted in the libelous letter to the police, Carole. Meanwhile keep working with Yahoo as best you can. Leah will help take care of that part of the problem."

"Greg, Roger Mussler has been so helpful and prompt. It would be nice if the Pompano police had any resemblance..."

"Right," Greg muttered quickly. "But call them about your police report on the Yahoo impersonation four days ago to find out when they'll follow up."

The spin-dry cycle of telephone calls to the police and to Yahoo was wearing me down. At least I now had two attorneys to help me. I exchanged more calls with Yahoo's CEO assistant and corporate counsel about the two "clubs," **Teens** and **Furniture**, which still showed my personal information. They were puzzled as to why. If they didn't know, what could I do?

The whirring round of calls to the Pompano police became more circular and more endlessly frustrating. The names kept coming: Chief Wright, Captain Drago, Captain Knight, Sergeant Montgomery, and countless assistants and secretaries. How many Pompano police employees did it take to follow up on one little case?

I went back to my computer to see if the websites were gone, and found an e-mail from John Zent of Yahoo, which indicated that he had no idea of my earlier telephone calls to Yahoo. More confusion.

Subj: RE: Fielder personal still on Yahoo sites
Date: 03/02/2001 2:48:29 PM Eastern Standard Time

I'll forward the other two for action....sorry you're unhappy, however the reaction time on this by Yahoo is far superior to that you would experience from its competition!

I was surprised at his defensive attitude. It seemed to take Yahoo an interminable period to simply shut down all references to me as *imasophistmaster*. In my internet ignorance, I didn't understand why they couldn't simply hit a "delete" button somewhere and eliminate my personal information instantaneously. They did finally eliminate the pages later that evening, which my attorney Leah discovered, but she didn't want to let Yahoo off the hook legally.

She e-mailed me, "I would like to go onto the Federal Court web-site for the Southern District of Florida this weekend to research all of the cases in which Yahoo has been sued in relation to a matter such as yours (for not timely removing materials on the web) to see if I can es-tablish a pattern of activity on Yahoo's part. I think that it was terrible that they took so long to remove the site from the web. I need you to put together a list of everything that happened to you from the time that you notified Yahoo of the problem until the time that all sites were re-moved. That is very important because it goes to potential damages."

She then tried to assure me that I didn't need to pursue the Pom-pano police for help on the website situation anymore. "I'm glad that you got together with Greg Starr. I met with him briefly and will pro-vide him with more details over the weekend. Hopefully, he can file his side on Monday. In the interim, I am handling the contact with BSO. Don't worry about that. I am also handling all contact with the State Attorney's Office. On Saturday, I will contact a local trust lawyer re-garding the portion of the trust that you sent to me to see if there is any way that we can do something about it in Florida. If not, I will contact the other trust lawyer that I know and help you find a lawyer in Vir-ginia."

Leah gave me more assignments: send copies of all the websites I found and printed out to her and to Greg; document all my police con-tacts; and document the slander and unprofessional conduct of the attorneys in Lynchburg, Virginia. That was a tall order, and not a pleas-ant one, but I spent the weekend working. She had told me before that eventually I'd need to document all family contacts as well, which I did chronologically as I sorted through my notes and files.

I took time out to e-mail my niece Kate Sammons, my sister Kay's teen-aged daughter. She had e-mailed me a thank-you for the eulogy of my father, her grandfather. I thanked her for the kind words, and told her of my own personal experiences in grieving many losses during my lifetime. I shared with her my current difficulty in being so terribly alone after the losses of my mother, my father, and my brother, and asked her to stay in touch. Little did I know then that I'd never hear from her again.

I finished the day by calling Barbra, and was pleasantly surprised to find her relaxing at home on a Saturday night. I told her of the progress with attorneys and Yahoo, but added, "No rest for the weary, Barbra, because now that my attorneys are finally moving, they've given me a list of assignments. But that means they want more money, too."

"More, already?"

"Each thing is separate. My attorney Greg thinks I have a great case for libel based on Laura's letter to the police, and the other one, Leah, is trying to talk to her old employer, the State Attorney here, to try to get a criminal charge filed against Laura for stealing my identity and posting those websites."

"Great. It *is* a crime, what she did!"

"I think the strategy is to make Laura come to Florida for the civil suit, then persuade the authorities to file the criminal charge against her when she's in town. They won't bother unless she's already in the State. It's all legalese rigamarole, if you ask me."

I explained that we needed a judge in Florida to force Laura to come to Florida, and a judge in Virginia that would agree. I worried that she and Betty would recruit our cousin the judge to help her weasel out of any responsibility for what she'd done. We might have to move into Federal Court, which would be more expensive.

"Carole, can you pay for that?"

"Probably not, Barbra. My attorneys want to make a big case of this, but I just wish my family would wake up and stop the insanity, cut their potential losses and mine."

"Do you really think any of them are that sane?"

That was a major question. And the answer was "apparently not." Barbra asked me about Kay, and I told her that she still did not speak to me, but her daughter and I had exchanged e-mails, and I was in process of documenting all family contacts in recent months. I told her, "If you plan to take any legal action on the trustee malfeasance, you need to do the same, especially your contacts with Kay. Leah is going to try to get a trust attorney lined up for me next week."

"Bob and I are still chewing on the possibilities, Carole. We just don't want any trouble from your nutty family."

"Neither did I, Barbra. Neither did I. But my choices are to go into debt for the first time in my life, or else to do nothing--be a victim and sit here and get robbed, maligned, libeled, stalked, or worse."

ؼ؈

By Monday morning, I was ready to send Leah the information she'd requested. I e-mailed her that I didn't plan to contact any more police, but "I am still angry that you have to spend your time and my $'s to get a court order instead of the police/State attorney issuing a search warrant or subpoena, as Yahoo's legal counsel indicated was very common throughout the country. *IF* the local police had done the normal thing, the website would have gone down immediately, and maybe you'd already have the name of the culprit and be moving ahead today, instead of needing the civil court order."

My concern for the money was growing, and I asked Leah, "Is the BSO just behind the times, or is their refusal part of the ongoing criminal investigation of me? If so, do I have recourse to recover some of my legal fees for this normally unnecessary effort?"

Little did I realize then what a foolish question that was.

I moved on to the next assignment, which was to clarify the trusteeship issues with Leah. I needed to determine exactly what Charlie Loving had done about the inventory of my father's personal belongings. I called Trevillian Auction in Lynchburg. The receptionist gave me the run-around at first, but I reminded her that I'd previously left a message and they had not called back.

"All I can tell you, Ma'am, is that we completed the inventory, but Mr. Loving has not gotten back to us about anything."

When I heard that distinctive Lynchburg accent again and realized it had been three weeks since my first calls to Trevillian, I flashed back to that awful day the police knocked on my door and I took it as an amusing mistake. I had not been particularly concerned about the accusations that morning because there were greater things on my mind that day: a puzzle surrounding Charlie Loving, my father's trustee whom I'd never met but felt I knew through conversations with him, Daddy, and Kay.

Charlie Loving, I understood, was the "reluctant" trustee of my father's estate. My father, who'd met him at church, had pressed him into the job last summer after Larry's last trip to Lynchburg, when he'd finally given up all hope on the Virginia girls' reconciliation. Larry had met Charlie and liked him. Although I'd never met him, we had talked by telephone many times, and his southern accent and Lynchburg twang gave me an automatic mental image of a typical good ole boy of the South. I knew he was retired, so I assumed he must be in his seventies. Daddy had talked about him often during the last two years, and Kay, who lived a ninety-minute drive away, saw him regularly, and told me he was "such a nice man, and right friendly."

When Daddy removed Betty's name and legally made Charlie trustee of his estate last summer, I called and thanked him profusely for taking on the job. Kay and Larry had also been grateful for the change. I remembered clearly one of the earliest conversations I had with him afterwards.

ৡৄৎ

"Carole Anne, I promise you that I'm gonna sit down with your father tomorruh and make him divide up all his furniture among you kids, and sign it."

I flinched a little when Charlie called me by both names, because the only other person who ever called me by both names had been Daddy, and then, only when he was angry with me. As a child, he usually called me "Butch," but if he said "Carole Anne," I knew I was in trouble. It was usually followed by, "I'm gonna tell you right here and now..." and he would "straighten me out." I assumed Charlie didn't know that.

Charlie had continued, "If I'm gonna do this thang, it's gonna be signed, sealed, and delivered into my hand right now. I've been atellin' him, and he's promised me tomorrow's the day. By cracky he's gonna do it, I assure you."

"Good for you, Charlie!" I had laughed. "He started asking us what pieces we wanted about four years ago. I submitted my list, but he said no one else showed any interest. I've asked him about it many times, but you know how he is." I never thought about it again, until after Daddy's death, when Charlie and I were talking, and I complimented him on his foresight. "Aren't you glad you got Daddy to take care of dividing the furniture when you did?"

"Carole Anne, I've gotta tell ya, he never did it. He jes' never did. What a job that's gonna be." I'd felt sorry for him then, as he seemed so beat. I'd offered to help out any way I could, given the limitation that I couldn't be there in person. Kay was the only one there for him to help sort through decades of accumulation in our parents' house.

Charlie and I had talked several times last year about my father's health, and we'd laughed together sometimes about his eccentricities, one being my father's determination to save money on the electric bill by refusing to heat the kitchen with a space heater.

"That's just plain the mos' inefficient heatin' method possible," Daddy explained to me. "Anybody who understands any physics at all knows that."

"Don't you think it's unhealthy to sit in a cold room to eat when you're not feeling up to par?" I tried to argue with him.

"I've tried to get that radiator fixed, but the fella who came out heah said no one today has the parts." Daddy had ended the discussion. And that was final. Comfort and health took a back seat to efficiency and saving money.

"Well, Carole Anne," Charlie commiserated with me, "you know Daddy will be Daddy. He's got his own ideas about how to do jus' 'bout ever'thang." Charlie always referred to my father as "Daddy," which jarred my ears, as I had assumed that he and Daddy were peers. Daddy's friends called him "Jack." Anybody younger, which was almost everyone, called him "Mr. Fielder." The familiarity bothered me at the time.

Sometimes Daddy seemed to use Charlie as an employee, or chauffeur. During one conversation, Daddy had criticized, "Well, Charlie seems to need to always be on the move. He drove me up in the country to Franklin County, but then wanted to come home after an hour or two. I'd wanted to see some other folks, but he *had to go*. No sooner 'n we get someplace than he wants to turn right around and come back."

Towards the end of Daddy's life, he became more and more critical of Charlie. It didn't make sense to me at the time that a recent "friend" to Daddy who had finally volunteered to be his trustee could deserve my father's deteriorating attitude towards him. It bothered me slightly, but it was obvious to me that Daddy's lifestyle ideas conflicted with Charlie's when he called Charlie a "playboy." I was shocked at Daddy's use of the term, and asked, "What do you mean that he's a playboy?"

"Well, he's always gotta be goin' somewhere to play something. He's goin' fishin' out yonder, or he's gotta go to a college football game someplace, seems like every weekend."

"Daddy, that's what he likes to do. He's retired. He wants to play, not work," I'd offered in conciliation.

"Well, pshaw!" Daddy indicated his disdain.

After that conversation, I wrote off Daddy's description of Charlie as a playboy as just a difference in their lifestyles, not in their basic moral values.

The last months of my father's life, Charlie hired someone to come in to clean up after Daddy, and make him at least one hot meal, five days per week. Daddy complained to me in every conversation, "She's just always wantin' to ask me somethin'. Where is this or where is that? I want my peace and quiet, and she's always botherin' me. It's an invasion of my privacy."

Daddy managed to make her quit after a couple weeks, much to Charlie's chagrin. When Charlie told me what happened, we teamed up. I did a lot of fast talking with Daddy about offering her more money for fewer days in his way violating his privacy, while Charlie did a lot of persuasive talking to get the woman to come back again. When they both agreed, Charlie and I verbally patted ourselves on the back.

It was not long afterwards that I received the call from Barbra to pass on the sad news to Larry's family, although we were still hoping against hope that he hadn't really killed himself. I knew that Daddy was spending the night at Kay's house in Salem, and I called to ask him about his recent contact with Larry, telling him only that Larry was in medical trouble.

The next morning, Kay delivered Daddy into Charlie's care back home in Lynchburg. He was just arriving when I called and told him that Larry was gone but had left a note. Daddy *immediately* said to me, "He killed himself, didn't he?" and quickly passed the phone to Charlie. I filled Charlie in on the details, told him what Daddy had just said, and gave him Barbra's telephone number. He never called her.

During the two weeks between Larry's apparent death and Daddy's, I felt painfully aware that my own health crisis prevented me from physically being in either of the two places I wanted to be: in Portland to help Barbra and grieve with her, and/or in Lynchburg to help my father and grieve with him. Whatever I could accomplish on the telephone was the only thing I could offer. I did my best to be supportive by long distance.

I remembered feeling grateful to Charlie for the help he had been to my father, especially since Larry's death, and I wanted to help him out any way I could with his new responsibilities following my father's death. He told me during one conversation that he didn't like to deal with attorneys, and didn't want to call my father's trust attorney unnecessarily. Barbra kept asking me what she should do about some of Larry's affairs and property.

Since I'd already spoken with trust attorney Lowry during Daddy's hospitalization, I called him to ask advice to pass on to Barbra and Charlie about Larry's "missing" status. Mr. Lowry told me that the court would have to establish a trustee for Larry's inheritance, unless his body were found, or seven years elapsed. Barbra might have to be that person, but it would be up to the court to decide, and he would advise Charlie about it.

During some of the stressful calls in January, I invited all three of my new long-distance "buddies," Mr. Lowry, Charlie, and Barbra, to come visit me in Florida, since I could not travel to see them. They all three seemed enthusiastic. Mr. Lowry stated that he had already planned a trip to Florida during the summer and would meet me then. Barbra and her husband might plan a getaway from the rainy season in Oregon. Charlie especially wanted to fish in Florida.

Shortly after the hectic activity during Daddy's final hospitalization and unexpected death January 17th, Charlie told me that he was going on a much-needed local fishing trip. That created a hiatus in our telephone conversations, which ended when I called him the second week of February to find out if he had returned. He was home, and told me he'd just gotten back a couple hours earlier. I offered to help do some telephoning to get information about preparing the inventory and appraisal of my parents' personal items and furniture, and I filled him in on Barbra's latest progress taking care of Larry's affairs.

That conversation occurred the night before the Pompano detectives knocked on my door.

After I called Barbra and spoke to her about the Pompano detectives' strange visit to my house the morning of February 9th, I told her about my call to Charlie and suggested she give him a call now that he was home again. I planned to help him as best I could by calling my Florida appraiser, who was already familiar with my father's work, to ask what she would charge to go to Lynchburg and do the job. I also planned to go online and search for Lynchburg appraisers, just to get some of the details out of the way for Charlie. I told Barbra, "It's the least I can do to help him out."

"Great Carole. I'm still kind of upset that he hasn't called me him-self, but I guess he's just worn out with your father's death and all. I can empathize with him on that."

After speaking with Barbra, I spent the entire day on the phone try-ing to do some of the footwork for Charlie. I got a good idea of the scope and expense of the job. In the late afternoon, I spoke with an old Lynchburg auction company, Trevillian's, whose owner told me, to my great surprise, that she had already inventoried the Fielder estate! She had already delivered the finished appraisal to Mr. Charlie Loving. I was puzzled and wondered why he had encouraged me last night to look into it.

I called Charlie, reported to him all the calls I'd made, and then asked him about Trevillian's finished inventory and appraisal.

"That lyin' bitch," he practically shouted at me.

I was shocked at his language. I couldn't imagine my father being around anyone who talked like that. It seemed so out of character for the image I'd had of Charlie. I guessed he was having a bad day today, or maybe he was mad at himself for his own failure to take care of the furniture division last year.

I made a quick decision: I hated to add to his woes, but the detec-tives who'd been to my house in the morning had not yet called back, and I might need Charlie sooner or later to deal with the sister that wrote to the police. I needed to talk with him as I would speak to my father.

"Charlie, I hate to add to your worries, but you told me I could talk to you just as I could to my father, right?"

"Yeah. What's on your mind?"

"This is pretty unbelievable, but the local police came to me today because one of my sisters in Virginia sent them a letter accusing me of doing something to Larry. They wouldn't tell me which one."

"Oh my...what the?"

"Actually, I should be getting a call back from them anytime now, because I asked them to check with the Oregon authorities, then get back to me and tell me which sister had done such a thing. I thought you should know."

"Well. Who ever...?"

"I'll call you when I know more, ok?" I concluded.

That day seemed like a lifetime ago, not just three weeks. By late afternoon I was ready to send to Leah the complete history of Charlie Loving's shenanigans in Lynchburg, beginning with that horrible day. Later that same afternoon I had verified through the owner of Trevillian Auction in Lynchburg, Sonya Minnix, that Mr. Loving was the one lying to me. I wrote Leah that Loving had been extremely deceptive on a number of issues, which led Barbra and me to try to hire an attorney in Lynchburg to intervene on our behalf with both Loving and the trust attorney Lowry, after they refused to communicate with us.

I e-mailed Leah that we had faxed information to the attorney in Lynchburg, including Larry's suicide note, set a telephone appointment, and then were blown off. I related how Kay and Barbra and I were in communication after Larry's disappearance and that there was no mention of disbelief in Larry's suicide. Then suddenly, in my father's obituary notice, in the standard statement that "the deceased was survived by...," all four girls were listed, and so was Larry!

The obituary error was doubly shocking because of my participation in the planning of my father's funeral services by telephone with members of the family and Charlie Loving. I wrote Leah, "Subsequent events belied the information and instructions I was given during that teleconference, at which I was the only one not personally present. The multitude of lies, misinformation, and deception among my family, and others present at my father's services, became very complex, and I only gradually learned the extent of them."

Memory of that agonizingly long Monday morning I waited for Charlie to call with news of how he and Lowry were going to take care of the mess created by Laura's letter came back to me. I wrote, "He never called, and later the attorney Lowry brusquely informed me that Mr. Loving did not have to honor my father's wishes concerning personal property, regardless of his expressed writings to me or the other heirs; that only the formal trust document need be followed."

I described to Leah how Mr. Loving cursed at me, told me that he had no intention of sending me the copy of the appraisal and inventory (as he had earlier implied was "in the mail"); that he didn't have to credit inheritance money for me or Barbra to buy furniture at auction; and that he told me to get an attorney and hung up on me.

"Since Mr. Loving refuses to communicate anything to either of us," my e-mail continued, "has refused to respond to Larry's attorney's requests for acknowledgment in writing; we cannot know what is happening with my father's estate in Lynchburg. What can you do in Virginia or in Oregon to sort this out?"

I felt overwhelmingly sick that my father had left such a mess behind. His conservative values, his sense of public propriety and privacy, his desire for continuity of tradition--almost every standard he lived by was being violated.

Following my Florida attorneys' advice, I had pursued what few leads I had for attorneys in Virginia. I contacted two in Roanoke: one sounded interested at first, but then backed off because Charlie had not yet done anything illegal that was easy to prove. Charlie *could* legally sell off everything personal and then present the heirs with a check for the proceeds, whatever it was. I couldn't bear to think of trading the work of my father's hands for cash, but I also wondered why I cared.

I envied Larry's not being here.

Chapter 10

"Thus the Lord passed before him and cried out,
'The Lord, the Lord, a merciful and gracious God,
slow to anger and rich in kindness and fidelity,
continuing his kindness for a thousand generations,
and forgiving wickedness and crime and sin;

yet not declaring the guilty guiltless, but
punishing children and grandchildren to the third
and fourth generation for their fathers'
wickedness.'"   --Exodus 34:6-7

Tuesday, March 6, 2001

I awoke with great pain and the sensation of snapping in my rib bones. The fall on my boat ten days ago had caught up with me. I needed medical help. Trying to get that kind of help was almost like dealing with the Pompano police, another spin cycle of telephone calls to my Primary Care Physician (PCP), to the customer service number of my Health Maintenance Organization (HMO), to the emergency room of a local hospital, and back again. I could hardly move my left arm, and a sharp pain shot through me if I breathed deeply, cleared my throat, or coughed. I gave up and stayed in bed.

In the afternoon, I learned by fax that Greg had sent Laura a list of "admissions," a standard stepping stone in the initial litigation process, and by e-mail that Barbra had made progress. Pamela Yee, Barbra and/or Larry's attorney, had written again to the Lynchburg trust attorney Lowry. She asked Lowry to send the personal property inventory, the date of the auction, and verification that Barbra would be recognized as Larry's legal representative and receive his share of his father's estate whenever the other heirs received theirs. She'd given Lowry a deadline of March 11, 2001.

Barbra added that Yee didn't much expect to hear a reply, given the past performance of the Virginia gentlemen, but that in itself would be evidence to add to the case I was setting up in Florida. Barbra didn't want any legal hassle. Her day was primarily devoted to celebrating new life--a new grandbaby born to a friend, her own niece's pending pregnancy, and best of all, time to share in her own pregnant daughter's ultrasound. Her Oregon world was the antipodes of mine in Florida.

99

To make matters worse for me, the day brought another shock: an e-mail sent to me by a nephew I did not know, half a world away in Germany. The chilling language of his hate letter insinuated that _he_ wanted my father's wishes carried out and that _I_ didn't. Marc Waddill, Betty's son, considered Charlie Loving, whom he could not possibly know personally, a man of "unquestioned integrity, honesty and judgment," for whom Marc had nothing but respect.

Marc then plunged into a defensive speech that he'd put up his own money for Charlie in a lawsuit, and invited me to sue him, Marc. He gave me his German address in Frankfurt am Main! Whose script was he following? Did Charlie Loving or Marc Waddill have anything to do with Laura's letter to the police and the websites on Yahoo? What did Marc know that I didn't, and from whom? His sister Karen, his aunt Kay, his mother Betty, or Charlie himself? He planted more seeds of suspicion and distrust. What an unforeseen blow from another blood relative.

I had only seen Marc two or three times in his life; the first was when he was a baby one and half years old, and the last at his mother Betty's house in 1992, when I was there as a guest of his sister Karen. But I remembered well the second time I met him, all grown up at age nineteen. I went to my book shelves and pulled out a photo album to find pictures of Marc, that second time I ever saw him, a day in May 1989 that I could never forget.

I was married, living in Sunnyvale, California, and had not visited Lynchburg in a couple of years. My husband and I were planning an East Coast trip, so I sandwiched in a five-day visit to Lynchburg that would include Mother's Day. I telephoned to ask Daddy to make arrangements for a noon dinner celebration at a local hotel. I had hoped it would be an opportunity for re-establishing some family contacts. I stared at the photos and remembered the whole thing so clearly.

※ ※

"Oh, that won't be necessary," Daddy pronounced to me when I asked him to call for reservations.

"It's Mother's Day, Daddy. It's a gift for Mother. I'm paying. Surely there must be a local hotel or restaurant that puts on a big brunch or lunch or something. Will you please call around for me? I don't have a telephone directory for Lynchburg."

"Aw, shucks, sure, it'd be long distance for you," he snorted.

"Do you know if Betty or Kay or Laura are planning to come that day? I'd love to see them, and they're invited too."

"Oh, uh, I don' know 'bout that. Betty's purty busy, and Laura cain't leave her animals overnight without hirin' someone to come in, so she won't come up heah. I'll ask Kay if I see huh."

"Sunday, even if it's just the three of us, we can have a nice meal and Mother won't have to do anything."

I'd telephoned Kay an invitation, but she said, "Sorry, but we're supposed to spend that day with Mac's aunt." Earlier that year, she had sent me Karen and Marc Waddill's addresses in college, so I wrote and invited them. Karen wrote back that she'd like to see me in Lynchburg. When I related that to Kay, she remarked, "I can guarantee you that Betty won't permit Karen to come."

I flew into Washington, D.C., visited some of my husband's relatives in the area, then several of my mother's family that I had not seen since the early 1960's. I learned, somewhat disturbingly, that none of them had realized how ill I'd been all my life, nor that I had to use a wheelchair to get around. I also learned from my mother's older sister, my Aunt Edith, that she had been diagnosed fifteen years earlier with psoriatic arthritis, when she was sixty years old, and suffered periodic, severe flare-ups. Moreover, her oldest daughter, and grandson by that daughter, had also been diagnosed with milder cases. We compared treatments, and wondered why my mother had never told either of us about the condition of the other. My parents visited them regularly.

When I arrived in Lynchburg late the Saturday night before Mother's Day, Daddy told me that I'd be hosting nine people for a champagne luncheon the next day: Betty and King were coming with grown children Karen and Marc; Kay, husband Mac and their five-year-old Kate would be there. I was amazed, but looked forward to this long overdue family reunion. The last time I'd seen Karen and Marc was 1972, when they were between one and three years old. Now both were in college.

The blackest Harold Pinter play would have been no competition for that luncheon. Kay and her husband Mac were gracious and polite. Their daughter Kate was bubbly and breathtakingly pretty. Betty's husband, King, said hello, then quickly moved away from me. I had not seen him since 1972, and had forgotten how tall he was. Probably 6'3". His son Marc was a towering 6'7", with straight, dark blonde hair. I tried not to stare as I searched for familial similarities. He had some slight facial resemblance to the men in my mother's family. Karen had an easy smile, striking looks, with her long, wavy, dark-brown hair. She bore some resemblance to Marc with her generous lips, dark eyebrows and brown eyes, but looked distinctly different from the rest of the family. She stood about 5'8", shorter than her mother, Betty.

Betty was much as I had remembered her from seventeen years before, still coloring her hair a faintly reddish blonde, statuesque, high cheekbones and even facial features. Always the glamour queen.

We met in a downtown Lynchburg hotel, where a huge banquet hall was arranged for Mother's Day celebrating, with large round tables in the center section, and smaller rectangular tables lined both walls. We could easily seat all ten of us comfortably, at one of the round tables, and the waiter was quick to start pouring champagne. I managed to seat my nieces, Karen to my left and Kate to my right. Betty immediately sat next to Kate and tried to engage her in conversation. It was blatantly obvious that Betty did not, and would not, speak to Kay, Mac, or me. I began speaking with Karen, excited to meet her at last, and as soon as she got engrossed in the conversation, Betty announced in a loud voice, "Karen, don't you need to go to the bathroom? Let's go." She then jumped up and hastened Karen out.

Kay and I looked at each other and shrugged. Mac and King vied with each other to talk to Daddy. Mother sat smiling, looking somewhat dazed, but happy, and didn't say much. When Betty returned, I talked to Karen again, and tried to include Marc, with difficulty. I also tried to converse with Betty, but she mostly acted as if she didn't hear me.

At one point during the meal, I asked Betty, "How are the cousins doing?" She ignored me, so I repeated the question, a little louder. She still looked down at her plate and continued eating. I asked Karen, under my breath, "Is she hard of hearing now?" Karen giggled and shook her head. I spoke again, loudly enough for several tables to hear, "I say, Betty, how are the cousins doing?"

She finally looked at me, and closed her eyes as she spoke, "What cousins?"

I chuckled, and said, just as loudly, "The Haley cousins, you know, the ones you have dinner with several times a year?"

"Fine, they ah jus' fine," she responded, eyes closed as she spoke. She then looked away and refused to say another word.

Daddy pretended not to notice. Mother didn't. Kay and Mac were giving each other a knowing look, and I turned back to Karen and Marc. Kate would join in from time to time, between trips around the table to consult with her mother. I, and the waiter, took lots of snap-shots, and before we departed the hotel, I pressed my brothers-in-law, Mac and King, each into taking a group picture, with the lobby fountain in the background. The perfectly beautiful first family of Virginia on Mother's Day. Those were the pictures I now stared at.

None of them would come back to our parents' house to visit with me that day. No one said to me the least thank-you for the meal, good to see you after all these years, glad you're feeling better. King issued, however, a softly-spoken throwaway invitation, "Come and see us sometime, you heah?" I was sure Betty didn't hear him.

৩৵৶

Neither Mother nor Daddy ever mentioned a thing about that luncheon. I never saw or talked to Marc Waddill again except for the short visit to Richmond in 1992. And now he was sending me hate e-mail from another country, another continent. What gossip had he heard, and from whom?

I read his e-mail again, and I felt numb, then nauseated, then grate-ful I'd hired two attorneys. I quickly forwarded it to Greg and to Leah and to Barbra.

Within the hour, Barbra called me.

"Oh my God, Carole! Is your nephew a pompous little shit or what?"

"I think the answer is a resounding yes, Barbra." The reek of my family's insanity had spread from Virginia to Florida to Oregon to Germany

"It's pretty clear he's been misinformed, probably by Karen, don't you think?"

"How do you figure, Barbra?"

"With the facts that he's been given, you seem to be trying to cause problems for no reason. I guess it's not fair to judge him, because he really doesn't know any of your side of the story, possibly no details at all. Of course, that hasn't stopped him from judging you."

"Really!"

"He trusts his sister and her information, which is a fairly normal brotherly thing to do. But shame on Karen for telling him what she wanted him to know so that he would think and react as he has. Manipulative. Runs in your family, Carole. But maybe it wasn't just Karen. Probably at Kay's encouragement. Larry told me they're pretty tight."

"You're right, Barbra. But will it ever stop?"

"Same twisted family tactics, new generation. Write a nasty letter, but don't call you directly. Karen, Kay, George, and now Marc don't have the balls to state their opinions to you in person, because you might respond and say something that might make them change their minds about you. And God knows they don't want to think that it's possible they are wrong or misinformed. Can't have that."

"I just feel so totally stupid and helpless with all this, Barbra. I barely know any of these people, yet it's obvious they all hate my guts."

"Carole, you have reason to feel cast aside again. Just like Larry. But hang in there. However this turns out, just remember that when it's over you never have to have any contact with any of them again."

"Gosh, Barbra. I didn't know I had any contact with them now."

"So, tell me about your cracked ribs." Barbra switched subjects.

"You were right. You told me so," I laughed. "But don't make me laugh, 'cause it hurts. I get my transfusion tomorrow, and maybe that'll put me on the road to mending."

Barbra then asked me if I'd developed the pictures of my vandalized yard, and if I'd gotten anymore phone calls from strange men. I had received another set of ominous phone calls today.

I told her, "Always around the lunch hour, till about two o'clock. If I answer, they hang up. Probably the porno-cruisers that see the websites just want to be sure I'm home before they bother to drive by. Isn't that just great?" I complained.

"And don't you press the star and "69" on your telephone to trace those calls back?"

"Yes, Barbra, I have. And they are never ever traceable. Any porno-cruiser is going to be smart enough to not give his identity away. I just need to screen all my calls with the answering machine." I shared with her my frustration that my nutty family had created this mess but probably didn't have a clue about the consequent terror they caused me.

"And would they believe it if they knew, Carole? If Charlie is ignoring me, and has decided Larry didn't disappear or kill himself, that you murdered him, don't you think he denies that your sister Betty is the mastermind behind all this?"

She had a point. By now Charlie and Mr. Lowry probably denied that they rushed to Daddy's hospital bed to change his legal documents to get rid of Betty's legal standing when she wouldn't go to Lynchburg to help him.

"Barbra, I have no doubt that by now maybe Kay and Charlie are polishing up the good ole family WASP image after all."

"You know how many times I had to ask your brother what that meant?" Barbra giggled. "I still forget sometimes: White Anglo-Saxon Protestant. I'm so glad I'm from Oregon."

Her remark reminded me again of the clash of cultures. Later that night, I searched online, not for WASP's, but for any Roman Catholic resources or expertise on American cults. Gratefully, I found an expert, a priest at the Rutgers University campus. I e-mailed him:

Date: Tue, 6 Mar 2001 7:34 P.M. EST
Subject: Can you direct me to resources?

Dear Father Stanley:

I am an active Catholic in a large South Florida parish. I am a convert (1973), and the only Catholic in my family of origin, and 3 generations back, and one forward. I am searching for resources to help me defend myself in a libelous assault by my own, estranged family members, at least one of which believes that the Roman Catholic church is a cult.

(My hometown is Lynchburg, Virginia, home of Jerry Falwell, President of the Moral Majority. I, also, grew up with distorted views of Catholicism, similar to those held in my community.)

This would be laughable, except one sister has sent a letter to the local Sheriff's Department in Broward County accusing me of being a cult leader planning mass suicides, presumably at my local parish church. That too would be a so what?--consider the source--except I am still under investigation based on that letter dated Jan. 29th, in spite of the fact that I am a regular lector, eucharistic minister, and have years of active experience in RCIA since 1987, both in California and Florida. The pastor

of my church did not feel that he could straighten out the Broward Sheriff's baseless accusations. Meanwhile, I am being bombarded by more
and more scurrilous verbiage, coming from family members not so estranged from me, and from a salacious website that someone--probably
the same sick sister--put up.

This afternoon, I received a vicious e-mail from a nephew living in Germany, whom I do not know.

I have had to raise $5200 to hire two attorneys to begin the legal process
to protect me--in spite of the fact that had the Broward Sheriff done
what most police jurisdictions do in cases of internet crime and of false
police reports, my tax dollars would have been adequate to protect me. I
have spent exhausting hours trying to hire attorneys to help me. There
will be a jurisdictional problem because of the conflicting State laws. I
am disabled and unable to travel out of my locality.

My question to you on resources: is there no help I can get from the
Catholic Church, as a very visible member of a large parish, when the
entire source of my endangerment assumes that my parish is a cult? And
I am its leader? (That's a good one--a priest follow a lay person's orders????) Unfortunately, this matter has passed into the hands of one of
the lead attorneys for Jerry Falwell Industries, and can be expected to
grow more, as it has already, in ever widening circles, since Jan. 29,
2001.

Any help or resources to which you can direct me will be most appreciated.

Sincerely yours,

Carole A. Fielder
St. Coleman's Catholic Church
Pompano Beach, Florida

Before going to bed, I checked e-mail again and chuckled out loud
at Barbra's excited report about seeing the ultrasound picture of her
daughter's unborn child. "Thank heavens for these happy things to distract me."
The generations of her family seemed so wholesome compared to
mine.

I answered her quickly with congratulations and the good news that my second attorney, Greg Starr, had just sent me the complaint. I wrote, "It is really very simple, as it should be, seven pages long, and repeats all the legalese three times, one each for Laura, Jane/John Doe a/k/a *Imasophistmaster,* and Yahoo Corporation. Asks for damages in excess of $15,000, legal costs and fees, and anything else the judge deems advisable. He's requesting a jury trial, has established some reference why the Florida court has jurisdiction--and that's the key biggie."

Another big issue was my credibility, not just in my family, where there obviously was none, but also among my friends and acquaintances. An example of the suspicious looks and funny responses came from a local, whose New Yorker sister I'd taken sailing. She told me that her sister frankly confided that without knowing me personally, if she had read Laura's letter and heard about the website, she would've thought I made it up.

I began to fear that anyone who heard some small piece of what was happening to me would think I was totally nuts.

I wrote Barbra, "This whole thing is so bizarre that it's impossible for me to get support from anyone who doesn't really get down to the nitty-gritty. And who can get their rational mind around all this? It IS mind-blowing. A suicide followed by a death, with one body missing! (I didn't even mention that in my e-mail to the priest at Rutgers.) Plus, Marc's crazy letter—who set him up? With Loving, Kay, Betty, Karen, as well as the two unnamed cousins, it's almost like a 10,000 piece jigsaw puzzle, isn't it?"

Generations of the same problems. When would it end?

The next morning I e-mailed my attorney Leah to say that I'd be getting my transfusion in the morning and seeing a doctor about my ribs in the afternoon, but I was anxious to hear from her.

"Have you made any progress with the BSO? As the e-mail from Germany indicates, this libel/slander is growing daily. Why does BSO still consider me a suspect???? Without the enclosures to Laura's letter, we cannot get at the sources of this spreading cancer."

It was a long day getting the transfusion in the morning and waiting for the doctor in the afternoon, but I found a pleasant surprise upon returning home. The priest at Rutgers had already answered me:

Subj: Re: Will you please direct me to resources?
Date: 03/07/2001 12:18:16 PM Eastern Standard Time

I am at a loss, Ms. Fielder, to understand how this horrible story has evolved. If, for some reason, your pastor is not able to assist you, I'd suggest you go to your diocese's chancery office. God bless.

R. Stanley

I immediately searched online for the Miami chancery office, and wrote to them, pasting the e-mail I'd sent to Father Stanley, and begging them for help to fight the libelous assault on me and my parish. I could only hope that Father Marin of Miami would be as prompt in responding as Fr. Stanley had been.

Chapter 11

"Your own friend and your father's friend
forsake not; but if ruin befalls you,
enter not a kinsman's house.
Better is a neighbor near at hand
than a brother far away."   --Proverbs 27:10

Friday, March 9, 2001

After a month of this nightmare I gave up on the local police for help. There was no one left in my family who would help. I hopefully awaited a callback from the church chancery office. I had scraped together enough money to hire two attorneys to work on the libel and defamation problem. But, I still couldn't understand what my father's trustee was doing to me and to Larry, who was legally represented by Barbra.

Charlie's job as my father's trustee was primarily that of communicator with the heirs, including me in Florida and Larry/Barbra in Oregon. He had never contacted Barbra and had suddenly stopped speaking to me. Surely he understood his legal and moral responsibilities to us when he agreed to become the new trustee in May 2000, at my father's request. Or had he planned his deception from the start?

Larry met Charlie just once, during his last, horrific visit to Lynchburg in March 2000, just before Daddy persuaded Charlie to become trustee. I never met him. I never heard my mother talk about him, so he must have been a relatively new friend, but just to Daddy, not to Mother before her mind deteriorated. What bothered me most was that my father, of all people, trusted someone who was very possibly not trustworthy.

I wanted Charlie to be trustworthy. My sister Kay liked him, clearly, because his presence took the worry off her shoulders. Did she really know him? Since she had strangely decided not to communicate with me since Daddy's death, was she contributing to Charlie's hostility towards me and Barbra? What did she have to gain? What did Charlie have to gain by treating Barbra and me so badly?

I walked outside among the flowers trying to answer these questions when I suddenly remembered the full horror of Larry's final visit to Lynchburg. He had talked to me about it, but not until several weeks

109

after his return to Portland, and long after I received a description from my niece in Atlanta, Karen Waddill Huckabee. She had e-mailed me about the bizarre encounter of that fateful day. I needed to read her account again. It was a year ago, but it should still be preserved in my AOL personal files. I found it and read it again with renewed horror and recognition.

Karen, Betty's estranged daughter, had sent me an e-mail dated Wednesday, March 22, 2000. It was a copy of a long e-mail that she had previously sent to her brother Marc Waddill in Germany, concerning her trip to Lynchburg.

She wrote about Larry's being there and how well they "really connected." She then listed a litany of his health problems. It was evidently the first time she knew of them. Since he had the same diagnosis of psoriatic arthritis as I, and was taking the chemotherapy drug methatrexate the same as I had for thirty-six years, it was surprising to me that she seemed so affected. In her e-mail she seemed both surprised and sympathetic. It was almost as though she never understood my situation during the few years we had a relationship—from 1990 to 1996. She never once mentioned to her brother that both Larry and I suffered the same genetic diseases. She did, however, emphasize all the other physical problems Larry carried, of which everyone in the family should be fully cognizant, based on his own correspondence with us many years before. (See **Appendices B, D, E.**)

Apparently, she never realized the extent of Larry's physical problems, or mine, nor did she seem to make the connection that both of us suffered similarly. She wrote that she renewed her relationship with her Uncle Larry, and said he was such a "wonderfully kind person. He shows tremendous compassion for Pappy," (her name for my father, her grandfather), and she continued, he "seems to reach him on a level that I haven't seen much."

She then went on to describe my father, and that he was "not doing all that great emotionally or physically." She talked about the amputation of toes on his left foot, and in graphic terms indicated the lack of healing. She indicated that "Pappy" was able to get around with his walker, but was very weak and unsteady, had fallen a few times but not broken anything. "He's very lucky," she wrote. "The worst part to bear is that Pappy is just so depressed about so many things."

She described his grief over the loss of my mother, his daily physical challenges, but most of all his distress about the "embittered relationships among his children. It's eating him up inside." She was evidently hearing for the first time what I had heard from my father for many years.

She wrote that the Saturday night that she spent in my father's house, along with Larry, she could hear my father moaning and talking to himself, and when she checked on him found him sitting on the side of his bed, his head hanging in obvious distress. When she asked if he were in pain, he'd answered no, that it was "about the kids." She talked to him awhile trying to comfort him and encourage him to try to sleep.

Like a melodrama, she explained in her e-mail that it was hard for anyone to sleep in my father's house that night because of an incident, which she proceeded to describe. She explained to Marc, that a cousin and his wife came to visit Larry that day, along with Kay, her husband and daughter. They had all gone out for dinner, came back to the house, when suddenly "all hell broke loose."

She described a "tremendous banging on the front door." Laura came storming in with her husband Wayne following. Karen had not seen her Aunt Laura since the previous Christmas visit to my father's house, at which time Karen and her husband both had met briefly with Laura and Wayne. Laura did not say hello to anyone, but strode directly up to Kay and half talking, half mumbling, threatened her with the question "so you gonna run away now, huh? Huh?Huh? You gonna get up and run?"

Karen then reminded her brother Marc about the slugging incident at my aunt Edith's funeral in 1997, when Laura accosted Kay at the aunt's home and almost broke Kay's jaw, for no known reason, and with no apparent reaction from anyone who witnessed it. Karen wrote that Kay's daughter, "Kate is terrified of Laura and she immediately went upstairs." Karen then tried to be polite and offered her Aunt Laura her seat. She and my brother Larry left the room to get more chairs, but when they returned, Laura was gone, and Kate had gone upstairs. Karen checked on Kate and saw that the teenager was starting to cry, so the two young women decided to watch television in my father's up-stairs bedroom to avoid the scene of older family members downstairs. Karen added that Kate was terribly upset by Laura and Wayne's behavior, as they "used to be like second parents to her." Obviously, that relationship had completely "deteriorated."

According to Karen's e-mail, Laura had pursued her niece Kate upstairs and "launched into profanities and threats when she walked in the room (saying things like, 'so you gonna run like your sorry-ass mama? the little bitch.')"

Karen told Laura to stop talking to Kate that way, and Laura then turned on Karen, saying, according to Karen, "You don't know anything. You don't know what's been going on. Oh, you don't know do you? You haven't talked to the Great One today. You'll find out. You'll find out tomorrow. …You're under mind control."

There it was! That same language as in the letter to the police! When I had read Karen's long e-mail the first time, I didn't know that Laura was referring to me. It was so totally crazy-sounding that I just ignored the details, and assumed it was more confirmation of all the gossip circulating among other family members that Laura was nuts. Larry and I hadn't dissected Karen's e-mail. He was much too depressed for the rest of his life after that trip, that horror, and I concentrated on trying to cheer him up. I avoided reminding him of that ill-fated, horrific trip.

Reading from my computer screen, I couldn't stop my tears. I could barely stand to finish, but I continued reading Karen's old e-mail. Karen characterized Laura's language as "crazy shit" and added that half of Laura's talk was mumbling, and the other half a string of profanities. Karen described Laura as having wild eyes that are "just always darting all over the place but not looking at anything."

Karen tried to protect Kate by placing her own body between Kate and Laura, in spite of Laura's pursuit and continuing threats to "beat that girl up" and "I'm going to get her." Karen confronted Laura and told her not to dare touch Kate. Somehow the trio had managed to get down the staircase, and Laura went back to the living room with my father and the other adults, while Kate ran to the kitchen. Karen later found Kate there crying.

Where had my sister and brother-in-law been during this threat to their daughter? What was my father doing? Larry? The cousins? Exchanging polite Virginia conversation in the living room? Karen didn't offer any explanation as to why no one called the police to take Laura away.

Karen's e-mail continued. Kate's father Mac finally took Kate home, and the two visiting cousins were "shocked at Laura's behavior." Karen wrote that the cousins heard Laura mumbling over and over,

"I'm gonna rape her, I'm gonna rape her..." But no one did anything about it. The cousins left and Karen went to the grocery store for some items my father needed.

When Karen returned, she walked in to see "Pappy" explaining to Laura and Wayne a comment he'd made about his displeasure at the "slugging scene" at my Aunt Edith's funeral. He was horrified by that incident between Laura and Kay, and he didn't want anyone behaving in such a fashion at his own funeral. Apparently Betty had twisted my father's comment, and told Laura that Laura was "un-invited" to his funeral. Karen openly wondered why Laura would care, since she had not attended her own mother's funeral. But Karen didn't seem to catch on that her own mother, Betty, had twisted a comment of my father's to further enrage Laura.

Karen wrote that the anger and rage coming out of Laura was over-whelming to everyone, that Laura was "on the very edge all the time, ready to burst into a fit of violence." She described Laura in the room with my father as he spoke. Laura never looked at him, but rather wrote continuously on a variety of pieces of notebook paper, taking one piece then another, in constant motion, and simultaneously mouthing unspoken words, rolling her eyes from side to side, apparently listening to voices inside her own head. Karen wrote, " She was having a con-versation with herself silently. I could totally watch it.... It was so bizarre. She's whacked out of her gourd."

Near the end of Karen's long e-mail to Marc, she wrote that she told Kay to get a restraining order and file charges against Laura. (Kay did nothing.) Karen added that Laura "could have been arrested that night for what she was threatening to do. This is very serious stuff."

I had been gratified when I originally read Karen's e-mail that at least one member of the family seemed to understand. Or did she? What had happened as a result? Nothing. Now, Larry was dead. Daddy was dead. This scene of family extreme dysfunction that Karen de-scribed had been swept under the carpet. Little did I know that Karen and Kay would together, much later, rewrite a new version of this his-tory and turn it into a pleasant visit for Larry!

Karen's e-mail continued, and she admitted that she thought it "odd" that Laura's husband Wayne sat around and did nothing when Laura was blatantly making threats in front of everyone. She wrote that Kay had asked Wayne if he could "do anything about this," but he just ignored her and turned away. Karen wrote, "He's whacky too!" At least she noticed.

Karen explained that the following day Kay, Larry and my father gathered in the living room and talked about my father's trust and the fact that he couldn't trust Betty as his trustee. He felt that his hands were tied, for some reason unspoken, and Karen wrote that he was "so distressed about the whole situation that he's scared to do anything." That seemed to be the family theme: "Do Nothing."

My father asked Kay to take over the responsibilities for his health, as a health care surrogate, but he seemed too afraid to give her the financial responsibilities, thereby leaving Betty in charge of all his assets. Kay refused, knowing that Betty would never co-operate with her in anything. Karen concluded weakly, "It's just one big mess."

The most amazing comment of the entire e-mail, however, was Karen's statement that she "really did have a good trip," and she felt "blessed to have strengthened my relationships with both Pappy and Larry." Really? I wondered if it was a hint of Karen's denial about the catastrophic effect that day had on both Larry and Daddy.

I did not know if Karen realized that my father had found that horrible scene so disturbing that he offered Charlie Loving a large sum of cash if he'd just replace Betty as trustee. Charlie could not have been a friend to my father without knowing about that day. Wasn't this event the reason my father insisted that he replace Betty as his trustee? And sure enough, a few weeks later, in mid-May, Charlie had agreed and signed on as trustee.

If Karen's relationship with both men was "strengthened," did she ever speak to Larry afterwards? I knew from Barbra how much unused medication she found in Larry's apartment, dating back to that trip. We both believed that trip and the way the family treated Larry motivated him to stop taking all his medication when he returned to Oregon, and to start planning his suicide. Did Karen have any idea?

How prophetic was her e-mail! It reeked of the family multi-generational malaise. I now wondered if the cousins visiting on that fateful day could possibly be the same cousins mentioned in Laura's missing enclosures.

I needed those enclosures.

Chapter 12

"My son, when you come to serve the Lord,
prepare yourself for trials.
Be sincere of heart and steadfast,
undisturbed in time of adversity....
Accept whatever befalls you,
in crushing misfortune be patient;
For in fire gold is tested,
and worthy men in the crucible of humiliation."
                                    --Sirach 2: 1-2;4-5

I got up from the computer feeling like I'd been hit by a truck. I had barely begun grieving the loss of my brother and my father when the police knocked on my door to accuse me of murdering Larry. Kay and Karen's betrayal followed closely thereafter. The hateful e-mail from Karen's brother Marc in Germany, whom I'd never even known, reinforced my growing realization of the wide-spread barrage of sudden reversals and losses, and tempted me to retreat from "all of those weird people." Now, the local verbal and physical attacks on my person and property, apparently the result of the internet invitations, demanded my response. I had no retreat, no place to hide. **I must do something**.

The e-mails from Kay and Karen, which sounded so similar, arrived after President's Day weekend. Before that weekend they had seemed supportive of me in my quest to find out who wrote the letter to the police. Afterwards, however, their e-mails appeared conspiratorial and accusatory. Karen had responded to an e-mail I sent to Kay, not to her, in which I'd laid out my civil legal options as I understood them at that point.

Karen wrote me a long treatise that began, "How disturbed and saddened I am by your increasing tone of spitefulness." She accused me of being just like her mother, Betty. She also wrote, "I fully support your following up with the letter." It was a mishmash of confused accusations and wishful thinking.

She wrote, "I am pained by what happened with Larry....But think back to when Pappy died. It hadn't even been 2 weeks since there was a notion that anything had happened. Charlie did the only thing he could have done considering the circumstances."

I jumped up from the computer pulling my own hair. "Notion? Notion?!" I screamed at the walls. How did Karen come up with a new history about the end of Larry's life and suicide? From Kay? From Charlie? What? "She was there last year! She saw how ill Larry was," I yelled at my computer screen. "She saw the crazy behavior in my father's house when Laura stormed in! She described it to me! Did she forget what she witnessed?"

She was present the day afterwards during my father's discussion about wanting to change his trust because he could no longer trust Betty, Karen's own mother. She had seemed to realize what that did to my father, after he spent a lifetime believing Betty and blaming everyone else for the hatred manifested in the family. Did she not have any idea that Larry had a heart attack after witnessing with her the insanity of that day? Didn't she get clued in when Charlie suddenly became the new trustee shortly after Larry's visit?

And what about Kay? She was there, too.

What could they mean that Charlie did the only thing he could? Lie about my father's distress? Lie about Larry's letters? Lie about Larry's health and history of threatening suicide? Lie about talking to me and my father about Larry's suicide? I couldn't tell if Charlie had fed Karen a line, or fed Kay a line who passed it on to Karen, but one thing was certain: Kay and Karen had decided they would not support me when I needed them most. I would probably never get to the bottom of it.

Kay wrote to me a day later with much the same language as Karen, accusing me of being hostile and bitter, yet defending Charlie's decision about the erroneous obituary. "ALL of us at the funeral home on January 17 agreed it should be so," Kay wrote.

So there it was! The origin of my nightmare. That statement made me realize that the whole change of history concerning Larry's suicide and its effect on Daddy began right there, in that room at Tharp Funeral Home, *after* they told me to write a eulogy for my father, and I hung up the phone. Unknown to me those people--Betty, Kay, and Charlie included--apparently decided they could more easily cope with my father's sudden death by denying the effect of Larry's suicide on him. In order to do that, it was necessary to deny Larry's suicide. And how better to do that than to deny that he was gone or dead at all? Laura had not been present at that planning conference: **what had they told her when she finally arrived?**

The discovery of Larry's suicide note and the investigation by Detective Mussler had been re-classified by Karen and Kay as a *notion*! Did Charlie Loving deny to them all that he had talked to me and Daddy about Larry's suicide? About Daddy's call to Barbra to get details? Did Charlie help Daddy contact the rest of the family after my call to him January 4th? Or did he just abandon Daddy in his hour of greatest grief? I now wondered if he had consoled my father at all. What kind of "friend" would suddenly pretend away the greatest tragedy affecting his friend?

Karen and Kay's e-mails, and later Marc's, evidenced their complete lack of understanding of what happened to Larry, to Daddy, and now, to me. They refused to talk to me, yet they imagined a dialogue between themselves and me. It had no bearing on the fact that the police were harassing me for capital crimes based on a crazy letter allegedly from Laura, and that I was suffering from trespassers and drive-bys and stalkers as a result of internet impersonation. Or that I was forced into civil action by a lousy local police force. I doubted they would care even if they knew.

Kay urged me to use "a loving Christian approach," and asked "What Would Jesus Do?" Karen, ignoring all investigative facts stated, "only God knows what truly happened to Larry and when." What obscene use of sacred words. They seemed to be living in their own worlds, with no connection to reality. And that's exactly how Larry had described them to me.

Larry was a witness and a victim that awful day Karen related in her long e-mail of March, 2000. So was Daddy. Karen and Kay were there. Did they forget it? Or were they so immersed in the family malaise that they simply denied it afterwards? Was that hideous day like a pebble tossed into the pool of this sick family, which created the ripples which were now becoming a tidal wave? Larry and my father were swept away. Would I be swept away too? All of those people who were there that terrible day--Where were they now? Where was Charlie Loving? Who threw that pebble? Which one was conducting the orchestra of disharmony whirling out everywhere now? Or was it ALL of them?

My thoughts ended abruptly when the phone rang. I was expecting a return call from one of the many attorneys I contacted about enforcing my father's trust. I had run into dead ends in Roanoke, Virginia Beach, and Richmond before finding Ross C. Hart of Roanoke, who asked Barbra and me to fax pertinent documents. Perhaps he was finally calling back with a strategy. I picked up the phone.

"Do you want me to pick up anything at the store before I come over, Carole?" It was a man's voice.

"Excuse me?"

"This is John, you know, we were just…"

"Who are you calling for?" I interrupted him, not recognizing his voice or name.

"Carole Fielder. Aren't you Carole?"

"Yes. And who did you say is speaking?"

"John. You know. John," he laughed slightly, "John Quarles. You do live at fifty-five fifty-five northeast fifty-fifth street, don't you?"

"Yes, but, what firm are you with? I didn't catch the name."

"Carole, didn't you just ask me to come over?"

"Who are you? I think you must be mistaken. Come over?"

"Yes, we've been chatting online for the past hour, and I'm on my way to see you…"

"I'm *sure* you have the wrong number…" I began, but the caller must have realized I was NOT the one he'd been "instant messaging." I heard the click on the other end of the phone, followed by my dial tone. I stood with the phone in hand, stunned.

My concentration on the trust issues, and my sadness at the family scene Larry had witnessed last year, was instantly forgotten. I rushed into the backyard, choked with fear. I saw my west side neighbor and hurried to the fence to talk with her. I couldn't get a word out before she told me that she had been burglarized three days ago, on Tuesday.

"Carole," she spoke with her German accent, hoarse from smoking, "you need to be very careful. We have been burglarized. While we were gone and you were gone. The police told us someone had been watching us—you, my husband and me--for a long time to notice when we would both be gone."

"Oh my god, Margot," I gasped as my heart pounded into my throat. "Again."

"Yah, yah, Carole, the police said he must have come into your yard and climbed the fence into our yard. He spent quite a time breaking into our sliding doors and sorting through all my jewelry. I lost over $20,000 worth, and worse, forty years of memories."

"Margot, I'm so sorry." Her loss momentarily took my mind off the strange phone call.

"Well, you know this is the second time for burglary for us in two years. But during the daytime, now. Do you think it's because of the internet invitation and all those men coming around here?"

Margot had sympathized with me about the loss of my brother and my father, had commiserated with me about the police accusations, and was totally disgusted by the internet impersonation. I had warned her about the vandalism in my yard and asked her to keep a look out for the backyard trespassers. She hated to deal with the police.

"Oh, uh, Margot, with all the callers and drive-bys screaming obscenities, the vandalism in my yard, and the men in my backyard and on the boat, I wouldn't be surprised. But the police have never sent anyone to investigate, so there's no way to know exactly." I didn't want to add to her worries by telling her about the phone call now.

"Well, I tell you, my guests lost all of their German deutsch marks. They have to wire money here from Germany. They are surprised how dangerous it is here."

"Yeah, Margot, it is for everyone here. I am so sorry for your losses. I don't know what else to say or do. I have filed a civil suit to try to find out who did the internet mischief, and to find out why the police accused me of murdering my dead brother. My lawyers are still working to force the police to give me the evidence I need to follow up. The police are still insisting that they are investigating me for being a cult leader profiting from organizing mass suicides."

"Oh Carole, how can they be so stupid? Why doesn't your church speak up and stop them? That's a big church, isn't it, and you're always there when you're not home!"

There it was, again. The obvious question. I blushed, embarrassed that I had no answer.

I chatted with her a little longer, then decided to call the chancery office of the archdiocese. Why didn't the church speak up on my behalf and call the cops off their investigation of me as a cult leader profiting from organized suicides at St. Coleman's? The absurdity of it had been amusing in the telling, but I found nothing humorous about the situation now. My neighbors and I were being terrorized in our own homes, with no help.

I called the telephone number for the Miami Archdiocese Chancery, Father Tomas Marin. After getting a recording, then a transfer, then an operator, and another transfer, I spoke with Anna Rodriquez-Soto, writer for the Catholic magazine. I told her I had e-mailed the office two days ago with the pertinent facts.

"I'm really out of money to fight this thing, and I need help from the church in the matter of the Broward Sheriff; at least I need to get the information they're withholding. There are more people implicated, most of whom adhere to the cultural ideas prevalent in that Bible Belt area around the Jerry Falwell empire, which explains the whole Catholic *cult* label. Lynchburg is my home town."

"Ah, well," she laughed, then continued with a heavy Spanish accent, "is there really anyone so stupid? That is absurd. But I will be speaking with Father Marin this afternoon."

Her amusement at my story summed up the problem that Barbra and I had in securing counsel. Nobody outside the narrow-minded, anti-Catholic enclave in that area of Virginia could believe it true that people anywhere in Virginia actually held to those beliefs. But all the people within that tight society considered anyone outside it suspicious, especially Catholics. Was I living the modern-day version of the religious wars waged by Christians among each other for centuries? Which side was more arrogant now?

I realized that I hadn't asked her exactly *when* I could get an answer, so I called back. This time, the person answering said Father Marin was out of town, and that Father Hennessy was in a meeting. I told the unnamed voice that I had e-mailed him two days before, and had spoken with Anna Rodriguez-Soto an hour ago. She then asked me to outline the problem. Again. I told her I was asking for help to get an authority of the church to vouch for me to the local police so that they would stop harassing me. That my local pastor couldn't help, and a Rutgers University chaplain had urged me to notify the chancery office, which I'd done two days ago, but I'd not yet gotten a reply.

"It would be better for you to call back again. Father will be back in the office on Monday."

I hung up wondering when I'd get a response. I grabbed one of my cats and sat down for a therapeutic purr-session, just to review in my mind what I knew to this point, to focus on my goals, to outline what I needed to find out. First and primary, as my neighbor just reminded me, and my lawyer Leah had originally stated, I needed to get safe. Obviously, I was under siege in my own home. (As was my neighbor.) I needed to stop the callers, the drive-bys, the vandals, the burglars, the trespassers. It was impossible to stop them without police help. I needed the local police department to investigate the three complaints I had filed February 27th, 28th, March 2nd; and to find out if my neighbor's burglary March 6th was related.

On my own without police help, I could screen phone calls, and avoid working in my front yard, so as to dodge the drive-bys. I believed Yahoo! had taken down the source of the problem from the internet, but how much time before that information would fade from the memory of the porno-cruisers or be deleted from their computers? Many more men might just show up on my property thinking they were invited.

Second, who was doing this to me? I knew for sure that Laura and Betty, with that crazy letter, had created the problems I had with the police. Based on the obituary notice, I surmised that Charlie Loving was part of the problem, possibly its originator. Somehow at my father's funeral services, he either lied or "Virginia-ized the truth" about Larry's suicide and Daddy's heartbreak. That triggered all the malicious speculation about me.

But someone was online still, impersonating me to local strangers. I had no idea how long it would take to find out. It could be Laura, Betty, Charlie, or the unnamed cousins. I needed the information in the missing enclosures to Laura's letter that the police still held. My attorney Leah promised to get them, but she didn't say when.

I hugged my cat, who then wriggled away. I felt helpless. It reminded me of being a small child victimized by Betty's long arms and gouging fingers. My father ignored her then, and now he had left me forever in this mess. I missed him. He had left Charlie in his place, so I would have to deal with Charlie, no matter what. I learned from one of my calls to Virginia attorneys that Charlie had four months to file any formal papers, so I may as well not expect any response from him until mid-April. I could only wait.

The days became a blur: one phone call after another, faxes, e-mails to attorneys, to the Miami chancery office, to Barbra. My attorney Greg Starr eventually e-mailed me that he didn't see anything "actionable" about my nephew Marc's hateful e-mail from Germany. I still wondered who told Marc such a story that prompted his hatefulness. Was it his sister Karen, or my sister Kay, or his mother Betty, or Charlie?

Then the next shoe dropped: Barbra called to say that Mr. Lowry, the Lynchburg trust attorney, finally responded to my brother Larry's attorney in Oregon, Pamela Yee, denying the validity of Larry's legal documents *simply because I had said he died.* In fact, a "power of attorney" only exists when a person is alive. Barbra and I knew that. We also believed Larry was dead, as did the authorities, but he was required by statute to be a "living missing person" for seven years, unless his body showed up. She had begged Larry not to kill himself and force her to find his body, but she'd not realized the consequences to herself of a missing body. That created a complication that Barbra didn't want: responsibility for his financial affairs for seven years after his suicide. She felt trapped. She had not bargained for the animosity from Larry's family.

Mr. Lowry and I had discussed this issue the week of my father's death. We both understood that Larry was "missing" in spite of the suicide. Barbra was acting on that legal basis.

"Barbra, it looks like you and Larry don't count for much in Virginia. I don't know what to say," I tried to console her. "What is it with them? First Larry didn't kill himself before my father's death; next he's missing; then I murdered him; next I reported him dead, therefore he is. Roger's investigation means nothing. Larry's suicide note is ignored; the missing body is irrelevant, the laws of the State of Oregon don't count."

"Well, Carole," Barbra giggled, "surely you understand those people better than I do. Nothing makes any sense to me."

"Did you call Roger about this?"

"No, is there any point?"

"Barbra, I do want to notify him, because now it seems that he is also being ignored, as though he never talked with Charlie. And I'm the one who asked him to call Charlie. I'll e-mail him."

I wrote Roger what had happened, and by evening received his response.

Subj: RE: Fielder : Case #2001-0441
Date: 03/14/2001 7:14:44 PM Eastern Standard Time

Carole, I am sorry for you and your family -- these things that are happening to you seem so hurtful, unnecessary and juvenile. I had not yet heard of this letter to Pamela Yee and I kind of wonder what her response

was. Nevertheless, in spite of the harsh and ugly issues being vomited up out of old Virginia, as you believe, the disappearance of Larry has been the crux of my investigation; the unpleasantness on the side, the east coast side, is apparently the culmination of years of study and I doubt any offerings on my part are going to make any difference. Still, until this should become a homicide investigation, I am willing to talk to anyone who is interested enough to call me - though I know little enough.

My FAX # is (503) xxx-xxxx, and it should be addressed to my attention. Anything you wish to send me I'll keep in Larry's file - but remember that it is Larry's file and also that it will be eventually a public record.

I wish I could help you get out of the loop, Carole, but it looks to me like you're in for the duration - unless you can somehow say to hell with this and with these people and just disentangle yourself from the whole maelstrom.

Incidentally, your attorney can contact Mr. Lowry and put him on notice that he is in error that Larry is deceased (in so far as is known to any certainty), and she can refer him to me and this investigation.

I wish you well.....and I'll talk to you later.

Roger Mussler, Det. WCSO

He was such a nice man, and he was absolutely right about the "maelstrom." The problem for me was how in the world to disentangle from it when the Broward County Sheriff was coming after me for capital crimes, and I was being pursued by strangers because of someone else's impersonation of me. I felt like a tennis ball being batted back and forth. Each time the internet crisis seemed to fade, the trustee issue arose; or another vandalism or burglary happened. The hits between Virginia and Florida only stopped at the net of Oregon's Washington County Sheriff. I was scared to wake up each morning to find out what else could happen.

Thursday, March 15, 2001

Half scared to face the day, I crept from bed to my computer and e-mailed my two local attorneys to tell them what Mr. Lowry had written to Pamela Yee in Oregon. I inquired whether it was libelous and pertinent to our case.

As the day wore on with no response from any attorney, local or Virginian, I decided to call and confront Mr. Lowry. I asked him why Charlie directed me to send Laura's letter to him. I asked if he recalled his discussion with me about Larry's missing body and the fact that it would take seven years to declare him dead, even with the suicide note. He seemed oblivious to our earlier conversations, acted hostile and announced that he'd had a call from my attorney.

"Who?" I was surprised and wondered what attorney had called him, but he wouldn't say, simply acted mysterious. When I pressed him about Barbra's status, he stated that he was going into court to make either Charlie or Betty Waddill the trustee for Larry's inheritance for the next seven years, as he had no intention of dealing with Pamela Yee or Barbra Milhaus.

So there it was. Betty was in the middle of it. I had suspected that she was somehow the originator of my nightmare, with Charlie's collaboration. It seemed like control of Larry's inheritance was the reason they behaved as they did. Laura was just a pawn.

When I told Lowry that my last conversation with Charlie included Charlie's swearing at me and directing me to hire an attorney, he told me that he didn't believe me and hung up on me.

It couldn't get any clearer than that. Charlie and Lowry had both turned against me. I would never know why or when exactly they decided to do that, but it certainly had not happened until my father's funeral service planning session. Betty was there. Laura was not. I was made aware of their antagonism towards me for sure after Laura's letter to the police.

I next dialed Charlie's number. He answered and immediately began what Barbra and I referred to as the "Virginia stupid act." I asked him the same question as I'd asked Lowry: why did he direct me to send a copy of Laura's letter? He refused to answer, but told me to write Mr. Lowry any question I might have. I asked him what Detective Mussler had told him, but he did a "Virginia twist" with words, told me to mind my own business, then announced he'd only deal with my Virginia attorney. When I told him I didn't have one, he insisted that I did, and that he'd gotten a letter from him that he was planning to answer. I wondered who he could mean, or if he were just making it up. He hung up on me, too.

"My poor father; to have trusted such a man," I spoke aloud to a sleeping cat.

Per Charlie's request, I immediately e-mailed Lowry the same question I had just asked both men over the phone:

Subj: Why did Mr. Loving want Laura's letter sent to you?
Date: 03/15/2001 4:35 P.M. EST

Dear Mr. Lowry:

I just called Charlie to ask him the above question, and he told me to ask you in writing. So again, I am asking.
Thanks.

Although I was emotionally wrung out from my attempt to get meaningful answers from the two Virginia men, I e-mailed Barbra. "What a couple of clowns. At least I've satisfied myself that *I* don't need a trust attorney, in spite of Mr. Lowry's hostility. Now that you know both Charlie and Lowry plan to ignore you, are you going to pursue any legal action if or when you hear back from the attorney in Roanoke, Ross Hart?" We had faxed him all the documents he wanted, but I never got a call back from him. I concluded, "This whole thing really stinks. Kay and Betty and Laura must have hated Larry the same as they hate me. Poor Larry. Poor you."

Just to make certain that I faced no trusteeship problem, I e-mailed my attorney Leah, and copied Larry's Oregon attorney, Pamela Yee. I related the two phone calls and explained that Mr. Lowry just declared to me that his letter to Ms. Yee did <u>not</u> state that he believed my brother to be dead just because I told him so. The letter he wrote to Yee stated, "I have been advised by Carole Fielder that her brother, Larry Fielder, is deceased." Did we all misunderstand the meaning of that sentence?

I also wrote, "Both men tried to dodge my question as to their understanding of my brother's disappearance/suicide as related by Detective Mussler. (???) Mr. Lowry pretended that Charlie Loving never told him about his conversation with Mussler. Charlie admitted to me reluctantly that he had spoken with Mussler and it was none of my business whether he communicated that to Mr. Lowry. So, do you think I still need a trust attorney in Virginia?"

✄✦✄

Saturday, St. Patrick's Day 2001

I still wanted to support Barbra in representing Larry. Charlie was described as "such a nice man" by some people, but we now knew that he had lied several times, maybe even to his attorney Lowry. Lowry had been very friendly and prompt in returning my phone calls before Daddy died. Charlie must have had a part in changing all that. But there were still missing pieces of the puzzle. Exactly what was Betty's part? Did both Charlie and Lowry know about that letter to the Pompano police before Laura sent it? Or did Betty create and send it and simply sign Laura's name?

My speculation ceased when I received in my regular mail an official "**NOTICE REGARDING ESTATE OF: ANDREW J. FIELDER.**" It was postmarked March 12 in Richmond, Virginia. Betty had mailed an official form to me, to Kay, to Laura, and, to Larry, at his previous apartment in Oregon. It was notification that she was the personal representative of my father's will, and would be "handling the deceased person's estate."

Did Charlie Loving know she was sending this? What about Mr. Lowry, who took the documents that replaced Betty with Charlie for Daddy to sign in the hospital on the Sunday before he died? Did she still not know that? I rushed to call Barbra, to ask if she were still picking up Larry's mail at the old address.

"Gosh, Carole, the apartment manager was holding it all for me for several weeks, but I told him last week to just forget it. But how can Betty not know what your father's wishes were? Do you think Charlie purposely forgot to tell her because he's scared of her, too?"

"Barbra, I don't make any guesses about any of those people. Whatever is the most twisted thing possible is what they'll do, and I can't think like that. You know that letter will go back to Betty as undeliverable. But she has to know that anyhow, so why did she send it?"

"I'm sure it's not good, Carole, whatever is in her twisted mind."

"Well, since I got through to Charlie and Mr. Lowry by calling them directly, I think I'll just try calling Betty and Kay again, and see if there's any breakthrough. But don't hold your breath waiting for news," I added, laughing. "Unless they're drunk on green beer for St. Patrick's Day, they probably still won't speak to me."

That Saturday evening, I called and reached Betty's answer machine, and left a message asking her, again, to please call me. I was surprised to reach Kay and her husband Mac at home, at 5:30. It was a stilted conversation, and she offered no explanation as to why Betty sent out the notice. I then basically begged her for her help in securing the safety of my own home and property. It was a wasted sixteen minutes. She "didn't want to be involved."

On Sunday, I attended mass and my next-door neighbor's barbeque. It was a relief that my German neighbor didn't blame me for her losses, although she felt strongly that it was all inter-related. She seemed more relaxed about her losses, and her husband joked about the expensive new necklace he'd bought her to make up for all the stolen jewelry and lost memories. It was a pleasant evening that sadly reminded me of my former real world.

The sense of normalcy did not last long. Two days later, Tuesday, March 20th, I attended my neighborhood Harbor Village Civic Association meeting. It was customary for local police to give a report at the beginning of each monthly meeting. Lt. Adkins was there from the Pompano police, and he warned us that there had been a rash of burglaries between January 25th and March 12th: five of nine of them were daylight break-ins through sliding glass doors. One of my neighbors asked if it were an unusual occurrence for the neighborhood, and Lt. Adkins told us that never in the history of Pompano had our neighborhood experienced so many burglaries in such a compressed time period. He gave out his telephone number and invited us to call him.

I felt numb. He listed the streets where the burglaries had occurred. I wondered if the salacious invitations on the websites that were targeting me had spilled over to my neighbors. What a horror. Someone else asked if there had been any arrests or recovery of property, but the officer answered "no." The unseen hands of unknown perpetrators of terror seemed to be multiplying and growing ever closer and more menacing. I thought of Kay's statement of "not wanting to be involved." I bet my neighbors "didn't want to be involved" either. I knew I didn't. When would it stop? Were the police going to do anything about it? Another wave of fear swept over me.

The next morning, I checked my e-mail and found a panicky note from Barbra. She wrote, "Where are you? I realize that sometimes you do not hear from me for over 24 hours, but I don't play on a boat by myself….so indulge me and just send a quick e-mail…"

I appreciated her concern and quickly responded that I'd spent yesterday at the doctor's office and getting my gamma globulin infusion, "which knocked me for a loop, but I dragged myself to a neighborhood meeting directly afterwards. I am waiting till the second the clock hits nine to call one of the cops who were there last night to give the neighborhood update on crime. Nine burglaries in two weeks. Will call you later."

The spin-dry cycle of telephoning began again. At 9:00 I called Lt. Adkins (786-4305) and spoke with his secretary Bonnie Van Dusen. She asked about the problem and wanted details of last night's meeting, then said she'd get Adkins to call me back right away. He didn't. That afternoon I called again, at 2:00. Bonnie acted surprised that I'd not already received a callback.

I dedicated the next hour to calling. I called several numbers looking for Police Chief Danny Wright, recipient of Laura's letter. I left a message with his secretary Gail, explaining to her that I needed enclosures to a letter he received several weeks ago. She suggested I call records.

I called records, and was given five different numbers with four transfers, spoke with three men and two women. Finally, at the last number, I begged the woman who answered to write down my four police report case numbers. She protested that she wasn't supposed to take any information, that I should call Strategic Investigations at 321-4200. It turned out to be a recording by Paul O'Connell, with a pager number to call. I left another message.

Next I called the State Attorney's office (831-6955) and asked for Michael Satz or Ken Farnsworth, who had never called me back. My attorney Leah Mayersohn evidently had not reached them either. I spoke with a man named Ed Walsh in person, who told me that he would call the police and ask when my case would be sent to them for investigation. Until the police passed the case on to them, nothing could happen.

I paused to catch my breath, to stop the spin cyle. After all those hours on the phone, I was still at ground zero: no detective had come to my house to follow up on any of my police reports, nor my neighbor's burglary. Absolutely nothing had been started by the police.

At 3:00 P.M. I decided to drive to the police station to get copies of all the reports. The lobby was empty. I used the red telephone at the front window to call the non-emergency police number and ask if anyone was there. I told the person answering that I was standing in the lobby trying to get reports and to find out what was being done about crimes committed in my neighborhood. The voice said someone would come out to answer my questions.

A woman appeared behind the reception windows, and I asked her about the reports. She wrote down all the report numbers I gave her, but said she couldn't find any of them.

Finally, a uniformed cop named Schnakenberg appeared. He knew nothing about any of my reports and wanted me to repeat, again, every little thing I had told over and over and over. I tried to give him a quick summary. He seemed interested only in the salacious aspects of the internet sites. He gave me no information, and no hope of follow-up. It was a complete waste of time, and a wasted trip. I returned home at 4:30 to discover I had just missed a telephone message from Major Rick Frey.

"This is Major Rick Frey from the Broward Sheriff's Office. My number is 786-4204. Colonel Wright asked me to call you."

I leapt at the phone to return his call, but reached his recording. I called the records department again, and they had found two of the four reports, but I'd have to drive back to the station to get them. I called Lieutenant Adkins again, but his recording rolled me to another number, where I spoke to a woman who promised he'd call back. Finally, I called another number that was given at my neighborhood meeting, a cop named Gary Hauter (786-4522). Another recording. Another message left.

All those calls accomplished nothing. Police help? In Pompano?

The evening brought more bad news in an e-mail from my attorney Leah:

Subj: Update
Date: 03/21/2001 6:21:17 AM Eastern Standard Time

I spoke to Gregg Starr yesterday after hearing your voice message. He provided me with a copy of the letter that he sent to Yahoo and a brand new Florida Supreme Court case (27 page opinion) which is not final yet. Unfortunately, this opinion is terrible for us.

In the interim, he communicated with the lawyer for Yahoo to try to get them to complete the interrogatories which would assist us in obtaining the identity of the yahoo user who posted the sites. I will send you more information on this later today.

What is the current status of your project to retain a trust lawyer in Virginia? Please keep me updated.

Leah

I downloaded the decision by the Supreme Court of Florida, No. SC94355:

JANE DOE, mother and legal guardian of JOHN DOE, a minor,
Petitioner,
vs.
AMERICA ONLINE, INC.,
Respondent.
[March 8, 2001]

I read it with total astonishment at the tormented, twisted reasoning of the five prevailing justices, and the outraged and reasonable dissent of the other four. One vote by one justice had thereby thrown away the "Communications Decency Act" Congress had passed to protect the innocent from cyber criminals and child molesters.

Instead, the Supreme Court used it to condone the murder of children, and to justify any obscenity, immorality, murder, or endangerment of innocent people by the cyber criminals of the world.

The case involved the murder of two Florida boys lured into a pornographic setting by internet pages, **after** AOL had been warned that children were being endangered by a known criminal offender using their web pages.

How could I, or anyone, ever be safe in our own home again?

What is the point of passing laws? So much for Congress' effort. What is the point of the judicial system? So much for justice in America. I felt utterly defeated.

As of March 8, 2001, the Florida court had decided that all the internet service providers, meaning Yahoo, AOL, Mindspring, Microsoft Network, and all the others, would not be held responsible for maintaining impersonating and dangerous web pages--even if they led to major crimes, including murder. Yahoo! Corporation's attorney Josh Russell had been the most helpful person to me after my horrific discovery of the websites. He told me I had to sue Yahoo! in order for them to remove the offensive material and to identify who had posted it. Leah had spent time researching other cases against Yahoo!. So much for getting Yahoo! to pay for the damages caused to me. So who could help me now?

I e-mailed Leah for details, "As for the AOL decision by the Supreme Court, what is the status of any legal action to recover my costs for having to privately do what the police refuse to do?" I felt helpless as I awaited an answer.

Much of the week became a blur of spin-dry phone calls and reading. I downloaded the Oregon State laws governing identification of dead and missing persons. I read the entire surprise decision by the Florida Supreme Court that rendered all the money I had expended on my lawsuit against Yahoo! Corporation wasted. Several days passed before I received any news from Leah. She simply e-mailed, "I am awaiting notification of whether or not Yahoo! sent Greg answers to the interrogatories. I am out of town and will return late on the 28th. I am still doing work on your case even though I am out of town."

I was glad to receive the e-mail, as I had left her many telephone messages, which remained unanswered. I e-mailed her in response and asked, "Is Yahoo going to identify the person or not? Are the police going to give up the evidence of the other sister's and two cousins' involvement in Laura Crews' letter or not?" I told her about my calls to the police and State Attorney and asked, "The police are either stonewalling me, incredibly disorganized, or are simply refusing to do their job. Which is it?.... Another 30 days have rolled by and I don't know if we are any closer to stopping this nightmare."

The next piece of news came in the U.S. mail, from my sister Betty. She admitted, "I received your message on my answering machine this past Saturday, March 17, asking about the notification you had received from me." She then proceeded to repeat the notice, ignoring my call and my question as to why she would send it when she was no longer responsible for anything. She had access to all the same information that I had. She refused to speak to me, and continued to act "Virginia deaf, dumb, and stupid." I studied the entire Oregon law on missing persons, and the most important statement to me was:

.... When a person is reported as missing to any city, county or state police agency, the agency, within 12 hours thereafter, shall enter into state and federal records maintained for that purpose, a report of the missing person in a format and according to procedures established by the authorities responsible respectively for the state and federal records.

Could that straightforward statement be twisted by Betty or lawyers somewhere to mean just the opposite? Could people in Virginia "decide" on a whim whether or not Larry was dead or alive, missing or not, and ignore what Detective Mussler had done, according to that law? Could the police in Pompano "decide" on a whim whether or not I was a murderer and a cult leader? Why were they still withholding the enclosures to Laura's letter, when they knew that the entire basis of her letter was a lie as soon as they read Detective Mussler's report? Why was there no follow-up to any of my complaints, nor to my neighbor's burglary? Why were they continuing to treat me like a criminal?

I sent a discouraging e-mail to Barbra telling her that Greg had dropped the case against Yahoo just days after Leah charged me to research other cases against Yahoo. The first $5000 was burned. Greg Starr had sent a one-page letter asking that Yahoo identify the person who'd set up the web pages. Did they have to answer now? Perhaps they would play the "silent game" that my sisters and my father's trustee and his attorney were playing.

I e-mailed Barbra, "I'm exhausted from the hatred and jealousies aimed across thousands of miles and decades of time. Nothing is worth all that. I guess I have to pursue the libel action to protect myself, my property, and my neighbors' property, but I'll be out of money soon, unless Charlie distributes part of the estate. Did you ever hear back from the Roanoke attorney? In one of my many calls, I spoke with another Virginia attorney who explained that Larry's interests will be passed over because of a Virginia law that states the original trustee gets to keep the share of a missing heir. Lucky ole Charlie. Good ole quick-tempered, smooth-operating, forked-tongue Charlie."

I recalled Daddy's misgivings about Charlie near the end of his life, although Daddy had come to rely on him for many daily activities. I could only speculate if Charlie had ever showed Daddy a sudden fit of temper such as he had displayed to me. Daddy never cursed anyone, and only occasionally used the word "damn." As for Kay's apparent loyalty and attachment to Charlie in spite of his actions, I could only guess that Daddy's distrust of her had been his premonition of things to come. The only thing he ever said was that she was just too much on the go, and that it was unhealthy for her daughter Kate, who seemed obsessed with horses.

Within a day Barbra e-mailed me that there had been nothing in Larry's mail from Betty before the post office stopped delivering it. She also had no response from the attorney Hart, but she wrote "If he thinks I have a snowball's chance in hell, I'll go for it. It's really bothering me that I might not be able to honor Larry's instructions as to who should be his representative."

She had obviously been thinking about the Charlie-Lowry-Betty-Kay-Laura connection, and wrote, "If that is taken from him then I will hold Kay personally responsible for dishonoring Larry's wishes. We both suspect that Charlie is listening to her and probably only to her. Charlie would have no personal reason to fight a legal paper from Oregon, would he, Carole?"

Did Barbra believe *any* of the people in Virginia were acting rationally?

She wrote, "If this happens, then virtually every one who Larry trusted and every one that he suspected that he could not trust will have completely dishonored him both in life and in death. After what has happened in the past few weeks, I have to tell you that my dearest fantasy would be for Larry to walk into that Virginia court and give each and every one of them hell for throwing him away. Then take his money and never speak to any of them again. I realize that would be perpetuating the family problem. But I think a time comes when personal survival should come first. I think the same for you. You have people who care for you, and though this isn't the same as family, your family doesn't know how to love. So grab the people who do love you and don't look back. Boy, how's that for unsolicited advice? Hope you do not mind."

Barbra signed off that she was going to go play a game of scrabble with her husband. What a wholesome concept. Nothing like that in my life. I was so glad she was in my life and had been in Larry's.

Chapter 13

Thursday, March 29, 2001

I needed to get the enclosures to Laura's letter. After the past three days of frustrating telephone calls to the Pompano police and lawyers, I had a list of names, but not much else. It was all so difficult. It took the entire police force to chew on it for weeks and weeks. I now understood what they meant by saying they'd call back "tomorrow." That was a code word for "never." Visions of the cattle on my uncle's farm chewing their cuds flashed through my head repeatedly.

For all my efforts last week, I had received only one return phone call, from Chief Rick Frey. If his call hadn't been on my tape recorder, I'd have thought I dreamed it.

I mulled over my contacts: Lt. Adkins had acted snippy at first, as though all my questions had already been handled by Chief Frey. After I gave him details of the specific enclosures I needed, he volunteered to look for them and call me back "tomorrow." When I finally reached the State Attorney Ken Farnsworth, he had received my earlier message via Ed Walsh, but he stated that he knew nothing of the case, and that I should keep complaining to the city authorities. OK. Who?

Paul O'Connell, the expert on internet pornography issues at Strategic Investigations, operated under a federal grant strictly for child pornography. He was sympathetic to me and fully understood the danger the websites created for me. He helpfully called Josh Russell, Yahoo!'s attorney, but afterwards concluded that if the local police refused to send a subpoena, I'd best quickly hire a private attorney to send a civil one.

Gee, what a surprise. My tax dollars at work.

I called Chief Frey back, and his assistant answered snippily that she had no idea when he'd call me back. For a change I followed up on my calls to the Miami Roman Catholic Chancery Office-- got the same unnamed person answering the phone. She acted as though I'd never called and left messages before, so I left the same message again. The bureaucracy of the Pompano police matched that of the Roman Catholic Church. I tried calling the Pompano police detectives directly, hoping that starting at the bottom again might be more productive than the top (Frey).

I spoke with a woman named Elizabeth, who told me she was a clerk who knew nothing and wouldn't connect me with a detective. After I spent some time on hold, she asked if I knew the names of any detectives. I rattled off Molamphy, Blankenship, and Montgomery. She then said that they were involved in "it," but wouldn't tell me what "it" was. Next, she admitted that two people named O'Brien and Harris would call me back, and that Montgomery had been transferred "downtown."

I kept hoping that someone, from the police or from the Catholic Chancery office, would call back with help. At 3:40 in the afternoon, a policeman named Dennis Howell called to say that I lived in *his zone*. My instant burst of hope he quickly deflated by stating that he knew nothing and wouldn't help me get the missing enclosures from Detective Blankenship.

So, why did he call me?

I quickly called his boss, Donald Harris, reached another snippy secretary who was unhelpful except for telling me that Harris worked for Adkins. I hung up and called Adkins, and his secretary Norma nicely admitted that he'd just walked by, and she'd ask him to call me. I took a deep breath.

I called Chief Frey again, and Bonnie took my message, remembering me from last week. I hung up and again called Wayne Adkins' number. He answered, but acted as though I had never before mentioned the enclosures to Laura's letter. He offered to go to Blankenship's office to look for the enclosures, but didn't commit to a definite return call. I called the criminal investigations unit once again; Dennis Howell answered and I asked him for an update. He refused to answer me, but told me Mitch Gordon was Blankenship's boss, to call him. I did, and left a message on his voice-mail about the missing enclosures Blankenship should have. I called Blankenship's direct number again, and got another recording. Whew! What's the use? Another thirty-five useless minutes in nonstop calling the Pompano police.

I decided to switch tacks, and at 4:15 called the Miami Roman Catholic Chancery office once again. The nameless woman with whom I had left the message yesterday answered, and she told me that "they" had told her to tell me to go back to the pastor of my church, Father Foudy. I held her on the phone long enough to explain how the problem was growing and becoming worse daily.

"But that's where I started six weeks ago, and he can't help me," I protested her brush-off.

"They talked to him already, and he *has* to handle it for you."

I hung up, stunned, and feeling hopeless and abandoned by my church, again.

Just as I put the phone down, it rang, startling me. I lifted it back to my ear and heard Chief Rick Frey himself speaking. **He quickly assured me that I had never been a suspect of anything.**

The nonstop calling had paid off! I felt a huge weight lifted, and wanted to feel exonerated and happy. My momentary relief was wonderful, but getting to this point had taken an enormous toll. I had never for one second thought of myself as a suspect of anything anyway. I had never before lived in fear, and the police failures that pushed me over the edge from fear to terror now pushed me to skepticism. I needed police protection from street criminals that beset me and my neighborhood, probably because of the internet invitations. I had a legal battle on my hands, and the police still withheld evidence that was crucial.

"Thank you, thank you. Thank you for telling me that! It has been seven weeks that members of the police department have continually repeated to me that I am a suspect in an ongoing capital crime investigation."

"Oh, Ms. Fielder, I assure you, you have never, ever, been a suspect of any crime."

"Does this mean that you'll finally give me the enclosures to the letter that I need as evidence in the civil suit I was forced to file?"

"Captain Montgomery doesn't think there were any attachments to that letter. He is as frustrated as you are."

"Then why didn't he call me back to tell me I was not a suspect?"

My question went unanswered.

He chuckled, "I repeat, you have never been a suspect of a crime."

"Then why has no detective been assigned to my case in the matter of the internet impersonation? Your officer believed it was created by the author of that letter. I still don't know why a police subpoena was not sent to Yahoo."

The silence was deadly. I continued, "Are you saying that anyone can steal somebody's identity and post websites that endanger life and property, with no penalty?"

"I talked with Paul O'Connell, and we wish it were a crime, but it's not."

"And you received a letter from out of State, that clearly indicated there were three enclosures, but they were missing? And you still sent detectives out to accuse a Pompano resident, me, of murder and profiting from organized mass suicides? Did you not even check up on the author of the letter? I have been up front as a lector or eucharistic minister at St. Coleman's Catholic Church, where lots of police officers attend and have seen me for the past nine years, but your men continued to accuse me of being a cult leader organizing and profiting from mass suicides there?"

He didn't speak, so I continued, unleashing weeks of frustration, "And ten days after your detectives accused me of murdering a dead man in Oregon, Captain Montgomery told me by telephone that I was no longer a murderer, but was still a suspect of being a cult leader, based on that letter. I asked him to give me the enclosures, and he told me in no uncertain terms that I was still a suspect of a serious crime, and that he wouldn't give me the enclosures. Are you telling me that he just made them up? That you have put me through this because of a three-page insane letter that was obviously missing the enclosures?"

I could feel the hair on the back of my neck rising, along with the heat from my flushing cheeks, as I comprehended his cavalier attitude about wrecking my life. I wanted to reach through the phone line and grab him by the throat and shake him. I stopped.

The silence on the telephone line was deafening. I waited.

"Well, maybe I'll call Captain Montgomery myself and inquire about that," Chief Frey said in a quiet voice.

"Thank you. I'd appreciate that, because he has not spoken to me since February 19th, when he said I was still a suspected cult leader and he was keeping the enclosures from me."

I put the phone down and cried. I felt no happiness that the chief of police finally admitted that he had never officially suspected me of anything. I cried, I screamed, I sobbed loudly. The pointlessness of the past seven terrifying weeks. Life lived like this was not worth living. Did Larry feel like this?

A few minutes later a local lawyer finally returned my call, and we spoke long enough for me to miss Chief Frey's second call. Chief Frey had found the attachments to the letter and would get them to me as soon as I called him back! I could get excited now. Maybe there *was* a point to life.

My heart was pounding in my throat as I waited for Frey to answer the rings, but his secretary answered. She could hear my joy, and she told me to call him back in ten minutes, that he was still there, but that she was just leaving for the day.

I set the timer on my kitchen stove for ten minutes, and began saying a rosary. When the buzzer sounded, at precisely 5:24 P.M., I called Chief Frey's number again, and it rang and rang. Finally he answered, told me that he was in the middle of a meeting, but that he wanted to verify that only I would get the attachments. He would advise Lt. Adkins to call and tell me exactly what time he'd arrive at my house with the papers. It would be tonight during the night shift, but he wasn't sure when. I thanked him profusely.

While the wait seemed interminable, I kept busy. I called my attorney Greg and left a message that the information was finally forthcoming from the police. I asked if Yahoo had yet identified the website creator. Then I called and left a message for Barbra to call me back immediately!

Within less than thirty minutes, the doorbell rang.

Thursday, March 29, 2001; 7:30 P.M.

After seven weeks of utter hell, the evidence I needed was finally thrust into my hand by a less than happy Lt. Adkins. There were all three enclosures Laura had included in her January 29, 2001 letter to Chief Danny Wright of Pompano. I thanked Lt. Adkins and began greedily devouring the pages with my eyes as fast as I could. I leafed through the first enclosure with a glance, affirming what I had already guessed: it was the eulogy for my father. (See **Appendix G.**) So I rushed to see Enclosure #2.

Hand-printed at the top of the page, Laura had written, "These are my cousins on my mother's side," with an arrow that pointed to the e-mail addresses of the two "mystery" cousins I had wondered about. Mystery solved at last! They were the two cousins I had seen for that quick Chinese lunch in 1995, my last visit to Virginia. They were the ones who had dined with Betty and King the night before, but had carefully failed to mention that fact to me. The ones I'd not seen in thirty-two years, not seen since I became ill in 1963. They never mentioned Laura, who was so much younger than they, yet here was the undeniable indication that they were on close terms with her, as well as with Betty.

My mouth dropped open in disbelief as I began reading, then my heart leapt into my throat as I continued. Unless all those people in Virginia were totally nuts, it made no sense to me that they didn't warn me about Laura, unless they were in full agreement with her. Had I really been a negative focus in their lives all those decades? It didn't make sense that they'd enjoy maligning me when I didn't even know anything about it. As I read, a black feeling of overwhelming nausea made it difficult to breathe.

From: "Laura Crews" <juliaericblair@hotmail.com>
To: HHaley@inna.net, margaret@inna.net
Subject: Carole's viciousness and Larry's "death"
Date: Fri, 26 Jan 2001 01:29:43 -0500

Dear Margaret and Helen,

Betty e-mailed me and told me that Margaret had been in communication with Carole (sorry to hear that, Margaret -- my caller ID showed she had called me on my first line xxx-xxxx, but apparently she doesn't have my barn line with an answering machine xxx-xxxx... and I certainly do not want her to obtain my e-mail).

In the right hand margin, adjacent to the next paragraph, was Laura's hand-written explanation, "This turned out to be Margaret's error--supposedly death was 2 wks before father's death. (Around Jan 5 '01)" It continued:

Don't you just love the news? So Carole is now saying that Larry died two weeks before Christmas? Be advised that as of about three weeks ago,

Larry was "missing." Not dead. He was "missing." Carole called Daddy and told him that Larry had "disappeared" and that no one knew where he was, and that he had left his wallet on his bed in his apartment and no one could find him and that Carole needed to know about Larry's bank account information--that is, to which bank was Daddy sending Larry money?

Daddy told Betty all this when Betty called Daddy. Daddy could not explain how Carole could know such details while she was sick in bed and dying in Florida. (But remember, Carole is The Mighty One and can be any place she says and she can also not be any place she says she is not, because she is The Mighty and All Powerful One... The True Giver of Truth and Integrity ... The True "New" Family Leader... Creator of the New World Family Of The New Age.... or whatever.)

Be advised that Carole is in better health than me. She is nowhere near death and is very capable of travel. There is a lot of profit to be made by obtaining the pity and handouts of others.

According to Betty and the Trustee for Daddy, Carole flew into a rage on speaker phone during the "planning" meeting for the funeral, because 1) she would be unable to conduct the service on speaker phone; 2) Laura might be at the funeral; and 3) Larry's name was going to be included in the obit (not an issue of alive or dead, but because Carole wanted him to be an Unperson who never existed at all).

Carole knows that I know what she is, and she is desperately afraid of me. I consider Kay as Carole's Oracle; and Karen Waddill is Carole's High Priestess. Karen, Kay and of course Kate (who looked like a painted, whorish freak with her heavily made-up face, pierced eyebrow and stringy hair hanging down), and husband Mac, as well as Joyce, Tommy and Shirley Bratton, all would not speak to me at the wake. Betty told me that she is sure the Brattons would not be taken under Carole's control, but would indeed believe anything sweet Kay would tell them.

Kay called my in-laws a couple of hours before the graveside service the next morning and yelled in a rage to Wayne that "If Laura threatens Kate the way she did last night at the funeral home, I will have her

ARRESTED! ! !" and slammed the phone down. My mother-in-law, who was at the wake, could not believe how Kay could POSSIBLY think that such a thing happened, in front of so many people. I assured Mom that Kay was only quoting what Carole had instructed her to say. The truth is irrelevant; if The Mighty One said that I attacked Kate in the funeral home, then it was so. The Mighty One had spoken and The Oracle had to repeat the magic words.

Carole faxed the Essay with a commandment to the funeral home that each and every person was to be provided a copy, and that it was to be read at the graveside. They weren't and it wasn't. It is very poorly written and I won't go into that, but basically she states -- four times -- that Larry is dead. Suddenly, he went from "missing" to dead. No evidence. But now he is an Unperson who never existed in the first place. She also states how she told Daddy Larry was dead and that she then was able to observe Daddy's life fade from him. (I can imagine her smug reflection on this.)

I think that Carole indeed did command Larry to go kill himself (which of course he would do without hesitation), with the idea that eliminating Larry would then make it, in theory, a 4-way split of the spoils.

-2-

Then she bombarded Daddy with phone calls telling him repeatedly that Larry was "missing" (not dead, remember).... and in glee saw that it really negatively affected Daddy. Then, with him eliminated, she could swoop in and empty the house of its valuables. But the trustee and the lawyer have changed the locks on the house. Karen and George Fielder (also not allowed to speak to me) had planned to stay in Daddy's house (imagine that) but were thwarted--they had to find some other lodging. I must stress that absolutely no one even mentioned "Larry's death" at the wake or at the funeral. The lawyer has not mentioned it, and the trustee did not mention it. If there was some definite evidence of Larry's death, I would think something would be said about it--and not just mentioned by Carole.

By the way, Kay eliminated references to me in Daddy's house, so that the trustee knew only that Jack had a fourth daughter, whose first name had been lost in time, but whose last name was "Crews".... so he went to the phone book to start calling the various Lynchburg Crews until he found one who might know of the mystery daughter. I do not think Carole will succeed in making Laura an Unperson.

At any rate, I don't see how there can possibly be any asset disposition until Larry's legal whereabouts are confirmed. So we shall see. Sorry this is so long, but I did want to advise you of this mess and to also remind you to be very, very careful with respect to Carole. Remember: there is no sincerity, no altruism, and always an ulterior motive in everything she does. She will take what information you give her and convert it to some sort of profit for herself.

Laura

My mind was spinning as I read the e-mails and simultaneously recalled the language of the website postings. The similarity of language tended to alleviate my fear, made me hope that no one else was involved in the internet. But the same New Age kind of lingo used by Laura to the cousins frightened me to the core.

Who, exactly, had all those people from my childhood become in adulthood? It was true that I had moved far away from my roots, by becoming a Catholic, marrying a Jew, living in California and France; but this, this craziness was off the chart of anything I could imagine. Larry's mental illness had shown up in bizarre behavior too. Now I wondered if all those "Virginia conservative Christians" lived in a never-never land of their own imaginings.

I rushed to read Enclosure #3, the e-mails between Laura and Betty. Again a blurry realization that Laura used the same language in her e-mails to Betty as was used on the websites persuaded me that Laura created the websites. My pulse throbbed in my temples as I began fast-reading the ten pages, which Laura's cover letter to the police had labeled "extended e-mail log of my sister Betty and me." (See **Appendix H**.)

1

Enclosure #3
E-mail excerpts

Here is excerpted e-mail correspondence:

> [On the right-hand side, Laura handwrote: "Be advised that there will be 'gaps' due to telephone voice conversations.]

From: Lwaddill@aol.com
To: Juliaericblair@hotmail.com
Subject: etc
Date: Fri, 05 Jan 2001 17:55:11 EST

Dear Laura,

I just called home and talked to Daddy. He had been to the doctor and he said the doctor's report was pretty good. He said that he is using the walker again - that Kay decided he needed to be in the walker, so he is using the walker again. He had been at Kay's since Tuesday.

He then asked me if I knew the latest about Larry. I said no. He said that Carole called him while he was in Salem [VIRGINIA] and said that Larry had disappeared. Daddy said that he talked to Larry about a week ago and Larry was bad off. But Carole said that Larry had disappeared. Carole wanted to know what bank Daddy was putting checks in for Larry. Daddy told her that she'd have to wait till he got back to Lynchburg because Daddy couldn't remember the name of the bank he deposited checks in from memory. (I didn't know Daddy was still sending Larry checks.) Carole said that Larry left his billfold and papers and some other things and disappeared. I asked if Carole had been to Portland. Daddy said no. I asked how Carole knew what Larry had left around when he disappeared if Carole had not been there. Daddy said that Larry had sent her a note. (If all this makes sense to you - good. It doesn't make sense to me at all.) I asked how Larry could get up and leave when Daddy had just told me that Larry couldn't get out of bed he was so bad off. Daddy didn't know.

Quite frankly, I gave up trying to understand the conversation. It is obvious that Daddy was very upset and concerned about Larry and all that Carole had told him. I do feel sorry that Daddy, who is in really poor condition now, has to listen to all this stuff. But evidently there had been a long discussion about Larry among Daddy, Kay, and Carole while Daddy was in Salem.

I just thought I'd pass this along. I called home a little sooner than I usually do because I knew that Daddy had had that fall. Usually Daddy doesn't tell me things, but this time he did.

Betty

From: "Laura Crews" <juliaericblair@hotmail.com
To: Lwaddill@aol.com
Subject: Re: Larry's disappearance
Date: Sat, 06 Jan 2001 14:54:42 –0500

Betty,

My first reaction to this was to think that this is a Carole double-whammy: 1) manipulate Daddy's panic/anxiety level to ensure that she does indeed have total control over him; 2) hack into Larry's bank account to further her assets.

Which leads me to ask if you can find out the bank. Banks and law enforcement agencies like to know when someone accesses someone else's bank accounts. We've been working with Tidewater civilian police departments on a ring down here that has accessed some $800K in stolen checkbooks and credit cards. So the subject is fresh in my mind.

The concept of Larry disappearing is rather realistic in my opinion. However, how indeed would Carole know about it before anyone else? Do Larry's friends (Milhaus or whomever) assume Carole is his "guardian" instead of Daddy? I would even consider the possibility that Carole has

2

Enclosure #3
E-mail excerpts

shipped Larry to Florida to better serve her. Just how is up to one's imagination... servant... sacrifice... nothing is beyond Carole.

Laura

From: Lwaddill@aol.com
To: Juliaericblair@hotmail.com

Subject: answer
Date: Sat, 6 Jan 2001 19: 10:13 EST

Daddy said that Carole and Larry are in constant communication and I believe that to be true. The other things that were said made no sense.

I also think that Carole wants the bank name to further her own nest. Daddy said that Carole was the one who told Daddy that Larry was bad off financially and to send money. I really can't see Carole asking Daddy to send Larry money if Carole doesn't profit in some way.

I am staying out of this. Totally out. Carole and Kay and Daddy are like a three ring circus. The only serious problem is that Daddy is not well.

Betty

From: Lwaddill@aol.com
To: juliaericblair@hotmail.com
Subject: Larry
Date: Mon, 8 Jan 2001 19:47:05 EST

I called Daddy on the way home from work. He sounds a lot better.

He told me that Larry had disappeared. That he had talked to Larry's friend, Barbra [MILHAUS (sp?)], and that Larry really has disappeared.

I asked if Larry took the car when he disappeared. Daddy didn't know.

Betty

From: "Julia Blair" <juliaericblair@hotmail.com>
To: lwaddill@aol.com
Subject: Carole on caller i.d. and the mysterious long-lost daughter "Crews"
Date: Tue, 16 Jan 2001 23:01:40 −0500

Betty,

Here's what happened on my end today: This afternoon when I was in the barn, I heard the phone ring seven times, which meant it was not line two which ends at four rings when the machine picks up. It didn't ring 20 times, so it was not Wayne. When I returned to the house to get ready for work, I checked the caller i.d. and saw it was "Carole Fielder (954 555-5555." It's very nice to have the phone number available for reference, but I was glad I didn't pick up in the barn (I couldn't anyway -- hands were full).

The other even more interesting item was this: Wayne called me (at home) to say his mom had called him (at work). She called him because Charlie Loving had called her because he was systematically going through the "Crews" in the phone book, and he apologized if she didn't know the answer, but he was trying to find out if anyone knew of a daughter of Jack Fielder whose last name is "Crews." That he didn't have any other information other than that Mr. Fielder had a mysterious, long-lost daughter with that last name (first name unknown), and he

3

Enclosure #3
E-mail excerpts

was trying to find some way to contact her to let her know that her father had fallen and was in the hospital, and that her brother was missing.

Mom Crews was totally shocked at the whole thing. Wayne was at that point asking me if I had talked with Betty. I said I had gotten some e-mails. He was horrified that I had not told him. I remained pretty casual about it. Wayne seemed ready to drop everything and run to Lynchburg. He called me tonite at work and said that according to the hard copy of the trust that Daddy sent some months ago, Charlie Loving has the power of attorney. Wayne also insists that I have met Charlie Loving. I am telling you that I have not. It seems rather noteworthy that Charlie Loving suddenly has found out that Daddy has some mysterious, long-lost daughter whose name has disintegrated with the passage of time!

Laura

From: "Julia Blair" <juliaericblair@hotmail.com>
To: juliaericblair@hotmail.com

Subject: Larry's cremains? / Carole's fear that Laura will be at funeral
Date: Wed, 17 Jan 2001 21:13:56 -0500

(originally sent to Betty but I forgot to put julia as BCC, so I yanked from ethereal memory)

Wayne called and told me he had talked to you this evening. You had not mentioned to me that Carole specifically asked if Laura would be at the funeral and then went ballistic at the prospect.... This could be rather entertaining. I am sure her fear concerns my being able to discredit her. Wayne thinks she might just show up to make sure that all her subjects and her possible prospects are not exposed to me.

I hope to see at least one person run screaming (so to speak) from the room at my mere presence... You must tell me yourself what transpired ref Carole and the lurid subject of Laura... Also, Wayne wants to have a recording of her phone message! I was rather surprised that he said that!

It occurred to me en route to work this afternoon: what if Carole has taken Larry to Florida to kill and cremate so that she will have something to go in the Lynchburg grave? There would be a lot of tricky aspects to take care of, but a tissue sample of some sort that could be kept on file in some manner would be similar enough in DNA to "prove" that the cremains in the hole are indeed hers... DNA cannot be extracted from the cooked and destroyed bones, but a sample conveniently stored beforehand and strategically produced as evidence later could come in quite handy. My desk sergeant said that she would still have to assume some sort of identity. With Karen as her righthand man, I would think that could be arranged. I am sure that Karen could be able to Double-Think that 1) Carole is dead; and 2) Carole is alive but with a different name.

This may sound absurd right now.... but has Larry's body been found yet? I do feel quite certain he is not alive... he would do himself in if Carole commanded him so.....

Let's just see where this goes....

Laura

From: "Julia Blair" <juliaericblair@hotmail.com
To: mond_world@hotmail.com
Subject: funeral
Date: Sat, 20 Jan 2001 08:52:43 –0500

4

Enclosure #3
E-mail excerpts

Ugly shit in Lynchburg. I am OK thanks to Wayne and his dad. Kay and Carole are insanely desperate in hate with me, grasping at straws and even beginning to look absurd to the most important people concerned now (the trustee and his wife, etc).

I am beginning to really think that Carole has moved Larry to Florida. The more I think about it the more plausible it seems (Betty says "ridiculous"). Carole wrote and faxed an absurdly stupid and poorly written essay on my father, which she commanded to be read at the graveside. They did not read it. I have one copy and must make more. In it, she said 4 times that Larry is dead. She says she was "tasked" with the job of informing Daddy of Larry's death, after which she watched Daddy get weaker and weaker and then die.

The most horrible thing she did was to demand that Larry's name be omitted from the obituary. She did not want Larry to be mentioned as one of Daddy's children. That, I think, was a bit of a slip-up for her. People were horrified that she wanted to make him an unperson. All she has told people so far was that no one knows where Larry is. She had not mentioned any confirmation of his death before....

I think it is time for me to contact Pompano Beach police in Florida. I have not heard yet from Portland Police.

I think the Lovings saw that I was not the monster that KC had told them I was. Kay claimed that I threatened the life of her daughter (Kate) at the wake. I spent most of the time at the wake talking with the Lovings.

Laura

From: Lwaddill@aol.com Save Address
To: juliaericblair@hotmail.com Subject: aftermath
Date: Sat, 20 Jan 2001 09:04:40 EST

Dear Laura,

I think that in the long run, Kay has done you a lot more damage than
Carole has or could. In fact, I think that most of the damage that Carole has
done you could not have been accomplished without Kay. My opinion.

Carole is considered suspect by a lot of people. But when Kay confirms
what Carole says, it makes what Carole said true. Joyce, Tommy, and
Shirley would never pay attention to Carole. But they do pay attention to
Kay.

I never heard anything about Larry's "death". That is Robert refered to,
etc. I didn't ask. If you know or heard any details, I'd like to know.

I was absolutely astonished at Kay's call to Wayne. Astonished. Kay was
making a Carole move. What did you do to Kate? Anything? Look at her
cross-eyed? This time, Carole is not making up the story. Either Kay or
Kate is. Do you think it was Kay or Kate? Kate refused to speak to me and
I stayed away from her. Kate is not an innocent.

I like Charlie Loving. But I blow hot and cold. I think you should always
think cautiously when dealing with him. I think he and his wife understand about Carole. I really do. But Kay is another matter. To Charlie,
Kay is helpful, wonderful, etc. Kay is the wonderful child who does no
wrong. When I read that Wayne had told Charlie about the phone call I
was delighted. Just delighted. Kay is still carrying out Carole's wishes.
Are you aware that Carole was calling Kay during the visitation for reports? Are you aware that Robert and Kay set up the microphone and cell
phone on Carole's orders. However, I have told several people about the
microphone/cell phone set up and their astonishment is total. First of
all, others find it funny. That is something that no sane person (is
Carole, Kay or Robert sane?) would do. Tell it as a straight story and
watch people's reaction.

5

Enclosure #3
E-mail excerpts

I think you owe your husband and your father in law a thank you. They did stay close by. I never saw you do anything to Kate. Wayne said he didn't see anything either.

I don't know about you, but the fact that you were there and you were "good" delights me. It delights me because I know how angry and upset it made Kay and Carole.

Betty

From: "Julia Blair" <juliaericblair@hotmail.com
To: Lwaddill@aol.com
Subject: Re:aftermath
Date: Mon, 22 Jan 2001 08:03:32 -0500

Kay follows Carole's orders. So does Kate. I am sure that Carole called Kay and told Kay that I had threatened Kate, and the fact that Carole said it meant that it was so. No questions. Wayne's parents were shocked at the phone call. Mom said that she just could not believe Kay would do something so "low." I reminded her that Kay takes instructions from Carole for Kay's every daily move.

I am sure that Carole was calling Kay during the wake in order to give Kay instructions. Kay, Kate, Shirley, et all stayed completely away from anywhere I was, and at one point they were gathered near the water fountain - I think in the hope of intercepting me. Wayne had me hold off long enough for them to wander away. Of course, I was terribly thirsty.

I didn't recognize Kate at first, sitting with Joyce. She looked like a painted whorish freak, with the tan face and the pierced eyebrow and stringy hair hanging down.

In Carole's stupid essay (which deserves an academic grade of "D" at best), she states four times that Larry is dead. I have no doubt that not only does she know for sure and is responsible, but that she knows where the body physically is. Time to talk to Florida police.

She even states that she was "tasked" with informing Daddy of Larry's death..... and that she subsequently watched Daddy go downhill and die afterward (I think with a bit of glee). Wayne felt that Robert diplomatically told her at the graveside that no one wanted to hear her anyway, and that is why she would just have to listen. I don't think so. I think he was apologetic.

I think she is really going to try something to get into Daddy's house. I told the Lovings so. She no doubt is going to be even more enraged to find that the house is locked tight. I expect she figured now was the time to make her moves: get rid of Larry, get rid of Daddy, rush in and grab before anyone notices.

Laura

From: lwaddill@aol.com Save Address
To: <juliaericblair@hotmail.com>
Subject: Re: aftermath
Date: Mon, 22 Jan 2001 17:47:24 EST

I'm at work, but I wanted to send a quick reply. Yes, Carole was calling Kay all during the visitation. The funeral home director had told us (King, me, Charlie) that she would be calling Kay to hear about things. And she did call - there is no question about that.

I didn't get near Kate. Kate refused to speak to me and I stayed away. Pierced eyebrow? Really? I never got that close.

I skimmed Carole's essay - didn't read it. I did realize that she said Larry was dead and that is probably why she got mad that I wanted him listed as a child. If she knows that he is dead, then I think it would be

6

worth it to find out where and when Larry died. Realize that George gets everything, per stirpes, if Larry is dead.

Re Robert: Maybe this is something I'll have to go into more detail later. Robert is worse than Kay and Kate in following Carole's orders. Robert tried, throughout the entire ordeal, to carry out Carole's orders. He didn't carry them all out because of Mr. Siegel - the minister at Fort Hill Methodist. Robert did really go through all the protocol as he was supposed to. Beware of Robert.

How do you know Daddy's house is locked tight? Since when? You might be mistaken on that.

At this point, I think the less you say to Charlie, the better. I know how he feels about Carole and you don't have to worry. It is Kay that he admires. Kay the good.

Betty

From: "Julia Blair" <juliaericbiair@hotmail.com
To: lwaddill@aol.com
Subject: Re: aftermath, status etc.
Date: Wed, 24 Jan 2001 12:07:06 -0500

The closest I got to Kate was when we first entered the funeral display room, and that was about 20 feet. I did not recognize her at first. She was sitting on a sofa with Joyce. I saw the flat painted tan face, heavy eye color, and the pierced eyebrow, and the long stringy hair streaming down the face. Then I realized it was Kate.

I did not know who Robert was at first, but it became apparent later. Mrs. Loving said that the house has been locked up and the locks had been changed the day of the funeral. I told her I expected Carole would have a moving truck there already, but Mrs. Loving said they had walked through the house and everything was intact. I have a hard time believing it will stay that way. They said someone would have to smash and break in, and would be in big trouble for doing it. Still, the items would be gone and no one would be able to catch Carole anyway.

Charles read her essay, as did several other people (including my desk sergeants). Their response: "You need to get a copy of this to the police." More later.

Laura

From: lwaddill@aol.com Save Address
To: <juliaericblair@hotmail.com>
Subject: Re: aftermath, status etc.
Date: Wed, 24 Jan 2001 17:25:28 EST

I didn't know the house was locked up and the locks changed. I am re-lieved. I never went there and I don't plan to until/unless called by Charlie Loving. I do think things are safe. But how would Charlie really know?

You read the essay of Carole's? I would not give her that pleasure. How do you have a copy? Did you ask for one?

7

Enclosure #3
E-mail excerpts

I am quite sure that Carole will contact every relative and friend, just as she did Margaret. I am tired of it all - Carole will play out soon. She won't have Daddy to call and harass at length. It will be someone else. but it won't be me.

I didn't recognize Kate either. When I realized she wouldn't speak to me, I just stayed away. Laura, I can assume that Kay will continue to do her thing against us with Robert Haley, the Front Royal kin, Virginia, etc. But do you care? I don't care anymore. I hate the nuisance. But for me, a lot is over.

I do wonder about Larry. I will get questions about that and I don't know the answer. The last I heard, Daddy had spoken to him a week to 10 days before he disappeared. Daddy never told me Larry was dead. Larry was disappeared. Larry left his billfold and everything in the apartment. And Barbra, when Daddy talked to her, was in the process of clearing out Larry's apartment.

Betty

From: "Julia Blair" <juliaericblair@hotmail.com>
To: lwaddill@aol.com
Subject: Re: Larry, aftermath, status etc.
Date: Thu, 25 Jan 2001 11:15:31 -0500

You didn't tell me that Barbra was clearing out Larry's apartment! That pretty much tells me that she knows what has happened. Otherwise, she is disturbing a crime scene. Of course, if she is under Carole's control, she will not cooperate.

Because of Larry's health problems, he should have been reported to police as "missing/endangered" and should have been entered into NCIC as such. I am capable of checking NCIC to see if he has been entered (that's part of my job), but to do so would flag the nationwide computer system that I have him in custody. So that is not an option.

Legally, I don't see how any property disposition can be done until the Larry question is resolved. I really feel that Carole's strategy was to eliminate Larry, which makes a four-way split; then eliminate Daddy, which would speed up the process. I think she intended to swoop in to loot Daddy's house while he was in the hospital.

Mrs. Loving said that when Daddy went in the hospital, everything was intact in the house. She said they locked it up and that they had the locks changed -- the day of the funeral. I told her I expected Carole was planning to send a moving truck and pack everything in the house into it. She seemed horrified, but also not surprised that I said that. She assured me that no one can go in except Charlie and the lawyer (and, I guess, her with them). She said they were concerned of the possibility of local criminal looting after people scan the obits.

We went by the funeral home before we left Lynchburg and got a copy of death certificates from Mama and Daddy, and also a copy of the essay. You really should read it. Lots of people should read it. I would not consider it as giving Carole the pleasure; I regard it as Carole incriminating herself. It is very poorly written: grammar, word usage, continuity, organization, parallelism, content - EVERYTHING!!! As an instructor, I would give her a grade of "D".... anyway, my friend Jackie said it was absurdly "flowery" like a romance novel or something. Other parts look

like a Sociology class term paper. Then you see her state, four times, that
Larry is dead. Not missing. Dead.

"Then two weeks ago, it broke my heart, and evidently his, when I had
the task of telling him of my brother's death. His pain and mine are
acute; he was alone, as I, in the horror and grief; I tried to share my
feelings with him, as best as possible by telephone. He couldn't. He never
had a vocabulary for deep feelings. But this final tragedy, that gave him
so much pain, sharpened his vision and understanding of the reality he'd
wanted to change, but could not."

8

Enclosure #3
E-mail excerpts

(Sort of sounds like she's trying to copy the style of Edgar Allen Poe, I
think.)

Pretty much everyone who reads the story stops at that point and ex-
claims that it looks like she told Daddy that in order to kill him.

Laura

From: lwaddill@aol.com
To: juliaericblair@hotmail.com
Subject: copy
Date: Wed, 24 Jan 2001 06:12:14 EST
I thought I'd send you a copy of an e-mail that Margaret sent me.

Betty
==================================
I thought I'd let you know that Carole called here last night after 10:00
p.m. We were asleep and didn't try to answer the phone! I don't know
about you all but it seems we go to bed earlier and earlier now.

Anyway, she wanted to know if we went to the funeral and if we did, did
we get a copy of her eulogy. She left her phone no. and e-mail address
for me to respond. I just finished writing her to let her know we did not
go--that we did send a basket of flowers (which Kay has more than likely

told her anyway) and I did not mention the eulogy at all. I told her I was sorry to learn that she was ill and, of course, expressed sympathy for the loss of your father.

From: lwaddill@aol.com
To: <juliaericblair@hotmail.com>
Subject: answers
Date: Thu, 25 Jan 2001 12:47:55 EST

I am the one who told Daddy that he should call Barbra. He said he had already talked to her and that she was clearing out Larry's apartment. Daddy told me about Barbra doing the clearing out.

It may be that Larry is dead and that Barbra and Carole know it and know details. I don't know details. I wish I did. Kay probably knows details. You and I might be the only ones who don't. The last time I talked to Daddy I said something like "maybe we'll hear from Larry" and Daddy said, "I don't think so." Everything is vague. Laura, I think that only you and I don't know details. I would assume that if we had an investigator in Portland, it would take about 1 hour to find Larry's death certificate. It may be that Charlie knows the details by now. You and I are the ignorant ones.

Larry's share goes to George, per stirpes.

Betty

From: Lwaddill@aol.com
To: juliaericblair@hotmail.com
Subject: from Margaret
Date: Thu, 25 Jan 2001 20:48:30 EST

Carole e-mailed me and sent the eulogy. I couldn't read it and it's no wonder no one wanted to read it!
I was so surprised and sorry to learn of Larry's death. She said he died two weeks before Christmas

From: "Laura Crews" <juliaericblair@hotmail.com

Following this page eight that simply dropped off with Betty's un-finished e-mail, and the one-line address from Laura, Laura had included pages nine and ten that were identical to her Enclosure #2. I began reading it again before realizing that it was the identical e-mail to the two cousins. Why had she included the same e-mail to the Pompano police twice?

My head was numb from all the information, the hideous mental processes so horribly displayed between my two sisters. There were so many people involved, apparently, that it was overwhelming. I rushed to the phone to call Barbra and fax her the whole thing. She asked me to read it to her.

"Not possible, Barbra. I can barely breathe. Just read it and call me back, please."

How many people did they implicate? I wondered who really knew about this, and if Charlie Loving were at the very center of it all. I believed the planning session of my father's funeral was the origin. I had felt bad vibes that day, but dismissed them as I hurried to compose the requested written eulogy. I now wondered if what I sensed in the awkward teleconference call simply emanated from an evil-minded man. I was so sorry that my father had trusted him, and I wondered if Charlie had encouraged Laura to notify the police. Was Betty just purposely stringing Laura along, knowing of her mental condition?

It was a long night. Truly, my sisters had constructed a Tower of babbling Babel.

Chapter 14

"God, you know my folly;
my faults are not hidden from you.
For your sake I bear insult,
shame covers my face.
I have become an outcast to my kin,
a stranger to my mother's children."

--Psalm 69:6,8-9

Horror, disbelief, shock, revulsion, fear, and terror of unnamed evil dominated my emotions for weeks and months. I read again and again Laura's letter to the police, the enclosed e-mails implicating some twenty-two other people, and the scurrilous Yahoo! Corporation websites. Sometimes I squeezed my head between my hands as I felt that a part of my brain containing the memories of my life was being turned inside out.

All those years of wondering, feeling twinges in my gut when some social exchange with a family member didn't seem quite right, that lifetime of feeling rejected and left out had suddenly been compressed into a pressurized bullet that exploded through the top of my head. What an epiphany! I wondered if Larry had experienced something like this.

Every time I looked at the web postings, or Laura and Betty's ravings, I gagged. I would have to find a way of detaching from it in order to deal with it. I had not yet talked to Barbra since I faxed her the twelve-page nastiness. Our exchanges always helped clarify things for me, but what could I say to her now?

I sat down with a cat on my lap to think it through. My eyes paused on the photo of Larry and me in 1978 placed on my piano. He looked like Chevy Chase twenty-three years ago. Suddenly a sense of Larry's hopelessness rushed into me, as it did whenever I ran across a reminder of him. I often thought about my two years of trying to relate to him after his inaugural visit to me in 1998. Our regular telephone relationship was so important to me. Before he died, I had felt a real sharing with him. I thought that finally someone could understand the intense suffering of my lifetime. But now, I doubted that he ever really related to me or my life. He probably had believed an imaginary concoction about me based on misinformation and gossip circulated in Virginia for decades. He had stayed in touch with "them" most of his life, while he had avoided me. And that made me sad for him, mad at him, and grievously depressed at the waste of both our lives so needlessly. But I wanted him back.

My eyes passed from Larry to the last photograph I'd taken of my parents. My lonely grief was swallowing me up. I remembered how I thought that Larry shared my grief for the suffering of our mother. I thought he understood that her suffering began long before her mind deteriorated to the point that she had to be institutionalized.

My mind drifted to my trip home in 1994 when I experienced another epiphany, four years before Larry decided to get reacquainted with me.

That was a trip I hated to remember. My husband had agreed to go with me, and although we were not getting along well, he turned into my best supporter when we arrived. We found my mother in a state of neglect, disheveled, staring alternately into space and at the various people in the room without recognition. She stood on one foot then the other, and turned in a circle without speaking, looking utterly bewildered.

My sister Kay had picked us up at the airport in Roanoke and drove us to Lynchburg. In the car, we invited her to come out to dinner with my parents, provided Mother hadn't already cooked something special for us. She acted slightly mysterious and said, "No, no, I don't *think* so."

"No, you don't think you can go, Kay, or no, you don't think Mother will have already prepared something?" I was puzzled at the tone of her voice.

"No to both things. Besides, I promised Mac and Kate, who are going to meet us there, that I'd make French toast, their favorite."

My husband's raised eyebrows and fast blinking signaled me his displeasure and surprise. Steak and potatoes, yes. French toast for dinner? No. Not a chance.

"Kay, really, can't we all go somewhere? We're treating!"

"No, you'll find out," she persisted mysteriously.

"We'll find out what, Kay? What's going on?"

"Oh, you'll see, you'll see for yourself."

And we did. When I greeted my father, I asked if he'd like to go out to dinner with us.

"No, no, you cain't take her anywhere. Look at her!" he pointed at Mother with contempt.

My heart burned as I quickly tried to talk to Mother, avert her attention from my father's insulting remarks. She smiled nervously at me, as though at a stranger, and to my horror, I noticed that an upper tooth was missing. She had never had a cavity in her life, and always displayed a dazzling, generous smile. I felt sick. My husband noticed my expression and shook his head with understanding and shock. We knew that Mother's dementia had increased. For several years she had refused to ever let Daddy speak to us on the telephone alone. But during the past year or so, she had never even come to the phone. Daddy always spoke critically of her, that she was always in her room sleeping, or watching television. Kay had told us that she was getting worse and worse, and that her doctor was concerned that she had lost twenty-five pounds since last Christmas. Nothing they said, however, had prepared us for anything like this.

My husband left two days later, and his parting comment to my father was, "Good luck with your decision, Mr. Fielder."

Daddy had looked puzzled. Sam and I had learned in two days all we needed to know: my mother needed twenty-four-hour per day care, and my father was unwilling to hire live-in help, and incapable of caring for her himself. I knew what I had to do, and that it would be an uphill battle. Before the trip, when Kay had hinted to us that Daddy was thinking that Mother would have to be institutionalized someday, I had been outraged.

"As long as there is a dollar left in my father's hands, my mother will live in her own home," I had insisted to my husband. "How dare they talk about putting her away!"

One of my friends, whose mother had died from Alzheimer's, had cautioned me not to be too adamant. She had asked me to consider three things before I went to Virginia. "How will you feel when your mother's teeth start falling out because she can't brush them? Or when she urinates everywhere because she doesn't remember how to find the bathroom? Or gets an infection from lack of cleanliness or smearing fecal matter everywhere?"

"Oh, that's awful!" I had exclaimed. "My mother is certainly not close to that point! She's got no memory to speak of, but I saw her at her sister's house two years ago, and she looked pretty as ever, and could still carry on a conversation."

What a difference two years had made. When Kay called me from Salem to tell me what day she was coming to Lynchburg to take me back to her house, I told her, "I really look forward to seeing you and your home, but also to getting some sleep. I've been awake ever since arriving here."

"Why, what's wrong?"

"Kay, how long has Mother been like this?"

"Oh, she's really getting worse all the time, now. Daddy doesn't think she'll be able to stay home much past next Christmas."

"Kay, I know why she's lost so much weight so fast. She doesn't know how to eat. She takes a bite of something, then gets distracted and forgets. She's starving. She also can't find the bathroom. The first night here, I had fallen asleep, but jolted awake when someone grabbed my leg. It was Mother, trying to climb into bed with me. She'd gotten up to go to the bathroom, but couldn't find her way back to her bedroom. She could have easily fallen down the staircase. No light was on. Plus, she'd gone to bed with layers of clothes and sweaters on, plus her shoes and socks, plus she'd pulled blankets over her. It was more than 90 degrees in that room, and she was soaking wet. She has to have twenty-four-hour care."

"I know it's getting bad," Kay began, "and Daddy did go look at that one place in Bedford, just last week."

"Kay, can he get her in there now?"

"Oh, no, they have a waiting list, plus Daddy's in no hurry."

"Well, I am. I'm on a plane out of here Monday, five days from now, and this has got to stop now."

"Daddy's planning to look at some more places. He'll do something by Christmas," Kay began again.

"No, Kay. This has to stop now. Now. The woman has to have care around the clock NOW! I am so tired I could drop. Daddy falls asleep off and on all day. He doesn't watch her even when he is here. He won't hire anyone to come in. Besides, she's past that point. How long has she been like this?"

"I told you you'd find out," Kay sounded pleased.

"So what have we got to do, Kay?"

"What do you mean?"

"Kay, I don't care what you think of her, or if you like her or not; I am not walking away leaving her in this situation. It has to stop now. Daddy has to get her twenty-four-hour care before I leave here. And I'm leaving next Monday."

"Daddy's not going to do anything right now, Carole."

"You know, Kay, I live winters in South Florida, where there are lots of old people. The television stations show cases like this all the time, almost every night there is another report about senior abuse, and..."

"Oh there you go! You're gonna get our father in trouble!" Kay started screaming at me. "It's not that bad yet."

"Not that bad? Not that bad? She can't feed herself, or go to the bathroom on her own, which is frequent, as I think now she's got a bladder infection. She's burning up in this heat, can't dress herself, can't bathe, and Daddy leaves her alone for hours at a time while he's gone. Not that bad? I wouldn't treat a dog I wanted to get rid of this way!"

"You're just causing trouble. Daddy will take care of it," Kay protested.

"Sure he will, Kay. Just like he always has. Just like he is right now. The man is well past eighty years old. He's not going to change anytime soon. When Sam asked him gently what he planned to do to take care of Mother in the future, he just jutted out that Saunders jaw of his, and said 'I can take care of her mahself just fine.' Right. You can help me, Kay, or you can fight me, but my mother is never going to be left unattended again. If I have to call in the authorities before I leave, I will. But I can't stay awake much longer."

Before that conversation ended, I guessed that I'd be cast out of Kay's life once again, and never get to see her home. Amazingly, however, by the next day when she came, she had completely changed her mind, and we together "hatched a plot" to convince Daddy. The next few days were some of the longest, most tension-packed of my life. We took Mother with us to Salem, and took turns alternately taking care of her and crying. We tried to cry out of sight of both Mother and Kay's ten-year-old daughter, Kate. Several times each of us had to make quick dashes into an empty room.

We worked well together as a team. "Here's what we'll do," Kay began. "I've already called Mother's doctor about it, and he said he was just waiting for an intervention. He'll be glad to talk to Daddy if we need him. We'll take Mother and Daddy to visit her remaining family in Front Royal, Saturday, to let them see how Mother is, and ask them to support Daddy in his decision. Then Sunday, we'll take Daddy by the old family graveyard, his favorite place in Franklin County, before we have a brunch at our lake condo up there."

"Oh, that sounds nice. We can spring it on him afterwards," I suggested.

Meanwhile, we called Betty, Laura, and Larry to tell them what was happening, and ask if the girls could come, and Larry call, to be with our parents on Sunday. Their 56th anniversary was that next week, so we could celebrate it early with them, and enclose checks covering the cost of a one month stay for Mother at an assisted living facility, with notes from each of us. The money would be our anniversary gift to them, for Mother to get the care she needed in an assisted living facility, while Daddy had time to rest and think what to do about her future care, without delay.

Kay was still close with Laura at that time, but she had no intention of calling Betty. They had not spoken for years. I agreed to call Betty, since I had been a guest at her Richmond home in 1991, at the invitation of her daughter Karen. Betty had carefully and strangely avoided talking to me then, and I could only hope that she would speak to me now. Kay and I made our calls and explained the situation.

Laura told Kay that she had a sick pony, so wouldn't come. Betty told me she was going to be busy that day and wouldn't come. We asked them if we could at least get together by telephone conference call on Sunday. They both agreed to that, and Betty wanted to arrange it. We called Larry, who also thought it a good idea. Betty would initiate two calls: a trial run of the conference call Saturday night at 10:00 P.M. to Kay's Salem telephone number, and a second one on Sunday, at 11:00 A.M. to Kay's condo number.

I told Kay, "Well, I suspect Daddy will want to just about kill us for pushing his decision, but he will be thrilled that all five of his children appear to him at the same time, even if it's just by telephone."

Saturday morning, Kay and I took Mother and Daddy to visit mother's remaining family in Front Royal. Mother's older sister, my aunt Edith, and all her children were there and so supportive and understanding of what Kay and I planned for the next day. They knew how hard the decision would be for my father, and that Kay and I would have to be very persuasive. They could see for themselves how worn out he was, and to what extreme my mother had deteriorated.

After the long drive back to Lynchburg to leave Daddy, we returned to Salem to await the conference call. When 10:15 P.M. passed without Betty's initiating the call, Kay and I tried calling first Betty, then Laura, then Larry. All the lines were busy. In our total immersion of caring for our parents, we had overlooked the fact that our siblings would probably sabotage any effort on our part. We looked at each other with the realization, and I said, "So we'll just have to do it ourselves. You write a note, and I'll write a note. We'll each write a check for half the total, then put it all in this anniversary card."

Kay and I could not at that time possibly comprehend the viciousness of the three of them. Six months later it became apparent what had happened, when Larry sent a letter to Daddy, showing his own confusion and the unfortunate influence Betty and Laura had on him. (See **Appendix D**.)

Sunday morning, Kay and I were both red-eyed and puffy-faced. We hid behind our sunglasses on the trip from Salem to Smith Mountain Lake in Franklin County, with Kate and Mother in the back seat. We met up with Kay's husband Mac, already at the condo, and awaited Daddy's arrival.

We planned to go directly to the Saunders family graveyard, a tradition with Daddy, a source of pride and instant trigger for his reminiscences of childhood. I'd told him that I wanted to do some gravestone rubbings to help figure out the stories my great uncle and my grandmother had told me when I was young.

In a phone conversation with Daddy before my trip, he had asked me to bring him the letters I had saved that were written by his uncle, my great uncle Brady Saunders. Before his death in 1968, Uncle Brady and I corresponded regularly, and I had saved his letters. Daddy was enjoying reading them.

One of seven siblings, all octogenarians, Uncle Brady Saunders had become the successor patriarch after his father's death, the respected Confederate Army colonel, Daniel Thomas Saunders, known only as "The Colonel." Uncle Brady, a wealthy industrialist with close connections to the politically powerful "Byrd machine," commanded respect from everyone, especially my father, whose first "father figure" had been The Colonel. The Saunders family graveyard was one of Uncle Brady's pet projects, and he expected my father to see to its care in his stead.

My father took his graveyard responsibility very seriously. My sister Betty and her husband King had helped Daddy clean up the weeds and re-glue broken stones during the summer of 1992, much to Daddy's delight. He'd sent me dozens of snapshots of the event, something he'd never done before. I knew how important it was to him. The graveyard was in good shape when we arrived.

Daddy looked relaxed, and laughed often as I did the rubbings, and began speculating on the relationships of the people buried there. He told us more of his childhood stories from the years he had spent with his grandparents, on this very property.

Afterwards, we all escaped the summer heat with a cold brunch at Kay's. Mac, on signal, took Kate outside, and Kay and I handed Daddy the card. After a quiet, infinitely long couple of minutes, my father's fury flamed from his ice-cold blue eyes when he looked up at us. Mother sat quietly, looking pretty and deceptively healthy, while we all discussed the inevitable, horrible decision. Kay called Mac to come in and talk to Daddy about it.

At one point, Mother finally spoke and asked, "Who are you talking about? Who's sick?"

My father glowered at her, his beautiful blue eyes glowing, "You are, Gladys. You are! We're talking 'bout you!"

"But I'm not sick," she protested like a child, bewildered.

Kay and I both dove for our purses to retrieve our sunglasses and hurriedly put them on.

"Let's go down to the lake," Kay gulped. "I promised Kate she could go swimming."

In the peaceful setting of lake and trees and shade, Mother and Daddy sat on a bench watching the water, and Kate, Mac, and me swimming. Later, I took a snapshot of them that would forever etch that awful day in my mind. They looked like the happiest, healthiest, still beautiful, senior couple. I still marveled that a beautiful photo could be so untrue to life.

Daddy refused to take Mother home with him that afternoon, and Kay and I didn't know what to expect. My plane reservation was for the next morning. It was a long night. Miraculously, Daddy called Kay at 10:00 A.M. Monday morning to tell her to bring Mother and meet him at an assisted living facility. He had found one where a client died that morning, and it was close to home in Lynchburg. The director had taken high school chemistry from my father, and was willing to help him out.

"You be sure and drive 'round to avoid lettin' her see home, now you heah?" Daddy had admonished Kay.

I made my plane in time, knowing that my Mother would never live "freely" again, but feeling that she would not suffer alone any longer. Kay had dressed her so beautifully, that no passers-by at the airport could have suspected the depth of our grief and sadness, nor the state of Mother's advanced dementia. I held my tears till they left, and cried through the whole flight.

Kay and I had planned how to proceed, and I volunteered to do all the long-distance telephoning of friends and family. By the time I landed in Florida, Monday, July 10, 1994, I had a fever and respiratory infection. I was sick in bed for a month. I made all the calls, however, and spoke several times daily to both Kay and Daddy.

During one of the calls with Daddy, he said, "Carole Anne, there was nothing wrong with Gladys until you came up heah." That added to the guilt I already felt from both Daddy and Kay's reports of Mother's protests and questions as to why they took her to the facility, and not to her own home.

Daddy eventually got over it, and decided that it was the right thing to do, and it was all his idea after all. Kay stayed in regular contact with me from then until Mother's death in October 1999. Where was Kay now?

Chapter 15

"Therefore do not be afraid of them.
Nothing is concealed that will not be revealed,
nor secret that will not be known.
What I say to you in the darkness,
speak in the light;
what you hear whispered, proclaim on the housetops.
And do not be afraid of those who kill the body but
cannot kill the soul;"   --Matthew 10:26-28

I gathered my courage to call Barbra and find out what she thought of the twelve pages of horrible e-mails. I wondered if the dark hatred of resentments and jealousies manifested by Betty and Laura was where Larry's imagination led him too, until he visited me in 1998. Did Larry ever realize what he'd done? He claimed to me that he had no recall of the letter he'd sent Daddy in 1995, which was a verbal attack on Kay and me, and critical of Daddy's painful decision. (**Appendix D**). I wondered if Barbra knew about it, and how it reflected both his sick mental condition and the influence Betty and Laura had on him.

When Betty and Laura later turned against him, I could understand his need for elaborate escape, to create his own kind of safety by planning a secret getaway of death. He knew what they were capable of first-hand. There was no way Barbra and her family, nor I, could possibly reach him and compensate for what he finally knew. The truth was too terrible. Whether our family members acknowledged it or not, we were connected, and the connections were deadly.

"Barbra? Have you read it yet?" I began our conversation.

"It's amazing, fascinating, and horrifying, Carole. Larry tried to tell me, but uh, I'm sorry, I just can't comprehend how people can treat each other like this."

"Do you think Larry ever believed I understood his situation?"

"Yes. You were the only one in the family."

"Did you notice that the underlying Big Lie throughout Laura and Betty's ravings seems to be that I was healthy, wealthy, and financially secure all my life?"

"Wow, Carole, that's an understatement. But there's something I've wanted to ask you for a long time. In fact, I constantly nagged

169

Larry to ask you. Did you or did you not inherit one million dollars from your Uncle Brady?"

Her question knocked the wind out of me. I was speechless.

"Carole, Carole, are you still there?"

"Oh yes, Barbra. Ohhhh. You're not joking, are you?"

"No, no, Larry always believed and told me that you'd inherited a million dollars from your rich uncle."

"Barbra, I can't imagine, *can not imagine* how anyone could possibly dream that up. He died in the '60's. Do you know how much money a million dollars was back then? My gosh, would I be living like I do if..." my mind was spinning with the implications of her question. My brain was on fire with speculation how such a story got started and why Larry would believe it. Of course—it had to be Betty, but did Larry actually believe it for decades? I wondered who else believed it. Certainly no one who knew me or my lifestyle.

I explained to Barbra the small fact behind the fantastic tale. My great uncle had no children, but he left a sizeable sum for that time, fifteen thousand dollars, to each of his nieces and nephews, including my father. It was more than twice his annual schoolteacher's salary. I couldn't remember exactly, but I thought the Saunders estate totaled about two million dollars. Most of it was donated to Lynchburg College after taking care of my uncle's widow. As children, Betty and I had spent some time at our uncle's farm during several summers. Uncle Brady had given my father money to help out with my medical bills before I left home. We had stayed in touch with letters even when I worked for IBM in Alabama. He did leave me a monthly stipend of one hundred dollars because, in the language of the will, I was "afflicted with an ailment."

Was Betty jealous of that? It seemed incredible, but there it was! I quickly calculated in my head what the total inheritance might be that I had received in thirty years—thirty-six thousand dollars, all fully taxable. It would be laughable if that was really the cause of all the decades of bitterness and acrimony. But, it was deadly.

"Gee, Carole, how disappointing," Barbra laughed. "I told Larry it didn't sound right, what he said. I kept telling him, just ask her, why don't you ask her? But he refused. He thought, and maybe Laura did too, that you just got lucky and rode off into the sunset leaving them behind."

"And what about my disability, Barbra? All those years in and out of hospitals didn't leave a lot of time for fun. What could they have thought?"

"I guess they never knew you were sick, Carole. Or didn't want to believe it. You left home a long time ago. Maybe they wanted to forget. The fact that you traveled places probably made them think you had gotten over being sick and, tee hee, were enjoying all that money. I'm sorry, Carole. I know it's not a laughing matter now. But it does seem that your whole family is all about money. I certainly know that from Larry—and your father, how he treated Larry."

Her comments resonated through me sickeningly. I suddenly recalled odd comments I'd heard from assorted relatives down through the years of infrequent contact. Since I traveled alone in spite of my illness, the family impression seemed to be that I must have been just fine. They couldn't comprehend how I spent my life forced to compensate for my physical handicap and pain. No one who has not had to use a wheelchair can comprehend the logistics, the discomfort, the abuse that goes with it. Life with long-term chemotherapy was another matter. I was a virtual stranger to all those people from my childhood. And my parents had not helped with their "Do Nothing" approach.

"Do you think Larry understood the facts of my life after his visit here, Barbra?"

"Well, I can't say for sure. But what happened to you when you were abandoned by your family and left disabled in Florida is how Larry saw his life, too. Especially the last two years. He was upset that Betty and Laura turned against him. He always prided himself on being able to get along with all of his sisters. He was the only one they would all speak to. Then they cut him off."

"Barbra, those e-mails, twelve long pages of hatred, lies, and innuendo—do you see that Laura and Betty are not alone in spreading it?"

"It's unbelievable how many names are in there, Carole. And not one of them has tried to give you any support. Just like Larry. It breaks my heart. Again."

"And it explains a lot about Charlie Loving. He was in it from the start. I wish you did have the wherewithal to take on Charlie. What kind of a friend stands by and does nothing with all this happening? I feel only contempt for him. I lump him together with lawyers, judges, cops, and HMO's. My father jumped from the frying pan (Betty) into the fire, when he picked Charlie Loving."

We ended the conversation in mutual dismay and sadness.

The day after I received the enclosures from Lt. Adkins, I e-mailed my attorneys that I'd finally gotten the evidence the police held up. I asked Greg if Laura had been served with the papers notifying her of my civil suit. I wrote, "I want to know if she's going to respond at all before we attempt to expand our civil action against the other people who, according to her enclosures, are part of her scheme to libel me."

I continued, "There are twelve pages of e-mails to and from two cousins and one sister, in which they discussed me and my "monster-ness"; and they imply feedback on the same subject from two other cousins, my father's trustee, the minister of his church, the director of the funeral home--as well as my sister Laura's husband and his parents. Since my communications with them all have been so curi-ous/hostile/nonexistent, the twelve pages validate why. Some of the terminology used is similar to the website, so my suspicions that it is the same person remain. But it is also obvious that the second sister, Betty Waddill, was "feeding" falsities to Laura Crews. Betty's e-mails give credence to what her daughter in Atlanta and my third sister Kay in Salem assumed--that Betty Waddill was the instigator behind Laura's writing the letter. She could also be behind the website creation. I do not know if any of this provides a *cause of action*. What is the plan now?"

My attorney Greg called me back Friday afternoon, and told me to fax him all the enclosures. He related to me that the process server company in Virginia serving the summons on Laura had called several times. They had gone to her residence, then to her place of employ-ment, and back to her residence. She kept dodging them. They then returned to the army base in Fort Eustis and saw her, but she ran away and returned with an army officer who told them that they couldn't serve a civil summons on army property.

"Oh, great, Greg. So nothing's happened?"

"Well, they say they've been in business twenty years up there, and have served thousands of papers on that army base, and this is the first time they were stopped. Your sister must have connections," Greg paused, then continued. "I didn't call you when they called me a week ago about the problems they were having, because they hadn't served her yet. They went back to her house, two more times. At some point, your sister had put up more locks, or gates, or something, so the proc-ess server had to sit in her car and blow the horn, to force your sister to come out. They knew each other by face by then. Ultimately, your sis-ter came out with a notebook in hand, and walked slowly around the car, bending over in back of it, writing down, presumably, the license plate number. When she got to the driver side of the car, the process server threw the papers on the ground and told her she'd been served, closed the window, then drove off."

"Laura and her infamous notebooks. I've heard about that," I mumbled, as I recalled several people describing her behavior at family funerals. She was always carrying around a notebook and writing in it-- even during funeral services, or at dinner tables. "So she *is* served, at least?"

"Yes, March 26th. Now she has twenty days to respond from that date, by April 16th. But there's more to the story, according to the woman process server," Greg was teasing me with the information now. "Your sister drives a pickup truck, and when the server departed, your sister drove after her, and rear-ended her car, a new Volkswagen. The server called "911" from her cell phone, while your sister pulled her truck around to the driver's side, rolled down her window and screamed obscenities at her, then made a U-turn on the side of the road and raced back home."

I burst out laughing. I laughed a belly laugh such as I had not ex-perienced in two months. I couldn't stop laughing for a full minute. Hit and run. According to descriptions through the years, at least Laura was consistent. Violent, loud, crazy.

Greg interrupted my laughter and said, "Gosh Carole, that's the first time I ever heard you laugh. Pretty funny, huh?"

My emotions were so raw, the relief laughter turned to tears as I told him, "I guess I haven't had anything to laugh about in a long time."

"I believe the highway patrol arrested your sister for assault with a deadly weapon. That may not be too funny for her."

"Good," I added.

Greg then explained that Yahoo's attorney had not yet responded, that with the terrible Florida Supreme Court decision, he was in a sticky situation. We needed to identify the creator of the web postings. He hoped Yahoo would co-operate, even though they didn't have to, now that the Florida Supreme Court decision was announced. Greg said he'd get back to me after reviewing all the e-mails. He warned me that the local police had wrongly used Laura's letter to accuse and harass me, but nothing could be done about that.

The laughter was gone too fast, and I once again sat alone review-ing the language in the e-mails, comparing it to the websites. How could anyone think someone other than Laura and Betty were the source of the websites? The use of the word "profit" in the context of Laura's e-mail to Margaret and Helen Haley, "There is a lot of profit to be made by obtaining the pity and handouts of others," was the same as *imasophistmaster's* profile that stated, "Hobbies:...turning others' misfortunes into my profits," and the "Favorite Quote: Your world is whatever you create it to be; you deserve the power and profit that others owe you!" (See **Appendix I** for sample web postings.)

I wondered how many persons were truly involved with Laura and Betty, as opposed to simply being mentioned by them. Surely all those people couldn't be fully aware of what Laura and Betty were doing based on their hateful imaginations. I went through the e-mails again, and made a list of the "cast of characters."

List of persons named/implied in Laura's Enclosures #2 & #3

1- Margaret Haley Ward, a first cousin my age
2- Helen Haley, married to a first cousin Betty's age
3- Betty Fielder Waddill (a/k/a "Lorraine"), my older sister
4- Charles Loving, Trustee for Jack Fielder Estate
5- Karen Waddill Huckabee, Betty's grown daughter in Atlanta
6- Kay Fielder Sammons, my next younger sister
7- Kate Sammons, teen-aged daughter to Kay
8- Mac Sammons, Kay's husband
9- Joyce Bratton, a first cousin my age
10- Tommy Bratton, a first cousin Larry's age
11- Shirley Bratton, married to Tommy (above)
12- Margaret Crews, Laura's mother-in-law
13- Cabell Crews, Laura's father-in-law
14- Jeff Thaxton, director, Tharp Funeral Home
15- Rev. John Siegle, minister Fort Hill United Methodist Church
16- Charles Lowry, attorney for Jack Fielder Estate and Trustee
17- George Fielder, adult son to Larry
18- Barbra Milhaus and family, of Oregon
19- Sgt. Chambers, desk sergeant, Ft. Eustis Army Base, Virginia
20- Earlean Loving, married to Charlie the Trustee (above)
21- Rev. Robert Haley, a first cousin somewhat younger than Larry
22- King Waddill, married to Betty (above)

I would have to wait for Greg to tell me if anything contained in the new material was actionable for legal purposes. Because the hateful things said in the e-mails were private communications, I wondered if there were a libel issue. It's not illegal to lie about people privately. If it could be proven, however, that the persons mentioned knew and encouraged Laura to send the letter to the police, and/or post the Yahoo impersonations, then they--Betty, Charlie, the cousins-- and their lies to Laura would become her best defense. But, they would legally become conspirators to commit libel.

My hope was that Laura would decide to do nothing and not even respond to the summons. Another "hit and run" for her. I would win by default in Florida and name my own damages. It would end. Then the last challenge remaining would be to hire a Virginia attorney to try to collect the judgment. Just because I won a case in Florida that included damages did not mean that Laura would pay for what she did. Winning a lawsuit was one thing. Collecting money awarded in a judgment was another, especially across State lines. I just wanted it all to stop.

Greg seemed happy at my comment, "If you summoned all those people to meet you in a central Virginia location for depositions, perhaps they would put pressure on Laura to fold. They would all have to take time off from their lives/work, and drive some distance across the State, and if they aren't stupid, would have to hire an attorney to go with them. I think that would make them furious at Laura and Betty."

I hoped the additional e-mail pages would eliminate the requirement for me to pay them as witnesses to show up in a Florida court. Surely depositions of all the people Laura mentioned would be enough, although still time-consuming and expensive. I also figured it was a good thing that my sister Kay and niece Karen were mentioned as if we were so close--after all, according to Enclosure #2, apparently Laura, Betty, Margaret, and Helen *agreed* that Kay was my "Oracle" and Karen my "High Priestess." Were all of them into that kind of strange language? I didn't know anyone who talked like that.

What if I could put Kay and Karen, with their inability to be direct or face ugly reality, in a courtroom to ask if they were my Oracle and Priestess? Ask them direct questions under oath in the presence of a glowering, glittery-eyed Laura. What a scene that would be! Unfortunately, that scene would probably never happen, as I worried how I'd come up with more money to pay Greg's next bill.

The reality was simple: whoever has the most money wins. Laura, *et alia* perhaps, had committed criminal acts--false police report, and internet harassment; and my tax dollars should have paid for the police to stop her/them. Failing that in Broward County, I might not have enough money to stop her/their criminal behavior with an expensive civil action. I worried about the number of hours Greg would charge me for looking at the mess of e-mails. I needed to protect myself in my own home and end this horror.

Greg advised me to go ahead and try to put pressure on any of the persons mentioned in the enclosures, to eliminate those who were "innocent bystanders" or persons unaware that their names had been used in Laura and Betty's great scheme. Who knew what, and when did they know it? Who encouraged Laura and Betty, and who simply shrank away from them, hoping not to "be involved?" If they **encouraged** Laura, then there might be legal conspiracy involved. Knowing what Laura and Betty were up to, and doing nothing to warn me or stop them, in other words, the "sin of omission," might be immoral to me, but it was not criminal or civilly actionable.

Perhaps Betty would pretend that she didn't know what Laura had done and wriggle out of any responsibility for the libel, and leave Laura hanging on her own. Perhaps some of the people would be disgusted that Laura and/or Betty had implicated them at all, and once learning the truth, would put pressure on the two women to cut it out. At any rate, my goal was to make them stop endangering me and my neighbors.

If I "aired all their dirty linen" under their noses, perhaps they would turn away. That would be my best security. Everyone involved with them needed to know what was going on, needed to know that the "secret" hatred was out and public, and their behavior in creating the web postings was dangerous to more people than just me. The oozing filth that lay beneath their pretty faces needed to be exposed to everyone near them. Stop the whispering. Shout from the rooftops.

∽∞∾

I devised a list of questions to send to the persons mentioned by Laura and Betty, designed to easily eliminate the person answering from any suspicion that he/she had any part in the libel. I would have to telephone each one in advance, explaining what I was sending and ask if they'd help me and themselves save money legally by answering the questions informally.

I reviewed the twenty-two individuals mentioned by Laura and Betty, mostly family members, but others, too. I decided that I should send the questions to eleven of them. My sister Kay, her husband Mac, and daughter Kate were maliciously slandered, and could easily "clear themselves," the same as Betty's daughter Karen Waddill Huckabee. Although they had unaccountably turned against me over President's Day weekend just two weeks after the whole horror began, I assumed they would help save me and themselves legal expenses, and answer the questions as an affidavit, without need of lawyers. That was four (4) of the twenty-two who would hopefully blast Betty and Laura's absurd speculations.

My cousins Joyce and Tommy Bratton, and his wife Shirley, had seemed friendly enough in 1995. I had dinner with Tommy and his wife. My father and I visited with Joyce briefly in Lynchburg as she was participating in a historical re-enactment of packet boats floating down the James River. The implication in Laura and Betty's e-mails was that they didn't like the Brattons. Also, Laura had displayed her psychopathic tendencies to Tommy and Shirley during Larry's last visit to Virginia in March 2000, as she ran after Kate Sammons threatening to rape her. I figured the Brattons would want to distance themselves from the mess by simple affidavit. That was three (3) more to answer the questions and be eliminated from any possible involvement.

The questionable behavior of two more cousins, Margaret Haley Ward and her brother Warren's wife, Helen Haley, left me feeling uneasy. They were the recipients of Laura's e-mail, Enclosure #2. They were quite obviously in the triangular communication loop with Betty and Laura. Were they frequent communicators? Were they witnesses to Betty and Laura's craziness, or did they possibly conspire with them to destroy me? One thing was certain: as soon as Margaret talked to me on the telephone, she e-mailed Betty. When Betty received Margaret's e-mail, she forwarded it on to Laura. Laura's e-mail to them seemed very familiar, as though it were just one of many exchanges. Those Haley cousins also socialized regularly with Betty at the "cousins dinners." Could they be a part of Laura and Betty's public defamation scheme to destroy me?

I had to admit that they were not trustworthy: they had deceived me in 1995 by their silence. A petty incident. I found my photo album with the snapshot of them, plus Betty and King, as well as another cousin and his wife, taken at one of their "Haley cousins dinners." They had dined together the same night I spent in Richmond. They all knew well in advance that I was coming from California to visit them for a reunion after thirty-five years' absence. None invited me to the dinner so that I could avoid all the driving.

Wheelchair and all, I drove all over Virginia to meet up with them, one in Fredericksburg, the others in Hampton. I saw my cousins Margaret and Warren, and his wife Helen, during a quick lunch at a Chinese restaurant. None of them even mentioned having dinner with my sister in Richmond the same night I was there. The only reason I found out about it at all was because Betty sent Daddy the snapshots. He immediately gave them to me when I returned to Lynchburg.

I suddenly remembered that my cousin Warren, Helen's husband, had a career in computers, and might be a whiz on the internet. I shuddered at the thought. Was it possible that the cousins, with Betty, dreamed up the idea of the websites as a joke at one of their dinners? I didn't want to think about the possibility, but I should give them a chance to distance themselves from the libel. I assumed that once exposed, whether they conspired with Laura and Betty or not, they'd answer the questions to exonerate themselves. Two (2) more questionnaires to send to the Haley cousins.

The director of the Tharp Funeral Home, Jeff Thaxton, and the minister of my father's church, John Siegle, neither of whom I'd ever met, had behaved strangely to me over the telephone--being friendly at first, then avoiding me. Laura and Betty's e-mails implied that they didn't know about Larry's death. Did my father's pastor, who'd gone to console my father about Larry's death, suddenly change the facts that day of funeral planning for my father? Even if he had been pressured by Betty and Charlie Loving, he would probably want to distance himself from the libel now. And Mr. Thaxton surely would not want his business tainted with such family scandal that originated on his premises. I decided to include them. So that would be two (2) more to quickly eliminate, a total of eleven (11) questionnaires to send.

There was no point in contacting the other eleven persons mentioned in Laura and Betty's e-mails. My cousin Robert Haley, the Methodist minister, who had co-officiated at Daddy's burial, was also slandered in Betty and Laura's e-mails. He knew first-hand the absurdity of their behavior, but he could add nothing legally. No point in bothering him. My nephew, Larry's son George, had already cut off all contact with his father and me. The last time I saw him in 1996, he had stated vehemently that he was changing his name from Fielder. He later made it clear he didn't want anything to do with any of his father's family. He was unlikely to have had contact with Laura and Betty during their creation of this defamatory scheme. I didn't know how to contact him anyhow.

On the other side, King Waddill, and Laura's husband Wayne and parents-in-law Cabell and Margaret Crews, were apparently all involved with Laura and Betty's efforts to destroy me. Charles Loving had been a snake in the grass, and presumably his wife Earlean went along. There was no point in asking them anything. They were clearly part of the slander. As my father's estate got settled, Charlie's legal intentions would become clear. So that was eight (8) on the list **not** to bother asking.

Three more non-family members, Barbra in Oregon, my father's trust attorney, Mr. C. G. Lowry, and the named desk sergeant, Chambers, of the Fort Eustis Army Base, remained on the list, but I saw no point in sending them a questionnaire. There were two names that tugged at my memory, however, and I reviewed the e-mails again.

I found this sentence on page six of Laura's Enclosure #3: "Charles read her essay, as did several other people (including my desk sergeants). Their response: 'You need to get a copy of this to the police.'" To what "Charles" could she be referring? I couldn't imagine how *any* lawyer could have read the eulogy of my father and considered it incriminating. Especially without consulting the authorities in Oregon. It seemed unlikely but disturbing if that "Charles" was Mr. Lowry, the trust attorney whose first name was Charles. I also wondered if Laura referred to Charlie Loving as "Charles."

Something else bothered me about the name "Chambers." When I was in shock about the police accusations not being resolved in a day or two, I had tried to reach Laura directly by telephone, at both her home and work numbers listed in her letter. I hunted for my phone bill, because I remembered making notes of the spin-dry cycle of calls to the Fort Eustis Army Base. My memory suddenly cleared and my body went on full alert.

Sgt. William Chambers was supposedly Laura's boss. On my first attempt to reach Laura, a Sgt. Bower spun me off to call the next day to

Chambers. The following day persons named Kellum, Demotte, Blackmore spoke to me, snickering and passing me along the line up to a Lieutenant Colonel Finnegan. He was reportedly the commanding officer and spoke to me directly, with a faxed copy of Laura's letter in his hand, and told me that she was an excellent employee, and the only thing he'd tell her was to **stop using Army equipment to send it out.** I could not believe that Laura's behavior was acceptable on that Army base, but there was nothing more I could do. Little did I know then that her certified responses to our legal interrogatories would not only list the above army employees, but also LTC Kerr, Chief Jellie, SGT Harris, SGT Patterson, SPC Henkel, and non-officers Felthousen, Chantal and Diven. There were fourteen (14) army employees, according to Laura, involved in her scheme to slander me. Eventually Army investigations involved many more names. It seemed to be a game of the military versus the civilians.

I couldn't get protection from my local police, and I was apparently under verbal attack by the army a third of a country away. What were the odds of my survival? I had to keep faith that the light would shine on the darkness if I just proceeded one foot in front of the other. One questionnaire at a time.

Of the twenty-two persons named in Laura and Betty's libelous garbage, half of them, eleven (11) could help cut through the mess by answering the questions I prepared.

1. What is your full, legal name, and current address?

2. What is your relationship to Laura Crews, and when and where were the last and next to last times that you saw/spoke with her in person?

3. What is your relationship to Carole Fielder and when and where were the last and next to last times that you saw her in person?

4. What is your relationship to Larry Fielder and when and where were the last and next to last times that you saw him in person?

5. When and how did you first learn of the suicide/disappearance of Larry Fielder?

6. When and how did you first speak with Mr. Jack Fielder concerning the loss of his son?

7. When, if ever, did you speak with the detective assigned to Larry Fielder's disappearance/suicide, his attorney, or his power-of-attorney in Oregon? Did Mr. Jack Fielder, Kay Fielder Sammons,

Carole Fielder, or King Waddill share with you their information received from the detective, the attorney, or the power-of-attorney for Larry Fielder in Oregon? If so, when?

8. Of the twenty-two (22) persons named in the enclosed case exhibits, did any of them relate to you a suspicion that the Oregon detective, the attorney or power-of-attorney for Larry Fielder were not telling the truth about Larry Fielder's disappearance and suicide note? If so, list and describe.

9. Did anyone at all relate to you a suspicion of foul play regarding Larry Fielder's disappearance/suicide? If so, list and explain.

10. Did any of the twenty-two (22) persons named in the case exhibits relate to you a suspicion that Carole Fielder caused the disappearance of Larry Fielder? If so, list and explain.

11. At the planning conference for Mr. Jack Fielder's funeral services, or during them, did any of the twenty-two named persons in the case exhibits indicate that Mr. Jack Fielder had not grieved the loss of his son two weeks before? If so, list and explain.

12. At the planning conference for Mr. Jack Fielder's funeral services, during them, or at any time afterwards, did any of the twenty-two named persons in the case exhibits, or anyone else, indicate to you that Carole Fielder (1) may have something to do with Larry Fielder's death/disappearance; (2) may be a cult leader capable of orchestrating mass suicides; (3) may be mentally unbalanced, or criminally insane, or easily enraged; (4) may have given orders to the funeral home, the cemetery, or family members; (5) may have secretly planned a trip to Lynchburg to steal all furnishings from the residence of Jack Fielder? If so, list and explain.

13. Describe in detail each act or omission on the part of any party named in this lawsuit, or any of the twenty-two (22) persons named in the exhibits, that you contend constituted negligence, or defamation of character, that was a contributing legal cause of the incidents in question.

14. List the names and addresses of all persons who are believed or known by you to have any knowledge concerning any of the issues in this lawsuit; and specify the subject matter about which the witness has knowledge.

15. Have you heard or do you know about any statement or remark made by or on behalf of any party to this lawsuit, other than yourself, concerning any issue in this lawsuit? If so, state the name and address

of each person who made the statement(s), who heard it, and the date, time, place, and substance of each statement.

That was it. Simple and straightforward. I assumed most of the recipients would have little to answer at all. All the questions were typed two to a page, to enable room for answers, and the last one was followed by the statement, "I hereby swear or affirm that my answers to the preceding questions are the truth, the whole truth, and nothing but the truth, under penalty of the laws of perjury in the State of Virginia and in the State of Florida." Then followed a line for signature and date, and a line for the notary public's signature and seal.

I planned to send a cover letter with the questions, and five attachments: (1) a copy of the legal complaint filed March 5, 2001, which included Laura's letter to the police and some of the Yahoo! websites; (2) a one-page list of the twenty-two persons named in Laura and Betty's e-mails; (3) all the e-mails of Laura, Betty and the cousins; (4) the letter Detective Mussler had sent my attorney Leah Mayersohn February 28, 2001, which laid out the facts and underscored the absurdity of Laura and Betty's speculations about Larry and me.

୧୬

April 5, 2001

I wanted to start out easy. My cousin Joyce Bratton had telephoned me on February 18th out of the blue, and asked me a few strange questions about Larry. It was clear to me that she had been talking to Kay, but she either didn't have any of the facts about Larry's suicide, or pretended she didn't know. Because of that call from her, I decided to call her first about the questionnaire. When she didn't answer, I moved on to her brother Tommy, who along with his wife Shirley, had seen Larry on that fateful last trip to Lynchburg, so starkly detailed in the long e-mail from my niece Karen. (See **Chapter 11**.)

Shirley Bratton answered my phone call, and I greeted her, then asked her to call her husband to the phone, but to stay on the line with him, as I wanted to ask them both the same thing. I had met her only once, on my 1995 trip. The three of us had dinner, and I made a videotape copy for them of the old Haley family movies we watched.

"Hi ya, Carole, wheah are you?" Tommy began in his slow Virginia drawl.

"I'm at home. And how are you tonight? Sorry it's so late," I apologized as I didn't get an answer until 9:21 p.m. We talked for more than an hour.

"Home? Are you in Lynchburg?"

"No, no! I haven't lived in Lynchburg in thirty-four years, Tommy. I live full-time in Florida now. Didn't you know?"

"Florida? Wow. That's a long way from heah. How d'ya like it down theyah?"

Shirley chimed in, "Ah always wondered what it's like in Florida. Is it hot?"

"It's subtropical," I began my tourist-oriented introduction-to-Florida-weather conversation. We spent some minutes comparing temperatures and rainfall and alligators and relative size of cockroaches, euphemistically renamed Palmetto bugs once across the Florida State line.

Eventually I turned the conversation to ask their permission to send some questions I needed answered. I described to them what had happened to me. I wasn't sure if they comprehended it all, but it would all be in writing for them to see.

"Wayulll " Tommy drawled even more slowly, "we'll be glad to hep ya' and ah'm sure Joyce will, too."

Then, just as I thought the conversation was finished, it took a bizarre twist.

"Carole, you know I know that Larry's not daid," Tommy announced.

"Excuse me?"

"Ya know, Larry and ah were verruh close, verruh close, verruh close....an' ah know he didn't go 'n kill himself."

"Really, Tommy? How do you know? Where do you think he could be?"

"Ah doan know about that, but ah know for **suhtin** that he's not daid. I jes' know that."

"Have you talked to Detective Mussler about this?" I was getting really uneasy.

"Nah, nah, I doan know wheah he might be, but he didn' kill himself," Tommy insisted.

"Well, Tommy, if you have anything that the detectives need to know, I'll be glad to give you their telephone number. But you really should talk to them about your relationship with Larry, if you have been so close to him. I didn't know that you guys were in contact with each other. Did you keep up a correspondence?"

"Naw, naw, we nevuh wrote letters. Nothin' like that."

"Did you telephone each other regularly?"

"Naw, naw, we nevuh called. But ya know, ah jes' saw Larry when he was heah, gosh, Shirley, wasn't it jus' last yeah?"

"We drove up to Lynchburg to see him at your father's," Shirley explained.

"Yes, I knew that, from several sources, in fact, and what a scene you two witnessed..."

"Yeah, yep. Larry was theyah and we talked a long time," Tommy interrupted me before I could ask more about that horrible day when Laura was threatening to rape her niece Kate, while all the family looked on.

"So did Larry confide his plans to you then?" I asked with disbelief.

"Naw, naw, nothin' like that. We jes' talked a lot."

"So, Tommy, when did you see Larry before that visit?"

"Ah, oh, ah guess it must be, prob'ly, wayell, ah guess the las' time afore that was when we were in school, and he came heah for the sum-muh," Tommy finished.

"You mean during college?"

"Naw, naw, I guess it was high school maybe, or eighth grade, somethin' like that."

I was speechless. My chest felt constricted like I'd just been put into a giant vice and squeezed between two huge iron plates.

"Hullo? You still theyah, Carole?" Tommy asked.

"Yes, uh, yes," I sighed weakly. "So, you think I should just go ahead and mail this package of papers to Joyce, too?"

"Shore, shore, ah'll be seein' huh to tell huh it's on its way," Tommy offered. "She's almos' impossible to catch on the phone. No point in callin' huh."

"Ok. Tommy, Shirley, thanks. Call me collect if you have any questions at all."

I hung up and started crying again, with all the pain of recognition at what Tommy meant by "we were very close." Was it a cultural phenomenon that all in our family were so disconnected from their own emotions that they were unable to connect with anyone else? I wondered if we all lived as isolated bits of flotsam and jetsam on the surface of a vast dark ocean. "Very close" but so far apart.

လ၁ၡ၂

I reached Tommy's sister Joyce a few days later as I was sitting in the clinic chair receiving my bi-weekly infusion of gamma globulin. As a medical technologist, she seemed to understand my health limitations, and we had a fun conversation catching up on memories and giggling like old times. She already knew why I was calling, apparently having spoken with her brother, and seemed glad to help.

Within a few weeks, I had contacted all the prospective recipients of the questions, and was ready to mail them. The telephone conversations with Reverend John Siegle and Mr. Jeff Thaxton had been strained, but they did say they'd co-operate.

Trying to catch up with my sister Kay Sammons in Salem, Virginia, and my niece Karen Waddill Huckabee in Atlanta, Georgia, turned into a type of hide-and-go-seek. They dodged my phone calls, but I faxed all the material to Karen at her place of employment--the Peachtree Presbyterian Church; and to Kay at her husband Mac's office as county administrator in Fluvanna County, Virginia. They could never use the "Virginia lingo method" to deny knowing about it and getting it. My fax machine carried a day and time stamp, and my telephone bill would prove I tried.

I received a by-now-typical hate e-mail response from my niece, Karen Huckabee. It made me wonder if she had read anything I had faxed to her. It appeared she was responding to a script in her head, almost as irrelevant as the e-mail her brother Marc had sent from Germany March 6th. She obviously did not know what my civil action was about, and appeared not to understand anything that had happened to me since February 9th. Her accusation that I was "threatening" her made me wonder if the mental illness suffered by Larry, and apparently Laura, had moved on down the generations. Only one thing she wrote made any sense.

She admitted, "For anyone to read Laura's words calling me 'Carole's High Priestess' and Kay 'The Oracle' and to gloat at the prospect of having 'at least one person run screaming (so to speak) from the room at my mere presence' during Pappy's funeral need read no further. The woman needs help. Desperately." The rest of her e-mail sounded like she took her script from her nutty brother. "Do whatever you want.

You can name me in whatever lawsuit you want and for all I care you can sue ME for being Pappy's granddaughter and taking the time to go visit him. If you continue your threats against me then you may be facing legal action yourself. But I guess that's what you live for these days. Whatever battles you have against Betty, Laura and Kay are your battles to fight."

She was clearly a confused young woman, but a product of her parents, and my parents, and on back into the darkness.

Trying to reach my two Haley cousins, Margaret and Helen, was a study in "dodge-ball" and "double-talk." I called Margaret Haley Ward, and got an e-mail response:

Subj: Hello
Date: 04/05/2001 11:13:22 PM Eastern Daylight Time

Hi Carole,

I got home a while ago and got your message. I've been gone all day and am really exhausted!

What's going on? How can I help you? I will be gone all day tomorrow and won't be back until after 8:00 p.m.
Hope you're doing well.

Margaret

I never got to speak with Margaret, but her husband, whom I'd never met, said they would gladly co-operate. He gave the impression that Margaret was too sick to return my phone call, but that he'd be glad to take care of it for me. I faxed all the material to him at his place of employment, as superintendent of schools in Mathews County, Virginia. His secretary confirmed that it all transmitted, and he called me back to say they'd do anything to help me out. He was sure that Helen Haley would help out, too.

Helen Haley wouldn't answer her home phone, and when I called her real estate office GSH Realty in Newport News, Virginia, I received a marvelous array of responses. She's on the other line. Call back in three minutes. She just stepped out. She'll call me. She isn't in yet, call back later. Finally, I simply asked for the fax number, and faxed all the material to her office. When I called to confirm that it had transmitted, I was told no, it didn't. I tried again. The transmission got interrupted. I called and was told that the machine ran out of paper, to try again. Eventually all thirty-five pages transmitted. I called back to find out when Helen would be in so that I could speak directly with her. That started another game.

I kept calling. Finally, Helen took the phone from the receptionist whom she had evidently directed to screen me. There were no niceties in that conversation.

"You are harassing me, Carole, and you'd better stop it," Helen began.

I was taken aback that she'd actually been there and had obviously looked at the material I faxed. I had not spoken with her since 1995 at the Chinese lunch. "So you are familiar with all this, Helen?"

"I don't know anything about anything. I never even looked at the e-mail your sister Laura sent to me," she huffed at me.

I had to suppress a scoff. What e-mail? If she never looked at it, how would she know?

"The only thing I know is that there's been a family feud going on for more than thirty years," she growled.

"Really?" I got curious. "With whom and about what?"

"I'm not going to answer any of your questions unless you talk to my attorney. You get your attorney to call mine," she hurried and hung up.

Her attorney(?), I wondered. What attorney? For what?

The most bizarre aspect of that conversation came later on my fax machine, on her real estate company's logo. It arrived May 5th, and was apparently written by Helen's husband, my cousin Warren Haley. It was labeled "Legal Questions." The Message lines were printed by hand:

CAROLE--WHILE HELEN & I ARE SYMPATHETIC TO YOU & YOUR FAMILY AT THE RECENT LOSS OF YOUR FATHER, WE ASK THAT YOU EXCLUDE US FROM ANY FURTHER CORRESPONDENCE REGARDING THIS MATTER. WE DID NOT READ THE ONE E-MAIL THAT LAURA SENT TO HELEN. WE SIMPLY DELETED IT. WE ARE NOT INVOLVED, AND CANNOT ANSWER ANY OF THE QUESTIONS THAT YOU RECENTLY SENT. REGARDS, WARREN & HELEN.

I laughed. Another belly laugh which I truly needed after all the effort I had made to eliminate some of the people from suspicion as conspirators. My cousin seemed to think that my legal questions to them were a social note! I concluded that Helen and Warren were as deeply involved with slandering me as Laura and Betty's e-mails suggested.

When I was ready to send the questions out to the Brattons, my cover letter to them told the story of my efforts.

Dear Shirley and Tommy,

Just a quick note to thank you for doing this. Laura Crews defaulted April 17, which means she admits to all that she did. Unfortunately, she has hired an attorney to try to dismiss the case before determining the extent of the damages. The more attorneys that get into the case, the more expensive it becomes. (All rather than talking person to person.) As you can see here, there are 22 possible witnesses to be deposed. What a waste of everyone's time and money, but Laura is calling the shots. And most of the 22 possible witnesses are apparently supporting her.

You expressed surprise that Margaret Haley would be involved in this. I am truly shocked and disappointed, as well. I still tried to give her and Helen Haley the opportunity to answer these questions, just as you are, but they refuse. So I have another attorney in Richmond to cover that end of the state. Kay also refuses to speak, so I've had to hire another attorney in Roanoke. Betty's daughter Karen, in Atlanta Georgia, was very supportive and encouraging up until February 21 or so, then suddenly turned on me and won't speak. (?) So I've had to hire an attorney in Atlanta to question her. I do not know why these people are averse to answering some questions, but sooner or later, either they will be forced to do so *subpoena*, or Laura will stop anyhow, and pay for what she's done. It just looks very suspicious to me that the very people that have complained about Laura's behavior for years, are unwilling to try to stop her.

As we discussed by telephone, my life and property have been endangered, my property vandalized, and my neighbors' property has been vandalized and burgled. There is no way to legally prove the events are related to the web site, but the "coincidences" are numerous and remarkable in the same time period. I will be forever grateful to the young man who had a "qualm of conscience" and told me about the website, and is willing to testify (under sealed order, of course.)

Hope to hear from you soon. Wish you'd consider a trip to visit me.

Love,
Carole

ॐॐ

Time told the whole story. Not one of the eleven persons returned the questionnaire. None of them has ever spoken with me again.

But while the days and weeks zoomed by during my attempts to get answers, I had much bigger problems to protect myself in my own home. And I was continuing to try to secure any memorabilia or furniture from my parents' home. Charlie Loving had been very busy, and my parents' home had been sold. He sent written instructions to all the heirs, including Barbra, after some more legal correspondence from Oregon, and gave a deadline for all of us heirs to decide who would receive which piece of my father's hand-made furniture. Another spin-dry cycle of telephone calls ensued, with Barbra and me trying to secure a Virginia attorney to protect our interests.

I seldom received news from my attorney Greg, except for short e-mail exchanges:

Subj: FIELDER v. CREWS, ET AL.
Date: 04/18/2001 5:23:29 PM Eastern Daylight Time

We obtained a default, but Crews retained local counsel who moved to dismiss. I will keep you posted.

I responded immediately and chastised Greg for the teaser. "What local counsel? Is it a done deal or not??? Please call me at your earliest convenience, or fax me the motion and default judgment."

My excitement that it was over was short-lived. It was just the beginning. I had to sit tight and wait for Yahoo! Corporation to reveal the name of the person, presumably Laura or Betty, who posted the websites. Meanwhile, Laura's attorney sent me lists of questions, called interrogatories, and requests to produce documents, to which I was required to respond. I was the one who had to do all the work, and prove myself, and produce my medical records of the previous five years, while her hatred and her malicious, criminal behavior continued to endanger me and my neighbors.

Worse, Charlie Loving's dishonesty to me early in this horror proved to be a mere foreshadowing of what was to come. Charlie and Mr. Lowry had sent a letter April 3, 2001 to all five heirs explaining the procedure for dividing the personal property:

"Each of you shall have until the 25th day of April, 2001 to return to Mr. Charles Wilmer Loving, Trustee, a written itemized selection of any item(s) you want and that item(s') value will be deducted from your share of the Trust.

I have listed each of your addresses at the top of this letter, and Mr. Loving requests that you each furnish him, as well as each other, your selections in writing by no later than April 25, 2001.

In the event any of you select the same item(s) it shall be up to you to agree between/among yourselves who will receive that/those particular item(s) and each of you notify Mr. Loving of your decision by the 9th day of May, 2001. If there is any unresolved issue as to who gets a particular item, including the coin collection, then, that/those item(s) will be auctioned by TREVILLIAN AUCTION CO. INC., located at 920 Commerce Street, Lynchburg, Virginia."

"AGAIN, I REPEAT, in the event any of you select the same items, then you are responsible for resolving the issue of who gets the item(s) and advise Mr. Loving of the final decision in writing by no later than May 9, 2001. This final decision is to be signed by all parties resolving the issue. If the issue is not resolved and signed by all parties selecting the same item(s) and Mr. Loving notified in writing of the agreement by the 9th day of May, 2001, then that/those item(s) will be sold at auction. There will be no exceptions to this procedure."

I had dutifully mailed my letter, return receipt requested, to all four other heirs and to Mr. Loving, April 10, 2001. That same day I received another letter with a corrected inventory from Charlie and Mr. Lowry, so I responded to that too. Laura had sent me a copy of the inventory with her choices underlined, but with no signature or prioritizing. Barbra had sent me her list for Larry. Nothing from Kay or Betty.

Beginning the evening of April 25, 2001, I compared the lists and sent e-mails to Laura and Barbra to work out our choices among us. I copied Mr. Lowry by e-mail on everything. Laura never sent her list directly to Barbra, in violation of the instructions, but we resolved our choices of most of the furniture.

It seemed like Barbra and I were operating in a vacuum, so I checked with my attorney Greg, "Is there some action I can take to force the trustee Mr. Loving to abide by the instructions that he sent to us two times? Is it a legal document or not? Did the statement, 'There will be no exceptions to this procedure,' mean what it says?"

I tackled additional problems which Charlie created. I was eligible to purchase my father's coin collection, because no one else wanted it. I remembered seeing my father sit at the kitchen table examining old coins that had been collected by my grandfather Fielder, who owned a grocery store. I was excited at the prospect of walking down memory lane, handling items that they had handled, although I knew nothing about coins. At least the collection would be a readily liquid asset: Charlie had appraised it at $6,482.95. He then made it as difficult as possible for me to get it. My dear friend Mrs. Barrett came to my rescue and personally picked it up from Charlie, packed and shipped it.

Charlie had written to us, "You will be responsible for the removal or transportation of any item you select and/or purchase at the auction." But his refusal to speak to me made it impossible to make arrangements for movers to make estimates on the resolved furniture choices.

Greg charged me for reading the instruction letters, then advised me to get an attorney in Virginia. There followed dozens more telephone calls to attorneys in Virginia. I wrote more retainer checks. After more of Charlie's shenanigans, he finally agreed that any furnishings the heirs chose or bought at auction would be deducted from our respective shares of our inheritance, and movers were finally allowed to go into my father's house with the list of my selected furniture to estimate shipping charges. Mrs. Barrett made arrangements to store some of my furniture selections temporarily at her house until the auction, so only one professional move from Lynchburg to Pompano was required.

The coin collection arrived safely, but I quickly learned its value was a hoax: local appraisers doubted the whole collection was worth six hundred dollars, and laughed when I told them I'd paid ten times that because of Charlie's "appraisal." More attorney calls, more fees, and more shipping charges later, I returned the collection to him to credit back into the estate the six thousand dollars he had charged me.

When the movers went back to pick up my furniture on the appointed day, they called to tell me some of it had disappeared from my father's house! Charlie still refused to speak to me, so I called the Lynchburg police to report the theft. With chagrin and disgust I learned that Charlie Loving had been a Lynchburg cop, so he could get by with anything. After all my efforts, Charlie decided to ignore his own instructions; everything was going to public auction.

I awaited the auction of the very same pieces of furniture my father had promised to give to me when I last saw him in 1995. The same pieces that, according to Charlie's instructions, belonged to me until Charlie unaccountably changed his mind. I couldn't bear to think of strangers taking my father's work, and I knew that my sisters had no room for any of it in their homes. Little did I know then how much Laura, Betty, and Charlie conspired to make me lose my inheritance in the auction for my father's furniture.

My father had lived his final years surrounded by secret hatreds and lies and innuendo, with his head buried in the sand. What a sad end to his productive life. But sooner or later, if I could endure it, the light would shine into those dark places and heal those sick secrets.

Chapter 16

"From within people, from their hearts, come evil
thoughts, unchastity, theft, murder, adultery,
greed, malice, deceit, licentiousness, envy,
blasphemy, arrogance, folly.
All these evils come from within and they defile."

--Mark 7:21-23

May, 2001

The days rolled by on the bumpy pavement of waiting and wondering what new trick or terror would appear around the next bend. Friends advised me not to act stupid or helpless. They cautioned me, "If strangers are breaking into the neighbor's house in broad daylight, watching your every move as well as theirs, sooner or later they'll be in your house, too." A wave of nausea and fear passed over me; I didn't know how to use a gun. Didn't want to know how. But that would have to change. I went shopping.

Before the end of the month, I bought a couple of handguns, signed up for the course to carry a concealed weapon, and got the license. I hated the idea of owning guns, but I would be irresponsible not to prepare to defend myself. There was no point in "calling the police for help." One for the car, one for my bedroom. At all times. I bought some pepper spray to carry with my keys. I felt a little safer.

The bills for my attorneys staggered the imagination. I was charged $200 per hour for everything. A phone call or an e-mail cost me $40 minimum. Leah and Greg were still waiting for Yahoo!'s answer before doing anything else. I was daily hoping against hope that any one of my sisters, or Charlie Loving, might have a change of heart, come to some kind of reasonability, and call me. That was a foolish dream.

The e-mails Laura and Betty sent to the Pompano police were apparently just the tip of the iceberg of nourished hatreds and resentments that Betty had spread like butter on everyone she contacted. Kay and Larry had been poisoned for years before they decided to re-enter my life. Perhaps such hostility was like an addiction, just something they did because they had to do it—or out of habit.

The phenomenon of suddenly cutting off all relationship and never

193

again speaking to a family member was a generational problem. I remembered the story that my own great grandparents never spoke to their first-born son after he committed an unpardonable sin: he married the enemy too soon after the War Between the States. He had the audacity to fall in love with a woman from West Virginia!

Now family secrets, which my ancestors traditionally swept under the carpet, were erupting like a volcano not only through the carpet, but out the family door into the community and onto the world scene. It was time to end all those generations of worry about "what people will think." The extreme avoidance of basic confrontation, of asking a direct question to get at the facts, had become absurd. My immediate family had involved both my extended family and total strangers in slandering me and endangering my community.

I felt morally obligated to stop it. But could I? Could the cycle ever be broken? I was having serious doubts because of the enormity of the whole scenario. This was not a matter of one crazy sister who didn't receive adequate mental health care. This was clearly **NOT** a family affair.

My whole community was damaged; friends in California, Oregon, Ohio, Indiana, Massachusetts, and New York were scandalized and wondering what was happening in Florida and Virginia. The quantity of lies and the extremity of imagination were the mere seedbed to create more gossip, more slander, more destruction.

The money was fast running out, and because of Charlie Loving's manipulations, I could not count on my inheritance to cover the legal bills. My credit cards could withstand no more. I had to give up.

I e-mailed Greg, with a copy to Leah, that I couldn't protect my inheritance and had run out of funds. I wrote, "Since we spoke, I have ascertained that many of the twenty-two persons named in the libelous materials were very much a part of the slander before I ever knew about it. They will refuse to be witnesses without subpoena. Many of them should rightfully be defendants. Their defamation efforts continue to grow. But the jurisdictional issue is cost prohibitive. I have retained three more attorneys (two in Virginia, one in Atlanta), as we discussed, in this matter. All to no avail. Virginia does not permit disabled persons access to the court system by speakerphone, contrary to the ADA as practiced in Florida and California."

I told them that I would try to find an attorney to pick up the case on a contingency basis, not knowing how impossible that would be. I continued putting together the documents due May 21st to Laura's attorney.

Leah surprised me with a quick response and stated, "I think that it will probably be difficult for you to retain an attorney who will handle your case for you on a contingency basis." Nothing could have been more true. She added, "I am also sorry to read that you are still having trouble with your father's trust in Virginia. I hope that the trust problems are resolved expeditiously for you. It is sad for me to read that the courts in Virginia are not ADA-compliant."

She was certainly right that lawyers never work for free, or *pro bono* in a case such as this. She was totally out of touch with my personal situation. She obviously did not know that handicapped persons living alone had no way of accessing the same "justice" guaranteed to able-bodied persons. I answered her the next day, thanking her for the note and telling her what Charlie had done with the personal furnishings in my father's residence. I wrote her, "The conspiracy to defame me among my sisters, the trustee, his attorney, several cousins, etc., is mind-boggling. I seem to be legendary in their twisted imaginations. Most of them I've not seen in thirty to forty years; some I've never met."

"When we first talked," I continued, "I thought we had an open-and-closed case against my sister, and that the trustee would recognize the truth once it lay before him. On the contrary, he was at the source of the scandal during my father's funeral services, and evidently knew about my sister's letter before I did. Now, I am out ten thousand dollars, have wasted four months of my life trying to defend my person and my property, can get no police protection, and have just learned that my 90-year-old father was taken advantage of by an ex-cop pretending to be his friend."

In my *naïveté*, I had never realized that trusts were so violable, and heirs who are not resident in the State of the trust had no rights. Trusts don't really mean anything when heirs can't inherit if they are not able-bodied nor able to get rid of a trustee bent on deception. I e-mailed Leah, "My missing brother (Oregon) and I have been deprived of our fair share of some $250,000 of fine arts and furniture, which our father specifically wanted to keep in the family. The trustee did a deal with an auction company, went through the motions of sending out to the heirs a fair procedure to divide up the belongings. It was a sham. When only my brother's representative and I followed his procedures, he abruptly changed his mind, withdrew the whole process, did a secret division with two of the other heirs in Virginia who had not participated at all in his procedure. What do you think he has to gain by doing that?"

I now wondered if Larry's representative and I would receive our fair share of the intangibles of a million-plus estate. If I couldn't find a lawyer interested in dividing that up, I'd have to give up. I ended my e-mail to Leah, "Please send me an itemized bill and refund any balance of the retainer."

She then sent me a one-liner, but no bill and no refund:

Subj: Re: Fielder vs. Crews
Date: 05/15/2001 7:20:26 AM Eastern Daylight Time

What about contacting law enforcement in Virginia--non-local, federal?

I was too discouraged to think about it. Without lots of money, there is no protection and no justice in America. I needed to face reality and get on with my life. I wrote Greg, copied Leah, and asked him not to withdraw quite yet, as funds left with Leah might cover him for a few days. I also wrote that I might get back retainers sent to the other five attorneys. Little did I realize then how silly that must have sounded to an attorney.

In my e-mail to Greg, I complained, "I thought you or Leah would get the name of the person posting the Yahoo site from Yahoo months ago. What is the status of your subpoena for that? It is essential information. I don't understand how $6000 was not enough to get information that Yahoo was willing to give me immediately if only the police did their job. But if I can't be sure of winning an obvious case, what is the point?"

❦

The police, my attorneys, friends who saw the letter and web pages, all suspected Laura posted the web pages, even if some of the other twenty-two persons named by her in the letter actually created them on different computers. I had verified that ten of the people named in Laura's enclosures were actively slandering me. I still had no idea why they "nominated" me for legend status. But I knew above all that if I weren't sick and unable to travel, this could never have happened. If I didn't receive my share of my father's estate because I couldn't get legal help, then I was at the end of the line financially.

It was almost comic relief when the day after I "threw in the towel" on the attorneys, the incoming water pipe valve in my bathroom toilet tank burst--plastic fatigue they called it--and flooded the entire interior of my home. What a mess. What an expense. I valiantly, and too strenuously, spent hours trying to vacuum up the water and dump it out. I thought I had done a pretty decent job, but the next day when I stepped out of bed, the water covered my toes. Far from the source of the flood, my floors and carpets were awash. The walls had evidently absorbed lots of the water, and as I had vacuumed the floors, I merely made room for the walls to drain. Much of my furniture was stained for a couple inches off the floor. What a metaphor for the spreading slander!

I reluctantly called my insurance company, and they urged me to get a professional flood-control company to come immediately. After several weeks of cleanup, the happy ending, or the way I interpreted what happened, was a check for more than $10,000 which came to repair the damages. I made only the more urgent repairs, and kept the balance of the money for legal expenses.

I re-hired my attorney, Greg, with the residual. Meanwhile, I had been working to prepare all the documents and answers to the interrogatories Laura's attorney demanded. I finally submitted them, including five years of medical bills, two years of telephone bills, and all the correspondence I'd had with all members of the family. The stack of paper measured over twenty inches.

June, 2001

The wait for Yahoo's response finally ended late in June. The information they sent, however, led to more questions, not answers, not Laura's name or Betty's name. Made-up, fictitious identities. I learned just what an Internet Protocol Number (IP#) is. I learned how to find out online what company owned which IP numbers. I was forced to learn more about the internet than I ever wanted to know. Leah wrote to me:

Subj: TERRIFIC NEWS
Date: 06/29/2001 12:58:14 AM Eastern Daylight Time

Carole:

This evening, Greg brought the information that he received from Yahoo to my office. I was able to assist him by taking to origination IP address and doing a search for it on the internet. When it did not show up on the Internic WHOIS directory, I figured that it must be a military address. Accordingly, I did a search for it on the military/ department of defense NIC website and confirmed that the IP address is a military IP address. I then called the department of defense NIC services and then the DOD Assist services and tracked this address to a computer on a Norfolk, VA military base. It is not from a classified computer. In the morning (it is now approximately 1:00 am), I will be able to contact some of the senior people in ASSIST who can provide me with even more specific information.

When I called to find out information about this address, I had to explain why I needed the information. The military personnel that I spoke with appeared very interested in why I needed this information. I have a feeling that I will have to provide them with even more specific information to get the final computer location. That should certainly impact your sister's career!

Once we confirm that it was your sister who set up the e-mail account and the profile, Greg can amend the lawsuit. Of course, that will have to be when he gets back from vacation.

I am very happy that we are close to nabbing your sister.

Call me tomorrow on my cell phone if you have any questions.

Best Regards,
Leah

My momentary elation was supplanted with disappointment that this was not the piece of evidence to "nail Laura." The actual pages Yahoo sent back created more legal questions. The only thing we knew for sure was that someone used a military computer located on the Navy base in Norfolk, Virginia. Laura worked for the Army in Fort Eustis, Virginia. Her husband worked for the Navy in Norfolk. Had her husband created all those web pages? Leah seemed to be on the track to get answers, while I was waiting for the auction of my father's furniture to begin.

༄ର

The anger I felt about spending my limited resources because the Pompano police had refused to help me kept growing. Finding out that Charlie Loving had worked for the Lynchburg police made me feel worse. I e-mailed Leah, "As for the libel, I will not be at all surprised if my sister's defense is to finger-point at the trustee as the originator of the whole idea: turns out he's an ex-cop. The trustee issues and the libel go hand-in-hand, but if the libel case gets thrown out of Florida, I am 'up the creek with no paddle' or Virginia counsel. So I hope your great news means the case will stay in Florida, and be finished sooner than later."

What did I really have for all the expense and months of struggle? I had spent money I couldn't afford believing that Yahoo's information would be the end of my nightmare. Instead, it told us that the person who invented the name "imasophistmaster," used on all the web pages, had registered with Yahoo Corporation's free service by giving out my name and an alternate name, "mond_world@hotmail.com."

My disappointment was palpable. I feared the prospect of more legal expense. Leah's excitement also ended when she ran into a dead end with the military.

I participated by telephone at the Lynchburg auction of all my parents' remaining personal furnishings. Unlike the other heirs who were local, I had been forced to send a cashier's check for $6000 to the auction company for the privilege of being allowed to bid. Kay didn't attend. It was open to the public, but quickly Laura and Betty bid against me to force prices into the stratosphere. I later learned that the local crowd was disgusted by the hatred manifested by Laura and Betty against me, and some of them left early. No one of the public dared participate.

Like a monopoly game, the auction included "funny money" bidding, since no cash would change hands until the estate was settled at Charlie Loving's pleasure. My inheritance was quickly used up in the bidding as I paid dearly for those old pieces of furniture I'd grown up with, which my father had promised in 1995 to give me if I wanted them. He'd been so disappointed that none of the others expressed any interest. Betty and Laura showed no other interest than to bid against me. In my mind's ear I could hear Daddy's comments of disgust and disbelief as I bid. "Are you crazy? Nothing is worth all that!"

If Betty and Laura were that determined to steal my share of the inheritance, so be it. Pay them off, buy them out. Maybe they'd feel they had "won" and leave me and my neighbors alone.

July, 2001

July 3, 2001 was a tropically hot, sultry day in South Florida, and I spent the day pruning bushes in my yard. In anticipation of the furniture that the auction company owner was herself delivering to me from Virginia, for a price, I needed to get rid of some of my own favorites to make room. I put one of my treasured dining room chairs, a distinctive cherrywood fiddleback on the driveway with a "Dining Room Set For Sale" sign. Anyone interested would instantly recognize the style and quality. I tied the sign and the chair to a folding beach chair and umbrella, and set up a table to sell mangoes, and potted flowers as well, to the passing motorists.

My neighbor on the north side of the street was working in his yard, too. I paused in the late afternoon for a few minutes to jump in the pool and rinse off. When I returned to the front yard, the dining chair had been carefully untied from the umbrella and the sign. It, as well as the beach chair, was gone. I had been inside less than ten minutes.

I ran across the street to my neighbor to ask, "Did you see who took that chair?"

"What? I just went in for a coke five minutes ago. It's gone?"

"Yes, yes, and the sign and the other things are lying there--as if a mockery of how well they timed it. You didn't see anyone stop or anything?" I was frantically wishing it were a dream, not another incident. Not another theft by another stalker watching me. Not again. Not after all this time.

"I can't believe it. I've been out there all day, just like you," my neighbor sympathized. "Whoever it was sure works fast. Must have been just waiting for you and me to go inside at the same time."

I felt sick in my stomach. Those were the same words that the police had used about the burglary on my west side four months earlier. I had to call the police. Again. The reporting officer practically scoffed at my question as to what he could do to track it down.

"Nothing, lady. Be grateful they didn't break into your house."

I did not celebrate Independence Day. I felt afraid, violated, imprisoned, emotionally paralyzed.

My neglected sailboat had developed serious rust problems in the engine compartment, and I spent the day working on it, cooped up for two and a half sweaty, dirty hours in a tiny area trying to get a pencil zinc unstuck from the heat exchanger.

I took a break at sunset and sent an e-mail to Barbra about the burglary, and the multiple calls I made to the local cops before they showed up, and their reluctance to file any report of the incident. I related to her the display of hatred by Betty and Laura at the auction. I wrote her, "Another public scandal. Glad Daddy is not around to witness it/them and Charlie's hand in it. Word is that even Charlie appeared embarrassed and trying to get away from Betty. Any news from Kay?"

The theft had unnerved me, and again I didn't feel safe. I had the guns now, but they didn't do me any good in this situation. The following Sunday, I called a local pet store to inquire about a dog. The Humane Society brought animals there for adoption on the weekends. Sure enough, there was a black and white cocker spaniel that looked just like the springer spaniel I had spent my childhood summers with at my cousin Joyce's house. I brought him home, and began the arduous process of learning how different a dog was from my cats. I later felt sorry for the dog, that he had come to such an inexperienced owner. I kept expecting him to act like a cat. To behave like the cats. To be neat and clean like the cats. To not exhibit so much hyperactivity and need for attention. He gradually trained me.

It turned out, unknown to me for awhile, that I was extremely lucky to get a recycled dog that had a beautiful disposition and had been well-trained at obedience school. He would transform my life, and the lives of my three cats. Installing fencing to lock him in the yard was another challenge, but I hooked into my neighbors' already-installed side fences, and knew that the dog was secured, but more importantly, no one would ever have any excuse to be found in my back yard without invitation. Eventually, the dog became an ear-piercing alarm system for anyone or anything (boats or bicycles, possums, raccoons, or iguanas) approaching my house.

Before the benefits of owning a dog became obvious, I was faced with tackling the dog's health problems. Barbra was a dog lover, and I e-mailed her the saga of treating my poor dog's heartworms, a major tropical disease transmitted by mosquitoes. I related to her the "getting acquainted antics" of my three cats with the dog.

I asked her if she had any notice about the auction proceeds, and told her that my furniture was supposed to arrive in a week. I wrote, "The chairs that Kay wanted but refused to get--I may have found a friend here to take. The poster bed that I thought Kay wanted is stacked against a wall. Since Kay would rather not speak to me than have those things, I guess the struggle to 'keep it in the family' is over. I'm not wasting anymore of my energy." I also related to her why and how much I disliked dealing with attorneys in the libel case that seemed eternal, as the fees increased with every passing month. I smelled a rat.

જ્જી

When the furniture arrived from Virginia at the end of the month, I welcomed the sense of connection to my lost parents. The pieces were so old, much broken and encrusted with years of dirt. My house was overflowing with furniture, so it seemed almost like a warehouse for my father's beautiful handiwork. The auction company owner had approached me frostily, but warmed up and admitted that Charlie Loving had made some outrageous comments about me, full of innuendo and suspicion. She didn't want to say too much, as he brought her business. It seemed he had a habit of "collecting" old people. I assumed that's how he built up his retirement income. She admitted that she knew the coin collection was worthless before he tried to "sell" it to me.

I believed more and more that all my suspicions about Charlie's behavior had been much too understated.

August, 2001
Near the end of the month I awoke one morning after a long dream, one that lingered with me, so that I wasn't sure I had dreamt it or it had actually happened the day before: I saw the name "mond_world" in two places, one in the e-mails Laura had sent to the police, and the other in the subpoenaed Yahoo documents. I practically could feel the tissue in my brain moving as I struggled to remember which documents they were, and why I had been looking at them in the dream. Nothing had been happening with my attorneys, and there were no more burglaries or trespassers after the dog and the fence were installed.

I was so puzzled by the dream that I went to look at the Yahoo documents to verify I'd seen the name "mond_world" there. Yes, it was the alternate name to "imasophistmaster." Whoever had made up the one, also made up the other on the Yahoo registration form. Why did I think I'd seen the name "mond_world" in Laura's e-mails sent to the police? I had not looked at that hideous mess in several weeks, because I filed it all away, after I'd sent a copy to my attorney and the initial shock and fascination ended.

I started reading the enclosures again, from the beginning. When I came to the bottom of page three of the #3 enclosure, there it was, in black and white, where it had been all along! Probably the reason I didn't notice was because the four-line heading was at the bottom of the page, and all the rest of the e-mails that were from "juliaericblair" were addressed to Betty, as "lwaddill." Clearly this was different! The body of the e-mail was located at the top of page four, and the language was just like all the rest of them, so I must have assumed they were all written to Betty, and in reading through all the garbage, I had missed this important clue. Who was *mond_world*?

From: "Julia Blair" <juliaericblair@hotmail.com
To: mond_world@hotmail.com
Subject: funeral
Date: Sat, 20 Jan 2001 08:52:43 –0500

4

Enclosure #3
E-mail excerpts

Ugly shit in Lynchburg. I am OK thanks to Wayne and his dad. Kay and Carole are insanely desperate in hate with me, grasping at straws and even beginning to look absurd to the most important people concerned now (the trustee and his wife, etc).

I am beginning to really think that Carole has moved Larry to Florida. The more I think about it the more plausible it seems (Betty says "ridiculous"). Carole wrote and faxed an absurdly stupid and poorly written essay on my father which she commanded to be read at the graveside. They did not read it. I have one copy and must make more. In it, she says 4 times that Larry is dead. She says she was "tasked" with the job of informing Daddy of Larry's death, after which she watched Daddy get weaker and weaker and then die.

The most horrible thing she did was to demand that Larry's name be omitted from the obituary. She did not want Larry to be mentioned as one of Daddy's children. That, I think, was a bit of a slip-up for her. People were horrified that she wanted to make him an unperson. All she has told people so far was that no one knows where Larry is. She had not mentioned any confirmation of his death before....

I think it is time for me to contact Pompano Beach police in Florida. I have not heard yet from Portland Police.

I think the Lovings saw that I was not the monster that KC had told them I was. Kay claimed that I threatened the life of her daughter (Kate) at the wake. I spent most of the time at the wake talking with the Lovings .

Laura

I found another interesting statement at the top of this same page three:

From: "Julia Blair" <juliaericblair@hotmail.com>
To: juliaericblair@hotmail.com
Subject: Larry's cremains? / Carole's fear that Laura will be at funeral
Date: Wed, 17 Jan 2001 21:13:56 -0500

(originally sent to Betty but I forgot to put julia as BCC, so I yanked from ethereal memory)

Wayne called and told me he had talked to you this evening.

When I read it originally, an e-mail *from* Laura (a/k/a Juli-aericblair) and *to* Laura, I overlooked the parenthetical phrase. Sometime since the end of March, I had learned that "BCC" meant "blind carbon copy." It was possible to send a copy of an e-mail to someone, without the recipient knowing to whom you were sending the copies. Blind Carbon Copy was a choice to click in a box on the computer screen for e-mails, but I'd never noticed it before.

"Ethereal memory" was a term I had overlooked. I now realized that it was a term used when computers were hooked up to each other, in an office setting. My brother had talked about "networking" the computers in his apartment, meaning they were hooked up one to the other. But I'd never known the term "ethereal memory."

The timing on the e-mails indicated that Laura and Betty were e-mailing each other during Laura's working hours. Laura worked at night. Evidently the army was paying her while she created these incredible monstrosities of attack against me and my neighbors. Her "ethereal memory" referred to the network of computers at the Fort Eustis Army Base.

It suddenly occurred to me that she probably had a whole host of e-mail accounts and names and aliases. I excitedly faxed the news to my attorney Greg, sending him the Yahoo material and the pertinent pages of Laura's enclosures to the police, pointing out the "ethereal memory" and the times of the e-mails that proved Laura was using her military computers on the job. I asked him to send me Laura's response to our interrogatories, in which she admitted writing the letter to the police but denied creating the websites. I wrote, "My urgent question to you remains: Is this enough proof that Crews is the culprit who created the websites? If so, isn't her denial a basis at least for perjury?"

Legally, it wasn't. Greg eventually initiated the process to send a subpoena to Microsoft Corporation, the owner of all the "Hotmail" accounts, to identify "mond_world." The legal action basically stopped until we had the name of a real person from an internet service provider. I didn't know why we had to go further, but Greg said we did.

Subj: FIELDER v. CREWS
Date: 08/29/2001 7:30:17 PM Eastern Daylight Time

Hi Carole. Again, sorry for the delay in responding. Good work on the investigation. I am going to subpoena records from Hotmail in an attempt to nail down your sister's identity.

September, 2001

For most of the United States, time stood still on September 11, 2001. I watched in horror as the second plane flew into the second World Trade Center building on television. For the rest of the month, I felt that the country had joined me in the terror I had been living for the previous eight months. It almost felt like the surreal circumstances of my personal life had suddenly spread to the whole population. Up was down. Black was white. Right was wrong. Life did not mean what it used to mean. USA, welcome to my world!

Chapter 17

"But to the wicked God says:
You give your mouth free rein for evil;
you harness your tongue to deceit.
You sit maligning your own kin,
slandering the child of your own mother.
When you do these things should I be silent?
Or do you think that I am like you?
I accuse you, I lay the charge before you."
                              --Psalm 50:16a,20-21

October, 2001

The days ticked by uneventfully as I awaited my first big day in the Circuit Court for the Seventeenth Judicial Circuit in and for Broward County, at Fort Lauderdale. A hearing was set by Laura's attorney. He moved the court to dismiss the whole complaint because the State of Florida had no jurisdiction over a Virginia resident. He further argued that even if the State of Florida did have jurisdiction, Laura had not written anything slanderous or libelous about me, because everything she wrote was either factual or her own opinion. And beyond that, even if the State of Florida had jurisdiction and she had slandered me, it wouldn't matter because she was truly an upstanding citizen just trying to help the police with an investigation, so her letter to them was "privileged." That meant that she was protected from any consequences of anything she said to them, and I had no legal complaint against her.

Furthermore, she expected me to pay for her attorney's fees for being brought into court.

I had had difficulty understanding the reasoning behind the legalese mumbo-jumbo. I had to accept my attorney's admonition that he could not predict the outcome. It was impossible to know how the judge would rule.

I approached the day with great hope, lots of prayers, and abject fear.

October 24, 2001

The big day arrived. I had prepared myself well in advance. I practiced getting up early enough to try to get my body functioning adequately to drive to the courthouse, a big trip for me. I would have to unload my wheelchair, its motor and battery and drive shaft, all separate parts that were awkward and heavy to lift. I could only hope to find the parking, the entrances, the courtroom.

I barely recognized my attorney when I entered the room, as I had not seen him but twice before: once, very briefly, the day I'd met Leah, my first attorney, on Ash Wednesday, February 28, 2001, almost eight months before, when he said hello on his way out; and the second time when he met me in his parking lot for me to give him the stacks of documents I had to produce for Laura's attorney, in July. All other communication had been by telephone, fax, e-mail and U.S. mail.

The moment arrived and we entered an almost empty hearing room. I was surprised to see that the woman judge assigned my case was not there. There was a substitute, instead.

Laura's attorney spoke first, and voiced his arguments why a Florida court had no jurisdiction. He was followed by my attorney.

"Your honor," Greg began, "my client has been accused of murder and heading a satanic cult, and of capital crimes."

He elaborated slightly, then picked up a stack of papers and asked, "I have here several cases...uh may I approach the bench?" He started towards the judge's desk as he mentioned one of them by name, FRIDOVICH v. FRIDOVICH, that had gone all the way to the Florida Supreme Court.

"That's ok. I have it," the judge interrupted him.

"You have a copy?" Greg seemed puzzled.

"Yes, I have it here," the judge waved a sheaf of papers at us. "And I'm going to deny the motion."

"Thank you." Greg responded, then said something to Laura's attorney and passed another paper to him.

It was over just that quickly. My head was swimming. What happened?

Greg motioned to me to follow him out.

"Did we win?" I whispered to him.

"He denied Laura's motion to dismiss," Greg answered without explanation. "The case goes forward."

"Oh, then that's good, isn't it!" I half asked. "Will you please make a copy of those cases for me?"

He agreed, and we parted company as quickly as if it had been a mirage. I wished I had someone to celebrate the occasion. I guessed it was a celebration. All those months of trying to find a lawyer, and all those lawyers saying I could never get it into a Florida court--wasn't that behind me now? The judge *would* hear my case!

It was weeks later before I read the cases Greg sent to me, and even then I could barely comprehend the legalese in them. The facts of my case seemed so simple to me. Laura and Betty were encouraged by the action or inaction of lots of people around them to do horrible things to me. Charlie Loving had been at the origin of their latest malicious lies, and he was the only person who could have stopped them in their tracks at my father's funeral. Instead he perpetuated the slander and libel by turning against me. The legal evidence read like an old Southern novel, like Faulkner, or worse, a Harold Pinter play, once the twenty-two characters named in Laura and Betty's e-mails were involved. What more could be said about it? Why did lawyers complicate it?

The case Greg mentioned was about several members of a family deciding to accuse another member of the family of murdering their father, some later time after his death. It was a story similar to mine. The family members conspiring to accuse their brother lived outside of Florida: the accused lived in Florida. And the Florida Supreme Court decided that it was Florida's business. It belonged in a Florida court.

I nurtured high hopes the nightmare would end as soon as we got the information from Microsoft, which would officially and legally identify mond_world@hotmail.com.

I had been out of touch with Barbra lately, but I e-mailed her the news that I'd won the first round. I wrote, "Only took 10 months and $12K to get there. So the judge disagreed that Laura was someone who 'has no contact with Florida.' Only 60 cops involved, 8 major burglaries of my neighbors, 3 minor burglaries/ vandalisms at my house, and about 150 other persons I know here in Florida involved so far. Whooppee! But what good is it? The case drags on for another year and more $'s."

I continued, "I never heard back from you about finding out who Larry's representative is for the next seven years. Did your attorney even inquire? I flat out asked the accountant to whom she had sent the check for $75,000, but she's playing coy and not answering, saying 'it's a legal question.' The life insurance check came, too. I wonder who got Larry's share????"

I changed subjects to fill Barbra in that I was facing the same crisis for medical care next year that Larry had faced just before he killed himself. I e-mailed, "Have been a nervous wreck thinking I had two possible alternatives, both horrendously expensive. As of today I have only one possibility. The future is bleak. I am so stressed about next year's health care choices that the legal matter has taken a bottom priority in my life. I haven't had a burglary since July 3rd, and the phone calls, cat calls, drive-by's, etc. bother me less and less. I guess one gets used to being stalked by sleaze bags. I'm glad I have a yippy dog, however, in spite of the added work he creates."

I was doing well physically, amazing in face of the legal stress. My doctor reduced the amount of gamma globulin I received from forty to fifteen grams every two weeks. I wrote Barbra, "I need to get completely off the transfusions by the end of the year, because I won't be able to pay for them next year, with the change of insurance. Just like Larry."

I ended by writing, "With fall in the air, I miss talking with Larry more and more, instead of less and less. The pain never seems to lessen. Maybe that's because I've not had anyone with whom to grieve in person. How is it for you now? I find myself thinking his thoughts ever so often. How lost, lonely, and terrified he must have felt."

My clock chimed and brought me back to the present moment. The pain of loss and loneliness loomed large in my quiet house. Larry was gone. Daddy was gone. I still grieved alone.

I felt another momentary flush of anger that Larry had left me. He had finally learned personally what I endured all those years when the family abandoned me sick and disabled in Florida in 1973. Didn't he know how delighted I was to have him share my life twenty-six years later, even though it was just by telephone? Why wasn't he here to console me on the loss of Daddy? And why wasn't Daddy here to acknowledge with me the effect that the decades of stuffed hatreds and resentments of those Virginia girls had on Larry, Mother, me, my neighbors?

I asked my cat walking by, "Why am I still here and they are both gone?"

I knew the answers, but I didn't like them.

To my brother, like my father, illness was not a challenge. It was an enemy to be licked, or at worst, waited out. Towards the end of 1999, I remembered, when I was telephoning Larry every few days, we often discussed the fact that no one in the family seemed to recognize the intense physical suffering that he, and I, had endured so long. We did not believe anyone, other than the two of us, had ever comprehended what our daily lives were like. Kay and Daddy, although they spoke to us, seemed to be completely oblivious to our respective situations, in spite of our efforts to explain in person, by telephone, or by letters.

❦

"Larry, do you think it's because neither Kay nor Daddy has ever been sick?" I had inquired during one of our telecons.

"Until now, yeah," Larry agreed. "Daddy is completely astonished that there is anything wrong with him after eighty-eight healthy years. I can tell by talking to him that he is really down about not feeling good, and not being able to take care of the house and yard the way he used to."

"Did I tell you about the conversation I had with him recently, when I kept trying to validate his feelings?"

"No, no, you didn't," Larry laughed. "I didn't know Daddy knew he had any feelings."

"Well, of course not, Larry," I snorted. "But he was complaining about raking the leaves, and how he got so tired hobbling around out there after an hour of raking. I couldn't believe he's already able to walk at all, much less able to spend an hour raking. Wow. Incredible resilience."

"Yeah, he's got that for sure."

"I haven't been able to stand up or walk for an hour, or even ten minutes, since I was nineteen years old."

"That's a long time, Sis."

"Anyhow, he told me how useless he is now. He couldn't climb a ladder three stories to clean the leaves out of the gutter. I just agreed with him, and asked him how long before the gutters would fall off the roof from standing water. He answered me that he wasn't sure. I then told him that once the roof was damaged from the falling gutters, he wouldn't be able to heat the house, so he probably should just move out now, before the winter sets in. Certainly there was no one he could hire to rake leaves or clean the gutters, so he ought to sell the house immediately."

"You said *that*?" Larry asked.

"Sure, more or less. I don't remember all the details, but I kept on agreeing with his disastrous predictions of what minor maintenance item would lead to the next crisis, until it sounded so utterly stupid that he stopped, and finally he laughed. He actually caught on to what I was doing."

"Gosh, Sis, that's real progress, for him. You think he really caught on?"

"Well, I'm sure it was just momentary. The idea of hiring anyone to do anything is utter anathema to him. You know that. And I don't think he's ever given a thought to the fact that I've been unable to do such things all my life."

Larry chuckled, "Oh yeah. I know it well."

"The concept that life might have value even when we can't do *anything* will never register in his head. He can't get past the fact that his life is finished if he can't mow the grass, rake the leaves, plow the garden, *et cetera, et cetera*," I finished somewhat angrily.

Larry and I had often had similar conversations, during which I would argue with him that he was valuable, and so was I, no matter how sick we were. That we had just as much right to be here as the healthy, powerful people. It was an uphill argument. He often expressed how disgusted he was with himself and his physical problems, and how useless he felt.

Larry's illnesses were no challenge to him, just an overpowering enemy. He kept waiting for things to "go away," or "get better." I could sympathize with that attitude; I'd entertained false hopes for many years at the beginning of my total disability. When did I stop that?

I had been an advocate for the handicapped practically from the beginning. When I testified before Congress (**Appendix A**), however, I didn't consider myself "handicapped." Was it when I finally accepted three years later, in 1978, one year after I was newly married that I'd have to use a wheelchair if I wanted to go anywhere?

More likely, acceptance of the challenge was forced on me. I had struggled for months in 1973 when I first arrived in Florida hoping that I could go back to work, constantly asking every doctor when he estimated I'd be able to do so. I refused to believe that "totally and permanently disabled" meant forever, because if I couldn't be "gainfully employed" I'd have no justification for living.

The pain of one of the many infections I suffered as a result of using methatrexate to control arthritis beat me into submission. On one of my regular trips to see Dr. Harvey Brown, the renowned arthritis specialist at the University of Miami Medical School, during an excruciatingly painful earache I just begged him, "Please, please take the pain away. I promise I won't ask you about going back to work again. Just, please, make it stop."

A little bit of me died that day. But somehow, the grace of God, or the Universe, or my newfound Catholic faith, or my passion for sailing, or something I might never understand, kept me alive. Life *is* difficult, and many times I didn't like living it. But something deep inside me accepted the premise that ***all life is precious***. I did not grow up believing that, however, and obviously Larry and Daddy--my family--never did. I suspected that the personal choice about the value of life was at the core of my family's dysfunction, just as it was the basis for the raging conflicts in society about abortion, euthanasia, and use of economic resources. My family history seemed to be a microcosm of those issues, and my choice about life made me their "odd man out."

And now that my mother, father, and brother were dead, my sisters wanted me farther "out."

I still had no idea why they expended any effort towards me after all those years without contact. Why *did* my siblings cut off their relationship with me when I was young? Was my chronic illness something they couldn't bear to look at? And if they saw an occasional photograph of me taken "looking normal" years later did they think I was no longer ill? How very many times I heard the left-handed compliment, "But you look so well!" What it really meant, usually, was "I don't believe you."

Larry told me his last trip home was motivated partly because he was sure the family didn't believe that he was so ill. He had been in contact with them almost all his life, and needed communication with them. I had tried for many years, but with no dialogue at all, I had given up.

That old family tradition of non-communication rolled on. The very thing that Larry tried so hard to fix was still broken, and now it tumbled into a courtroom of sister versus sister. What could possibly be behind Betty and Laura's public hatred of me, a virtual stranger to them after thirty years?

Any answer was purely speculative. Surely Betty's sibling rivalry of me as the second-born wasn't the whole answer. Perhaps the fact that I was able to get a college degree in five years in spite of my handicap, while her choice of an early marriage made her pursuit of a degree continue for sixteen years, contributed to her jealousy. Perhaps it was the small inheritance our great uncle left to me and not to her, although we had both spent time on his farm as children. Perhaps it was because I "stormed in with Kay" to take care of our mother in 1994 when Betty, as the eldest, should have taken the responsibility.

My two cats suddenly raced across the patio, the larger one chasing the smaller one. He outweighed her and arrived at my house first, although they came from the same litter. I laughed aloud at their antics, recognizing the usual pattern of their behavior and how well they had established their "pecking order." He was first, and she m st never forget it!

Their antics made me wonder if I had somehow violated the family pecking order.

The speculation could be endless. I looked at the handsome photograph of Larry in 1978 and I wondered what he would think. Then I looked at the only snapshot I had of Laura from 1974. Larry and Laura had been close until the last year. His letters to her (**Appendix E)** indicated that he knew what was bothering her, but no one could engage her in dialogue about it. He was only one of many who witnessed Laura's rants against Catholics, and I had personally heard some of Larry's anti-Catholic remarks. Could that be it? Perhaps my Catholicism was a convenient trigger for Laura's vengeful public display.

How and why did all this happen to me? Was I simply caught up in the karma of generations of family jealousies and resentments? Or perhaps my journey through life included some kind of cosmic spiritual battle that had originated in previous centuries of religious wars, in which I needed to take a stand. Certainly my family's subliminal anti-Catholicism, as well as Charlie's and Lowry's by virtue of their Bible Belt culture, contributed to their active dislike and distrust of me. But to go on so far, so long, and so publicly?

Perhaps my family was again a microcosm of society at large, where it was now unfashionable to admit to religious prejudice, but the undercurrent was still there. "Mackerel snappers" was whispered now, instead of shouted.

My cat's meow broke into my thoughts. I would never know anything about people I never saw, and who refused to communicate except through libel and through lawsuits. It was human nature to assault each other with gossip, but the most powerful weapon used to destroy relationships and create wars (and lawsuits) was total refusal to communicate. Larry must have felt totally alone. I also felt alone, but I knew that the phrase "dysfunctional family" so popularly used meant that I was not alone in feeling alone.

My family's gossip was deadly, and so was their refusal to communicate. My mother escaped it by entering her valium-addicted world until it killed her mind, then her body. My brother's recognition of the devastating consequences of gossip and my sisters' hateful refusal to communicate with him, I believed, forced him to take the only escape route he felt he had. Then his suicide led to more gossip. My father's final recognition of the deadly gossip that had swirled around him for years finally sucked the life out of him. The gossip circles rippled outwards.

Gossip kills. That's why almost every civilization has warned about it. Father Foudy reminded us parishioners in at least one homily per year about the importance of asking three questions before speaking about anyone. First, is it true? Second, is it necessary? Third, is it kind?

I truly understood the ninth commandment, or the eighth, depending on how one counted, as stated in the book of Deuteronomy 5:20: "You shall not bear dishonest witness against your neighbor." I had recently discovered that Catholics and Protestants don't even agree on how to number the Ten Commandments. Maybe I lived in that California state of mind too long, where I grew to believe that America was truly a melting pot, and that there was tolerance for everyone. Perhaps I had been obtuse to think that choice of religion was not that important anymore. I certainly had been ignorant of the dangers posed in modern society by the latest "toy," the world wide web. There, gossip could flourish and damage instantly and universally.

My cats wanted their dinner. I looked at their expectant blue eyes, then turned to the photos of my family, then cast a glance at my innocuous-looking computer. Identity theft on the Internet may be the latest weapon in the arsenal of Evil. What happened to me could happen to anyone. I would have to face the challenge, just as I had faced others. I doubted that Betty or Laura ever expected me to dig deeply enough to defend myself, to challenge their attacks, or to "spill the beans," of their lifetime of hatred.

I daily hoped and prayed that there would be some small justice in this world. But whatever happened, I knew that more would be revealed. In time. The light would shine in the darkness and heal the wounds.

And thus it was throughout the world in the year 2001, the new millennium: Some things never change.

Postscript

2003

What happened after the court decided to hear the case? A long, expensive, stupid process still continues that appears to have no ending. After subpoenas were sent and received from Yahoo!, Microsoft, and Verizons Corporations, we learned that Laura Crews had slipped up and included an e-mail to a fellow conspirator in her letter to the Pompano police. Her enclosure that she designated "my e-mail log with my sister Betty" included an e-mail that was not to Betty, but to the person who registered as both "imasophistmaster@yahoo.com" as well as "monde_world@hotmail.com."

That person apparently used a computer hooked in to the computer server located on the Navy base in Norfolk Virginia to post the impersonating web pages.

The e-mail address "monde_world@hotmail.com" belonged, according to the subpoena return from Verizons Corporation, to one Harold McCachren, a retired navy employee, who lived in Virginia Beach, Virginia. He defaulted in the civil action by failure to respond at all. He admitted, however, on the telephone, to owning a hotmail account, and that his daughter Lisa and her boyfriend/husband also lived with him and had access to his computer.

After information passed between the lawyers, the police, and the Criminal Investigation Departments of both the Navy and the Army, it was further learned that Laura, as well as her husband, had access to that same computer, officially owned by the Department of Defense (DOD). It was a "cache server" that connected hundreds of military computers to the internet, including those at Fort Eustis Army base. Sadly, DOD at that time had no log-in system whereby the individual user could be traced in-house, so the military brass used that as an excuse to cover up this embarrassing and dangerous incident.

I urged the Pompano police to follow up. That was as futile as any previous attempts to get help or protection. I appeared at eleven Pompano Beach City Council meetings explaining the police problem and the jurisdictional complications, and begging for help. Those meetings were televised locally, and many residents became concerned, especially as they realized that anyone, anywhere is endangered by employees of the military bases. That yielded no help either, however, in a City that was immersed in much bigger corruption and political scandals at the same time.

Finally, I attempted to get help from the Governor of Florida (Jeb Bush), as well as from my Representative to the U.S. Congress (Clay Shaw).

The request to the Governor made a circle back to the Pompano police department of the Broward Sheriff's Office (BSO), where the Chief of Police, who had been so apologetic to me when he discovered the "missing" enclosures to Laura's letter and sent them out to me March 29, 2001, wrote an e-mail in response: he implied in the e-mail dated December 12, 2002 that I had made up the whole incident. Several police officials, all the way to the Broward Sheriff's Professional Compliance Office, took a stance that there had never been an incident that I reported, and that Laura had never sent a letter to them, and there had never been any record of any report about anything.

In the first quarter of 2003 I finally obtained from opposition attorneys for Betty and Laura a copy of the police report, which was fifty-two pages long and signed off February 19, 2001. It had a case number sure enough. It included Laura's letter with all its enclosures, Oregon Detective Mussler's original thirteen-page report about my brother's suicide, as well as a copy of Larry's suicide note. The BSO had simply harassed me and run me in circles for two years, wasted the time of countless hundreds of people in the community and in State and federal government, and spent thousands of taxpayer dollars to cover up their actions.

The police failure to co-operate with the United States Department of Defense in a timely manner to arrest or otherwise impede the actions of Laura Crews and her fellow conspirators on the military bases in Virginia, means that they are still free to use military computers to commit internet crimes. Eight of the nine burglaries in my community that occurred while the internet pages were posted were never investigated. Coincidences? Or a dangerous situation waiting to happen again in Florida or elsewhere.

The Congressional inquiry that Congressman E. Clay Shaw initiated, based on the three returned subpoenas to Yahoo, Microsoft, and Verizons, plus the letter to the Pompano police that included Laura's e-mail to "monde_world@hotmail," was blown off by the military in Virginia, as the rumblings of the Iraq War took priority. Written proof of the crime meant nothing to the military. They had bigger problems.

As for Betty Fielder and Charles Loving: their apparent conspiracy to defame me and to deny me my rightful inheritance also goes unpunished. Betty, a/k/a Lorraine Waddill, can still be found online as a legislative assistant in the Virginia General Assembly and as a board member for John Tyler Community College. Family rumors abounded that Charles Loving got paid $150,000 by my father to replace Betty as trustee. So far, no one knows if he acted in conspiracy with Betty out of guilt or fear. He never made any apology for taking advantage of an elderly man, for participating in maligning the family name, or for conspiring with my sisters to harm me, a physically disabled person in another State.

In 2003, I secured an old e-mail between Betty and Laura expressing their plan to scheme with Loving to divide my share of the inheritance. In it they planned to bid up the price for my father's handmade furniture at the auction in June 2001, exactly what I had in fact witnessed. Still later in 2003, Betty belatedly signed an affidavit that "The letter to the Pompano Beach Police Department that the plaintiff complains of was not signed, sent nor authorized by me." A day late and a dollar short, as the saying goes. Another belly laugh.

Easter Week of 2002, my poor brother's body was found washed out of a drainage pipe underneath a six-lane highway a short distance from his apartment. The gun was still clutched in his skeletal hand. Even that discovery has not slowed the family dysfunction and rage that continues to play out in the courts. Additionally, Laura Crews continued to post messages on a Yahoo club declaring that I had murdered our brother, profited from my satanic cult, and that the Broward Sheriff's Office was foolish to have failed to prosecute me. The official records in Oregon meant nothing to her. She proceeded to post messages about what she intended to do with my skull.

As for me, I try to live quietly, one day at a time. I do not have the health to move and try to hide. I still talk to my Aunt Madeline and cousins, to my dear friend Mrs. Barrett and her children. I had my identity stolen again in 2002, but for economic crimes—somebody ran up $1700 of charges on a cell phone company in my name. That makes me one of the million Americans, estimated by American Express and CNN, victimized each year.

Identity theft for economic crimes is nothing compared to the nightmare terrorism I endured because of internet impersonation, and the devastating consequences of gossip in all its forms that continues to spread and grow. Gossip kills. I often think that my brother made a wise decision. Who would want to live under these circumstances?

Is there any solution to the problem of identity theft and internet impersonation? Yes. The Internet is national and crosses State lines and needs national legislation. Impersonation needs to be a federal felony, not a State misdemeanor defined by fifty different legislative bodies. Police need to rediscover the basic values of the community and stop harassing citizens in need of help. The U.S. military need to stop treating the internet abuses by their employees as a joke. It is serious and it is deadly. There are already laws on the books that make the use of military equipment to commit any crime a federal felony. So prosecute the culprits!

People have asked me what I hoped to accomplish by telling my story. Besides reform of the laws and enforcement of the ones already there? Besides exposing the lies spread by Betty and Laura and the Pompano police? I hope to spare anyone else from this terror. Anybody can be a victim of internet impersonation, even if their family is not as dysfunctional as mine.

But there are more reasons why I wrote this. If one person contemplating suicide because of family hatreds and malicious gossip reads this and changes his mind, that's why. If one person whose identity has been stolen and who has suffered the insults and insinuations of the police or banks gets some consolation, that's why. If one person who has stopped speaking to a family member reconsiders and decides that life is too short for such hatreds to destroy the brief gift of life, that's why. If one person who belongs to a Bible Belt fundamentalist Christian religion reconsiders that Catholics are just human beings like anyone else, that's why. If one Catholic realizes that many non-Catholics are not "protesting" anything, that they are good people raised in a tradition that enables them to live life to the best of their ability—and it has nothing to do with the Catholic religion, that's why. If one Catholic cleric, or bishop, or archbishop, reads this and realizes how devastating their arrogance and homegrown myopia is to "little people," and to society at large, that's why.

Finally, if anybody reads this and understands that doing nothing in the face of gossip, malice, or ill-will towards another is equivalent to participating fully in it, indeed equivalent to being the originator of it, then the pain of writing this is worth it.

Gossip kills. Will you be next?

Appendix A

Author's Testimony to Congress in 1975

National Commission on Arthritis and Related Musculoskeletal Diseases

Report to the Congress of the United States

Volume IV, Part 4:
Public Hearings

April, 1976

DHEW Publication No. 76-1156

U.S. Department of Health, Education, and Welfare
Public Health Service
National Institutes of Health

St. Petersburg, Florida   December 8, 1975

SUBMITTED STATEMENT OF
CAROLE FIELDER COX, PATIENT
DELRAY BEACH, FLORIDA

Ladies and gentlemen of the Commission: Today I am here to do what I can to improve the desperate plight of millions like me. This is my first trip away from home since I became totally disabled from psoriatic arthritis two and a half years ago. I feel that the physical hardship of being here, the increased pain and the risks from exposure, will be worthwhile if you, by gathering testimony, can get this country moving on this devastating issue.

I was asked to explain how arthritis has affected my life, both physically and emotionally. My original response was that I could not bear to relate it. But in view of the purpose of the Commission, I decided to briefly indicate to you how arthritis has affected my life. I am emotionally able to tell you only because I am a professional writer and have forcefully disciplined myself to be detached in the telling.

I am 31 years old, single, living alone in Delray Beach, Florida. I was declared totally disabled in June 1973, after a six-month period of rapid deterioration following complications from the flu and from my regular medication, methatrexate. As you undoubtedly know, methatrexate is a strong poison, known as an anti-cancer drug, which produces many grim side effects.

I have been taking methatrexate consistently to control my arthritis since January 1964. I am currently in a very weakened condition from the use of methatrexate, and am unable to tolerate a large enough dosage to successfully control the skin lesions and joint swelling. I also take Motrin, the anti-inflammatory, for arthritic pain. I use a great quantity of topical ointments, usually steroids, to soothe the worst skin lesions. Although I keep strong sedatives on hand, I have always avoided taking painkillers until the very worst requirements.

Through the years I have changed doctors when they advised me I could not continue my education, or was unable to pursue my career, or when they refused to write a prescription for methatrexate. I underwent acupuncture, with limited success, rather than retreat to the world of codeine, Darvon, or Quaalude, as suggested by my doctors. Most physicians declare that it is impossible that my liver has not stopped functioning. But alas, here I am, still.

I will not go into the gory details of methatrexate's effects upon the body. I will not go into the impossible financial situation created by weekly medication that costs some $25; or laboratory tests and doctor's visits monthly or more often that cost at least $30. I am fortunate to have been as active as I have; to be able to walk unaided many days, usually with minimum pain during the high-sun hours (about noon to five).

Procuring groceries, preparing meals, dressing, bathing, applying ointment, general house maintenance are difficulties for me, varying in difficulty from slight to insurmountable depending on the hour, the day of the drug cycle, the week of fluctuation of my disease, and the side effects of methatrexate.

How has being a victim of psoriatic arthritis affected my life emotionally and in relationship to others? I will answer first in general terms. As though the pain of crackling, inflamed bones were not enough torment, many people add unwittingly and ignorantly to the pain. People seem to be able to deal with dramatic illness and recovery, or even death, much easier than they can face the day in and day out dragging on of endless worsening. Endless complication. No death to ease the agony. Endless half-life, endless dying. I have had many years to observe persons' reactions to psoriasis and psoriatic arthritis, and for brevity's sake, I will categorize these reactions into three groups: strangers, or infrequent contacts; acquaintances in social or professional contact--regular, but casual and superficial; and intimates, including family, close friends.

The first category of reactions is easiest for the arthritic to accept after the first year or two of suffering, for strangers and persons in infrequent contact cannot interfere, usually, in the actual daily living of the arthritis victim. One becomes immune to the glaring ignorance contained in such comments as: "I've heard that arthritis is all in the mind. You have to adjust your thinking;" or, "Be thankful you don't have something serious, like cancer;" or, "Oh, what a shame! I know all about arthritis because sometimes when it's rainy my shoulder acts up. Do you have an electric heating pad?" or "Oh, no, you don't! My mother-in-law bitches all the time about her hands, but then, when she wants to, she gets out in the yard and lifts pots of flowers like nobody's business. So if you've got a problem, don't tell me it's arthritis, or *'rheumatism,'* as she calls it."

On the other hand, the arthritis victim learns also to be wary of the unctuous sympathizer who happens to thrill to medical case histories and true confessions, and who pumps for information in order to pass it on to the next person. This sympathizer usually gets the last word with something like this: "Oh, well. I'm really sorry for you. But let me tell you about my second cousin Tillie, who used to have dizzy spells, and she ...." *et cetera, ad nauseam.*

To editorialize about this first category of reactions, I will assume that the stranger to arthritis doesn't really know anything about it, is sure that it isn't serious or fatal, and he or she will be damned before he or she is allowed to be confused by some facts.

The second category of reactions includes those of acquaintances of regular contact with the arthritic, who see a frustrating inconsistency of pain, health, and decay. If the arthritic is seen on one of his "good days," the acquaintance may remark, "Oh, I see you finally licked your problem. Good for you!" The next time that same acquaintance sees the victim on a bad day, then he becomes skeptical: "Oh, no, not again. I thought you'd given up all that business." The acquaintance is confused by arthritis' inconsistent manifestations, so he assumes that the arthritic simply must be "putting on" sometimes.

In the case of work and career, the employer who hires the handicapped arthritic, who has honestly declared his case on the application, decides after employment, "Well, you don't look sick to me. You've outperformed our standards many times. Now that the busy season is here, I fully expect you to work at least 15 hours overtime a week without pay just like all the others. You want to keep your job, don't you? I expect you can do it." The employer's skepticism is obvious in his smirk.

Similarly, fellow employees who see the arthritic performing above standard one day suspect him of being a slacker the day that he does not meet standard, even if in the long run he is competitive and productive. Neighbors who see the victim mowing the grass one day are very skeptical when they see him soon afterwards hobbling along on crutches or asking for help to trim the hedge.

In summary, acquaintances and work associates who begin by being sympathetic, soon tire of the inconsistency of the arthritis victim. The inconsistent physical appearance, and ability *versus* disability, lead to skepticism and distrust. The reasoning of such acquaintances often becomes thus: If the arthritic's body can't be trusted then probably the arthritic's character and personality are defective, too.

The third category of reactions is the cruelest and most painful to delineate: the rejection of the arthritis victim by intimates. It is not unusual that human compassion has limits. As I remarked earlier, it is infinitely easier to deal with the finite, whether the end be good or bad, but just so there is an end.

The parents who first hear their child complaining of pain in the knees may first suspect "put-on" or manipulation. After medical diagnosis and treatment, when the affliction begins moving from joint to joint, these same parents may become sincerely sympathetic. But what about the expense involved? What of the neglect of siblings of the arthritic child? It becomes unfair to everyone in the family, with siblings resenting the arthritic's overwhelming share of family income and attention, with parents becoming oppressed from the burden.

For the young adult approaching majority, or attempting some means of self-support, he may be faced with the parent's attitude: "When are you moving out? I hope it's soon. And when you leave, be sure and pick up that stack of unpaid doctors' bills." The single, young adult arthritics face a bleak social life, if social existence is possible at all, for they must plan around "bad days," or drug days, and thwart the worst of their disease in order to put their best foot forward with the young lady or young man

Often, the single person out of school becomes socially isolated, as no one wants to date a "sicky." On the contrary, if a partner or companion is finally found, the young person may be faced with a loving fiancé and a horrified pair of prospective parents-in-law, who may warn openly: "Son, she's a real nice girl, but don't you get too serious. Don't you know that disease she's got will take every penny you ever hope to earn?"

In the case of arthritics who are already married, the marriage needs to be more than perfect to survive the strain. The understanding husband may go on for weeks, months, perhaps years, waiting on his invalid wife; but often the sacrifice looms too large. Why should two people waste their young adult lives only because one of them has a problem? A man or woman aged mid-thirties to mid-forties is supposed to be at peak productivity. The urgency of living life fully is felt. If the wife needs a Southern climate, but the husband's career demands location in the North, what are they to do? If divorce ends the marriage, then the arthritic faces the additional stigma and isolation of the divorced, single person living in a married world.

For the arthritic who is faced with the choice of deterioration to final invalidism or a move to a more favorable climate, he or she or they, in the case of the elderly, may choose the move, away from family, old friends, established community life; and afterwards, the old friends and family conveniently forget the plight of the arthritic: Out of sight, out of mind. For those left behind, it is a convenient escape from the infinite reminder of infinite dying of spirit and body. Easily, the arthritic is suspected of being a selfish loner, and is dismissed with the thoughts, "I wonder why she wants to live way down there in Florida?" or "Gee, they have it made now. It must be nice to live in Florida."

I have spoken in general terms, but I have experienced all these things without the humor. I will now be specific and personal about how arthritis has affected my life throughout the past 12 1/2 years.

In pre-arthritis days I was ambitious to have a legal career, planning to attend the College of William and Mary for both undergraduate and legal work, in Williamsburg, Virginia. I was a sophomore at William and Mary when the disease began. I was 18 years old, enjoyed academics, modern dance, and being a drum majorette. From August 1963 to January 1964, I gradually deteriorated; and, as most arthritics experience, I ran the gamut of some 20 medical doctors who misdiagnosed my case. One outstanding local orthopedist saw me at a time when I looked like I had the beginning stages of leprosy (severe psoriasis), and my left knee was the size of a football. He had been prescribing cortisone and was draining my knee for the fourth time in three weeks. He announced, "Dear, it's not painful; it's just a nuisance."

At the end of that six-month period of being plucked out of the Technicolor world of the living and dropped into the gray world of the sick; of confrontations with doctors, hostile because of their helplessness; of being quizzed weekly by a psychiatrist who kept asking me what was bothering me, he refused to accept the answer that the pain and crippling and hideousness of my skin that prevented my return to college were the problems.

At the end of that bleak stretch of aspirins and Darvon and cortisone and sunlamp and tar baths, I was lucky enough to accidentally be referred to one Dr. Robert Irby, at the Medical College of Virginia in Richmond. He had been at the National Institutes of Health during the original experiments of methatrexate therapy on psoriatic arthritis patients. He made an immediate diagnosis and called the Institute of Arthritis and Metabolic Disease Chairman, the late Dr. Joseph Bunim. After an additional 30-day period of waiting and deteriorating, I was admitted to NIAMD, where I remained for four months and began intramuscular injections of methatrexate, a dosage of 100 milligrams per seven-day period.

I want to mention here two doctors whom I met there who have subsequently been helpful to me, and who restore my faith in medical mankind. They are Dr. George Alepo, later of the Georgetown University Medical School; and Dr. William O'Brien, now at the University of Virginia Medical School in Charlottesville.

When I reentered the world of the living in the summer of 1964, it was at less than half pace. I relearned to walk, resumed taking courses at the local college in Lynchburg, Virginia. My routine was this: one day per week at the hospital for liver and blood tests; one day per week waiting in the doctor's office for the intramuscular injections of methatrexate; then usually four days more spent partially in throwing up in reaction to the methatrexate; on the seventh day I'd start that routine again. Needless to say, there was little energy or time to enjoy extracurricular activities or to have a social life, although I was fortunate to have a special boyfriend throughout those years.

In 1967, one year later than my original class, I graduated *magna cum laude* and valedictorian, with a major in economics. I had not considered job offers seriously as I was unable to work any regular hours, much less 40. My hard-sought academic scholarship, won from the University of Florida Law School, was suddenly taken away from me when the State took drastic measures during a financial crisis; so, following the general medical advice to move South, I accepted a fellowship from Louisiana State University in graduate accounting.

The change of climate from central Virginia to Baton Rouge, Louisiana, proved beneficial; but more importantly, I was accidentally referred to a dermatologist, Dr. Carpenter, who urged me to try oral tablets of methatrexate. That being successful, I started upon a new freedom of activity. During the school semester I interviewed with visiting representatives of many companies. The fact that living on $200 a month was penurious, and the fact that my special boyfriend of the previous three years was over a thousand miles away, prompted me to accept a lucrative offer by a company in the aerospace industry in Huntsville, Alabama.

Aerospace and defense contractors win "brownie points" from the government for hiring the handicapped and minorities. I was a double "brownie" as I was both handicapped and female, entering a predominantly male profession, financial analysis. I was most fortunate to be able to work during the next couple of years and to marry that special boyfriend. Returning to Virginia to be married proved to be devastating immediately to the state of my health. In order to be able to function at all I had to move southward, a move which sounded the death knell to the marriage.

I will not recount the days of physical agony spent at work during those hours or minutes I could literally drag myself there once the rapid deterioration began. I will not recount the many problems of secondary illnesses resulting from the methatrexate, and I will not recount the conflicts with doctors over the taking of it rather than giving up my job to become a drugged, painless zombie. I was responsible for paying my own way, and I knew what the Social Security laws were. My request for a transfer to Florida was denied for economic reasons until 1973, when I was granted a medical transfer. It was too late, however; and after being forced to experiment without methatrexate for several months, I was given up as totally disabled and returned to methatrexate therapy. Prior to the move to Florida, my husband returned to his parents in Virginia, ending an eight-year-long relationship.

I will not recount the petty financial disasters of moving to south Florida alone, seriously ill, and being female, during the impossible housing shortage of early 1973. I will not recount the emotional disasters of discovering that being disabled, divorced, in financial straits, and located in a hitherto unheard of, probably uncivilized region (south Florida) was beyond respectability in the eyes of my family; therefore that relationship was severed.

So here I am, telling you today some things that I don't like to recall, things which I don't often think about. I have tried to gloss over what seems like too much melodrama. My intent is to demonstrate the cruelty and the devastating social and psychic harm done to sufferers of arthritis. The villain? Ignorance; ignorance on the part of doctors who do not keep up with the latest diagnostic techniques and treatments; ignorance by the 90 percent general population of the horrors endured by the 10 percent arthritic population. Of course I want to be cured! Of course I'd give just about anything to be relieved of the pain! But, being realistic and recognizing economic facts of life, I know that research takes money; and money, like oil, goes first to the squeaky wheel.

A person with arthritis usually has the patience of Job. Like Job, the arthritic is a victim of innocent suffering, enduring years-long physical torments that create spiritual aches as well. I have previously treated that delicate question, innocent suffering, in a book, published in 1974, titled *Hesse, Goethe, Jung· You and Me.*

[A copy of the book was submitted with this statement.]

During 1975 I have been dedicated to the effort of spreading information about arthritis primarily through my work in a federated women's club, the Deerfield Beach Junior Women's Club, which is sponsoring a benefit for the Arthritis Foundation. Today I am attempting to turn my negative experiences into, hopefully, something positive for others who suffer like me.

Isn't it time that this nation became aware of the facts of arthritis? Isn't it time we lit a candle in this awesome darkness of ignorance? Education in the mass media, in medical journals, in public schools, I feel, is the foremost step to be taken. If enough people learn about arthritis via television, radio, newspapers, magazines, public education health classes, then the letters to Congress will begin. If everyone who gripes about the "F.I.C.A." deduction from his paycheck knew that there are millions like me who want to contribute to F.I.C.A. -- would gladly do, rather than siphoning off that money, they would support research into finding a cure for arthritis.

I think that the first step the National Arthritis Act should encourage is the step that will teach people not only the facts of the physical pain, the facts of the economic loss to all, but that will teach mankind to be less unkind to the victims of this unglamorous, ungodly disease. We, as a society, need to learn how to cope with this seemingly endless problem. If we face it--in 1976?--then perhaps in 1977 we will conquer it. Thank you.

TESTIMONY OF
CAROLE FIELDER COX

COX: Ladies and Gentlemen of the Commission: I am 31, living in Delray Beach, alone, totally and permanently disabled since 1973. I have psoriatic arthritis, and have used the anti-cancer drug methatrexate consistently for the past 12 years to avoid complete invalidism.

I was asked to explain how arthritis has affected my life, physically, emotionally, and in relationship to others. I prepared the 12-page presentation submitted to you, reluctantly, because of the intense grief in recalling 12 1/2 years that must seem impossible melodrama to anyone who didn't live them. Please refer to that paper for additional details, or to this book for my treatment of the philosophic problem of innocent suffering known so intimately to arthritics. (Book is *Hesse, Goethe, Jung, You and Me*, by Carole F. Cox.)

I feel that I can speak with authority on other persons' reactions to the arthritis victim. I have demonstrated in that paper the way that strangers to the arthritic cruelly display their ignorance by being sure that arthritis isn't serious--or fatal. Acquaintances and work associates may be at first sympathetic to the arthritic, but upon seeing the inconsistency of his ability from day to day, or week to week, soon become skeptical, and distrust not only the arthritic's body, but also his character and personality. The reactions of family and intimates of the arthritis victim usually end sooner or later in rejection, whether for financial, spiritual, emotional, or geographic strains. People can cope with dramatic illness and recovery, or even death, much easier than they can face the day-in-day-out dragging on of endless worsening, endless complication, endless dying. I know because I've had 12 1/2 years to observe, was left by a husband who ended an eight-year-long relationship rather than move South. I was completely abandoned by a large, ultra proper, WASP family, for whom my being suddenly disabled, divorced, in financial straits, and located in a hitherto unheard of, probably uncivilized region (south Florida) was beyond respectability and Virginia gentility.

But I am a lucky lady. I've lived longer, more productively than any doctor told me I could do, even at NIH. My liver should have stopped functioning by now, and me, too, but I am still hanging in there. As a popular commercial saying goes, "You've come a long way, baby," and I have. It's been a damnably long way from being a healthy, athletic, honor scholar, blazing her way to a legal career, to being a disabled Social Security recipient. But during that 12 years I did finish college with honors; I did work as a financial analyst in one of the nation's top companies; I did get married. Even now I am somewhat active during my few good hours: published one book, am working on another; work with church groups and a federated women's club. I have snapshots circulating to show what that's doing. And I am here.

I am here to state that there is an enormous villain hereabouts that wreaks cruel, devastating social and psychic harm to the sufferers of arthritis. The villain? Ignorance; ignorance of doctors who do not keep up with the latest diagnostic techniques and treatments; ignorance of the 90 percent general population about the horrors endured by the 10 percent arthritic population.

Since the National Arthritis Act funds are but a drop in the bucket towards an ultimate solution or cure, I feel that the first priority of expenditures should be on education in the mass media, in medical journals, in public schools. We need a Betty Ford and Happy Rockefeller to do for arthritis what they did for breast cancer. We need TV specials during prime time, on the "Today" show in the morning, on the "Tomorrow" show at night; we need newsprint in the glossy magazines and in the newspapers. We need to invest now towards getting future monies to finish the job of research. It pays to advertise.

If all who gripe about that FICA deduction from their paychecks learn that there are millions like me who want to contribute to it rather than siphon it off, they will support research; maybe even write their Congressmen to say so. The education should include the facts of the physical pain and suffering, the economic facts that do make it everyone's problem; and the realization of mankind's unkindness to victims of this unglamorous, ungodly, unending disease. We, as a society, need to learn how to cope with this seemingly unending problem. If we learn to face it first, then soon we will take appropriate steps to conquer it. Thank you.

POLLEY: Thank you very much. If you hadn't gone to the trouble of making this testimony available, we wouldn't have it. It may have been an ordeal for you to do it, but we really appreciate it.

COX: Thank you.

Appendix B

To: Mother and Father   May 15, 1990
    Betty and King
    Carole and Sam
    Kay and Mac
    Laura and Wayne

I know that I have not written to any of you in a lot of years. I do not like form letters usually, but this is one that I think all of you should have so that all of you will get an idea of what has happened to me over the last 5 years.

In January, 1986, I had a nervous breakdown and landed in the hospital in Atlanta. I was in the hospital for a week (it did not do much good, though) and then in a day-care-clinic from the end of January until the first of April, 1986. I was doing much better with the help found at the day care clinic, but I was a long way from being enough better to function properly. The nervous breakdown was caused by serious events that occurred to me in January, 1985. That is when the company that moved us to Atlanta closed their offices and terminated my two year contract after only 6 months. At that time, we had two house payments, two car payments and a host of other things that put a lot of stress on Mary and me.

In January, 1985, I started looking for another job, but that was not easy because I did not know about companies in Atlanta (other than trucking companies), and I had no contacts. I looked for months, and during all of this time, my health was diminishing. I finally got a job with Source EDP in May of 1985 and thought that perhaps things would turn for the better.

I lost that job in September, 1985, and started seeing a psychiatrist. Things seemed to go from bad to worse and then in January, 1986, I had the breakdown as mentioned.

In April, 1986, we sold our house in Atlanta and moved back to Portland. I thought that that would be the best thing to do. It was the right idea to get Mary and George back to Portland where they had friends and family. I tried to get my consulting business going again, but was not totally successful. I went through 6 different doctors (and $4,000) before I found one that could really help. He was so expensive that I had to switch to the County Mental Health Clinic. At that time, they seemed totally useless, and could not even prescribe the right medicine to me. It seemed like all I was doing was sinking further and further into the "black hole".

I had several assignments with my consulting work but found it very hard to do (as if my knowledge had disappeared) and I was not able to get very many assignments. I had work for about 5 months, but found myself unable to get more clients to continue my consulting work.

It is now November, 1986 and my depression was worse and I had to go back to the doctor that charged so much because he seemed to be the only person that could help me. Although I was unable to pay him at the time, he said that it was ok and that I could pay him later when I had a job and was once again on my feet. Unfortunately, I was still unable to work and could not sleep which made all the problems even worse. But, it did seem that the drugs he prescribed made me feel better. Not a lot better, but at least some better. I thought that that was a step in the right direction.

In January, 1987, I got what seemed to be a bad cold that I could not seem to shake. After several doctors, different types of medicine, and almost 4 months, it was determined that what I had was ASTHMA. So then, I went through several different types of medicine to get the right combination to conquer the asthma. Finally, we hit upon the right medicine to make the asthma controllable.

In June, 1987, I started a small home repair and remodeling business. It worked out for a while. I had fun and made some pretty good money. Unfortunately, the depression and the asthma made it difficult to work and by September, I had run out of projects to do. I continued to advertise but ran into a streak of bad luck and did not get any additional projects. At this time, my sleeplessness was really taking a toll on me and I had no energy for anything.

In October, 1987, I went to work for Edelen Custom Doors as a consultant doing operations work, computer set-up, and sales of home improvement products. This seemed very good and I felt a lot better. Unfortunately, I was always extremely tired and I did not know why. My asthma doctor decided that I should have a sleep study done to see why I did not sleep very well. This is a test to monitor your sleeping habits. What came out of the sleep study was I had a disease called SLEEP APNEA. This disease causes you to never have REM sleep and thus, never be rested. My sleep apnea was so bad that my heart completely stopped beating for more than 30 seconds 283 times during the study. They said that that was extremely bad. This caused total sleep deprivation and that is why I was always very tired and was sick a lot. The answer to this problem (at the time) was major throat surgery.

In January, 1988, I had the throat surgery and missed two weeks of work at Edelen's, but that was ok because I explained what was going to happen prior to it actually happening. It was the worst surgery I have ever had. They removed my tonsils, tissue in the throat and other things to make the breathing passage clearer. Unfortunately, the surgery did not work. I had another sleep study test done after the surgery, and I was not any better. The next option was a tracheotomy, and I refused to have additional surgery and have a hole in my neck.

During all of this, I was still going to my psychiatrist and working at Edelen's. Because of my sleep problems, I was falling asleep at work in the afternoon, but I never knew it was happening. In May, 1988, Edelen's terminated my contract because I was falling asleep. I also had fallen asleep driving the car and ran off the highway (at 55 mph) and wiped out a whole lot of bushes in the center median. I safely got the car back on the highway and no one was hurt and there was no accident.

2 days after Edelen terminated my contract, Mary said to get out of this house and never come back.

So there I was ... No job, no money and no place to live. This put me into a tailspin and I got extremely depressed. Not only did I have no job, no money and no place to live, I had MANIC DEPRESSION,

ASTHMA AND SLEEP APNEA. All of this made it almost impossible to carry on life.

I was lucky to find a place to live without a job and I continued as best that I could. The struggle continued but it was even worse than before.

All during this period of time, I had been seeking social security, welfare, food stamps and unemployment. I received none because I was a white male with no dependent children living with me. I was denied any type of aid and felt that I could not go on any more. And truly, I do not know why I am still alive today. I finally got a free attorney to take on my case. He said that it may take several years before anything will happen so try to be patient. It was worth the shot so I did it.

The first of June, 1988, I found a place to live (as mentioned above) and I started looking for work. I was so depressed most of the time that I could not even seek out an interview. In fact, my disease made it seem like the words "Don't Hire Me!" was written across my forehead in bold letters. Time went on and I had interviews but no job offers. This was very distressing, but I kept on trying.

Finally in August, 1988, I got a job selling micro-computers and peripherals to the end user market place. It was not spectacular, but I was successful at it. I was successful except for early morning meetings and in the office in the afternoon. My sleep apnea took over during these times and I would fall asleep at work. I was not aware that this was happening until I was terminated for falling asleep at work. In November 1988, I was terminated from the job.

After this event, my depression got worse. It became difficult to even get out of bed on many days. By December, I was able to send out resumes and look for another job.

In December, I interviewed with Georgia Pacific at the branch. I thought that this may be the building block that I needed. The first and the second interview went extremely well. In January, 1989, Georgia Pacific hired me as an inside salesman working in the branch. This was great and I felt a lot of internal encouragement. I knew I had a sleep problem so I did everything I could to defeat it. I would go to bed at 8:00 or 8:30 pm and get up each morning at 6:30 and have breakfast. I tried to get the perfect schedule, if you know what I mean.

Things were going well and I got to the point of selling over $14,000.00 per day. This was very good for an inside salesman who was just learning the accounts. Unfortunately, I was not winning out of my sleep apnea. Despite all attempts (including taking NO-DOZ to stay awake on sleepy days), the sleep apnea made me fall asleep at meetings and even behind the computer terminal. In May, 1989, I lost my job with Georgia Pacific. Things were very bleak now and I went days without getting out of bed, eating or talking to anyone.

In June, 1989, I was able to start looking for a new job. But I knew this one had to be the type where I did not have the opportunity to fall asleep. So I got a small job at a friend's company called Quality Bird Toys. I also worked out an arrangement with Edelen Custom Doors to sell their products on a commission basis only. I worked the show room some and also got customers on my own. I became very successful at this so that Edelen decided to change the terms of our agreement. By doing this, they made it impossible for me to make much of a living with an agreement with them. So I spent more time working at Quality Bird Toys making parts and also finished product.

At least working at QBT I would always make some money (not much, but it was much better than nothing at all). The Edelen deal fell through the cracks because I was unable to negotiate a good enough agreement for me to earn money.

It's now September, 1989, and I was still busy with two jobs. Most of the time it was with QBT. I became very close friends with the family that owned QBT. I had met them through Cub Scouts and George's Baseball and Basketball. They have a son in the same class with George. Their names are [Bob and Barbra Milhaus]. They are my best and closest friends and know about my medical problems and help me out a lot.

One day I was telling Barbra about my sleep apnea problem because I was very tired. I found out that her father has sleep apnea and he was on a C-PAP machine to help him sleep. I thought that that might be something that could help me. I checked into this with my doctor and she wanted me to have another sleep test while on a C-PAP machine to see how well I would do. This sounded great except for the fact that the sleep study costs over $1200. Since I did not have the money or the insurance to cover the test, I put it on the back burner. Barbra helped me find a way to get the cost of the sleep study written off at the hospital. This was done and I had the sleep study in late October, 1989.

With the use of the C-PAP machine during the sleep study, I slept through the night for the first time in over 12 years. Evidently, my sleep apnea has been with me for quite some time and the lack of sleep is very hard on the body and the mind. We now knew that the C-PAP machine would help with my sleep apnea problem.

The cost of a C-PAP machine was $1500 and that was impossible for me to handle. So we knew what to do, but it was not possible to do because of its cost.

I told my psychiatrist about the study and the evaluation of the machine and its results. Through my doctors and Barbra, they were able to find a foundation that would rent the machine for me. This was great and around Thanksgiving, I received my C-PAP machine. The machine pumps air down through your nose and down your windpipe so that your throat stays clear and you can breathe properly. Finally, I started sleeping through the night. The only trouble I have is if my sinuses are stopped up or I have a cold.

Right after Thanksgiving, I went to work for Toys R Us as a sales clerk for four nights a week. By doing this, I was still able to work for QBT. And with the machine, I wasn't always tired. The Toys R Us job was fun but it did not pay very much. But at any rate, I was earning some money at both jobs.

I am also writing software (computer system) for QBT and it's coming along really well. They are both a manufacturer and a wholesale distributor, so the software is quite complex. But it is fun to do and tuning up my skills quite a bit.

Barbra Milhaus has been instrumental in getting food stamps and general disability for me. Without her help, I never could have done it. Also, now after 4 years, my disability case is in the hands of a judge. A year ago, I got an attorney to help me get the SSI disability. My hearing should be coming up soon.

Barbra has also tried to get me housing assistance, but so far, it has been unsuccessful. It is really weird. If you can pay for your rent, they will help you out. If you are unable to pay your rent, they won't help you. Sounds like a bank to me! In March, the Milhaus helped me pay the rent and I will work off the debt over the next few weeks. With their help, I believe that things may work out.

I have tried everything possible that I could think of to get out of this HELL hole that I am in. I do not know if I will ever make it out, but I am going to continue to try.

Hopefully you will understand why I won't move back to Lynchburg. One of the key reasons is that my doctor thinks it would be very bad for me and secondly, George is here. Without George, I would have been dead a long time ago. In addition:

- My friends are here.
- Bob and Barbra are here.
- My psychiatrist is here.
- My asthma doctor is here.
- My other doctors are here.
- My C-PAP machine is here.
- My medicines are closely monitored.
- The latest in medical technology is here.
- My computer and belongings are here.
- My work with QBT is here.

There are other small reasons. But this list of reasons for not moving back to Lynchburg is significant.

Just last month, April, I had a terrible episode with the gout. It settled into my right knee and right hip and for more than a week, I was unable to get around. The pain was so much that it hurt just to roll over in bed. I couldn't work. I couldn't drive. And Barbra took me to the hospital to have the leg looked at. At the time, no one knew that it was the gout. The hospital drained a lot of fluid out of my knee and sent me to an orthopedic doctor. He drained more fluid out and said that it did not seem to be an orthopedic problem.

I went to another doctor (one I had gone to before) and he took more fluid off the knee and the fluid had also built up in my right ankle. He checked the fluid and it was a severe attack of the gout. He is now treating me with different drugs and hopes to have it under control before too long. I am not supposed to be on my leg and do no running until June. I can be on my leg a little bit but not too much. One of the drugs he put me on, he says that I will be on it for 2 to 3 years.

Now you know why I haven't written in years. The last five years have been extremely bad physically and emotionally. In addition to the above account of my life, we sold our house in Portland and in Atlanta; we've spent $20,000 on medical bills (and I still owe a lot more); I have lost almost everything; Mary and I are divorced; etc.

And as a post note, just the other day a man ran a stop sign and ran into the right rear of my car, and that is going to have to be fixed.

I had hoped to get definitions for the diseases I have. But I have not taken the time to go to the library. The diseases I have are:

> Manic Depression or Bi-polar disease.
> Sleep Apnea.
> Asthma.
> Gout.
> Arthritis.

Thanks for taking the time to read this. I wish everyone well, perhaps now, you can understand why I have not written and do not phone. I love you all. Take care and good-bye.

Love,
Larry

Appendix C

[Reprinted here from *SAN FRANCISCO* and *SAN JOSE* magazines, by permission of the author. The January, 1990 cover included the teaser: *Conquer the open sea with Carole Kahn.*]

PEOPLE

Smooth sailing in the Charter business
by Pam Woodside

Success for Carole Kahn, owner of CAK Charters, began with what she refers to as "a piece of cloth on a stick"--the stick being the mast, the cloth being the sail that hung on a non-motorized boat.

Friends, Ken and Delores Harmon of Boca Raton, Florida, didn't realize they had opened a whole new world to Kahn--a spirited young woman who compensates and lives with psoriatic arthritis, a rare and debilitating condition.

During a visit with them, "The Harmons asked me to join them on a family outing. I didn't know starboard from the port bow--and I didn't think poop was a nice word. I was terrified. It seemed so completely beyond me, but I wanted to be with the family. So I went. I saw two teenage girls swiftly maneuvering a small boat. They slipped the mast, raised the sails, turned the boat in the right direction and sailed off in their sailboat. I thought, if they can do it, so can I."

And, she did.

Kahn soon discovered that her intellectual curiosity and love of nature added to the joy of sailing. From that moment on, Kahn became an avid sailor, in spite of her disabilities. This condition has caused Kahn to adapt in her daily activities.

Walking and standing cause her pain. Removing jar lids and medicine bottle caps are her nemesis and many fine motor skills are difficult, but playing the piano exercises her hands and wrists. When pulling lines on a boat, she uses thick gloves to build up her grip. To keep the rest of her joints symptom free, she swims faithfully.

"I've got to do my laps," Kahn said about her daily swim.

I Feel Equal on Water

On land, Kahn experiences her disability; but on water, "I can be equal," (to those without physical limitations). "It's wonderful. I feel a great sense of accomplishment. I can swim miles, climb to the top of a mast and sail all over the world," Kahn said.

Her adventures have taken her to the outer islands of Tahiti in the Pacific, the Saronic Gulf islands and the Peleponesian Coast of Greece, the Virgin Islands, along the French Riviera, to the Florida Keys, and to the Channel Islands near Santa Barbara, California.

All these travels could not have happened without Kahn's tenacious attitude toward handling her illness. When she began losing the use of her right hand, Kahn thought she'd better make use of her strength before she lost full use, so she began taking sailing lessons on a full-keeled sailboat, with auxiliary motor, in Redwood City, California. As one thing led to another, and her confidence increased, she decided to buy her own 32-foot Ericson sloop, which she docks in Sausalito.

Sailing her sloop, or yacht as she calls it tongue-in-cheek, is the "love of her life," to be enjoyed on waters across the globe.

While on a European trip with her husband Sam, Kahn discovered one of the most beautiful sailing meccas of the world, the French Cote D'Azur. It was a dream come true and a challenge to be met. So she bought a flat and moved to France. For six months of the year, she lived on French bread, fresh fish, and sailing the Mediterranean daily.

But even living a dream has its problems. Commuting between continents has its very own--airline hassles, long walks to
gates, waiting, etc.; however, with a great deal of physical planning, Kahn has adapted to make her life easier. She uses and
manipulates her own wheelchair with attachable motor, and carries an emergency bag of basic necessities and a portable folding
stool for long waits.

Another Challenge

Thriving on challenge, Kahn pursued another. After accruing
an appropriate number of sailing hours, she applied for a Coast
Guard ocean-going (vs. inland bay waters) license. This license
allows Kahn to operate or navigate a passenger carrying vessel in
the Pacific Ocean.

Although she loves an intellectual challenge, preparing for the
exam presented Kahn with an unusual course of study.

"I had to memorize every light, signal, tower, and building in
or along the bay, and understand every bell, whistle, and gong. I
drove and sailed up and down the coast checking out all the
points and ports."

Few applicants get through this exam, consisting of 12 to 20
separate tests, in less than a year, let alone pass. Like other
professional exams, there are waiting periods if the person does
not pass the various levels. Kahn was among the first female
applicants on the West Coast to take the exam and receive her
license within a few months.

Passing It On

However, achieving was not new to Kahn. Early on in her sailing experience, she took on the role of instructor.

"Learning something new and communicating it to others is
what drives her," said Ron Raffensperger, student. "Carole enjoys
passing on the thrill of what she gets out of sailing. She is very

thorough and wants you to understand every procedure. You practice until you get it right. She's conscientious and evaluates everything before she does it."

Even more challenging for Kahn are her foreign students who speak little English. Teaching friends and visitors from Italy, Germany, and France is a regular occurrence.

"I've also skippered for business meetings, weddings and 21st birthday parties. I'll even provide a catered lunch," added Kahn.

Whatever the occasion, Kahn conveys confidence and clear directions to students and passengers.

"Carole was really open about telling us what to do and getting us to try different tasks, from handling the mainsail to driving the boat," said David Stanton, San Jose State University student and experienced water skier. Stanton was impressed with how she operated the 32-foot boat. "She never had a hard time with any of her maneuvers," said Stanton. "My first experience was great, but I have more to learn."

Kahn believes one proving ground is right here in the Bay Area.

"If you learn to sail on the San Francisco Bay, you can sail anywhere," Kahn said.

Her course has prepared many students in seamanship, (knots and hitches). They learn safety, weather and currents, chart reading, take-off and landing, how to identify parts of the boat and sail, and practical maneuvers such as tacking and jibing.

"Once you know the ropes, sailing is a lot of fun," said Terre Mathiasmeier, fellow sailor.

But as Kahn's husband Sam said, "It's like learning to drive a car; don't learn from your spouse."

After a few times out, he found that sailing can be perfectly safe and pleasant. Kahn urges women to take a few lessons "so they don't get stuck in the galley or hauling out the anchor." Then sailing will be enjoyable.

Mathiasmeier also enjoys sailing, finding it relaxing, especially in the winter months. "Despite the need for extra layers of clothes, the wind isn't as high and they can often be shed as the day progresses," said Mathiasmeier. Her favorite excursions include sailing under the Golden Gate, observing the herring harvest, and catching a glimpse of a whale. She especially remembers when she and Kahn sailed in Greece on a 40-foot Sunfizz sloop.

Mathiasmeier looks back at that experience with a feeling of accomplishment, but that's what Kahn feels every time she launches her boat out of Richardson Bay in Sausalito.

Whether it involves many hours of maintaining her boat, or the extra preparations for a trip, Kahn has met another challenge.

Appendix D

Dear Dad,

Hi Dad! How are you doing? I really appreciated the phone call the other day. I was surprised, but really pleased. I have been meaning to write for some time now and just never took the time to sit down and put it in a letter. Now I am going to try to get everything written down that I can.

How is Mom doing in the home? Betty called the other day (after the funeral) and said that Mom recognized people and was fully aware of the situation at the funeral. I know it must have been very hard on her to have been there. I know that you also stated that it was very sad for her. But don't you find it interesting that she was cognizant of what was going on? What does she actually have? No one has ever told me for sure what she has. Laura and Betty say one thing and Kay and Carole used to say that it was something else. Of course, I never hear from Kay (even though I used to call her every couple of weeks) and Carole only calls if there is some type of disaster happening.

I try to send a card or something to Mom every few weeks just to let her hear from me. I don't know if she knows who is sending the cards but I will continue to do so unless you think it is detrimental. I sent her a sympathy card last week and will try to send something cheerful next week as spring approaches. I know you must spend a lot of time at the home (or somewhere) because I have often called and there is no answer. Betty says that you stay up late so maybe I'll try at night (after 10 pm your time) instead of early in the morning.

I appreciate the Christmas gift very much. I want to thank you for everything else that you have sent to me and for everything that you have done for me. I know that I do not write nor call all that often. There is no excuse for not writing because it only costs 32 cents to mail. On the other hand, calling costs quite a bit more and I really don't have that large of a budget to make a lot of long distance phone calls. I try to call Betty every so often and likewise, Laura. And then I also try to call you once in a while to see how you are doing and to see how

Mom is doing. This means that I have to split up when I call whom so that I do get to everyone who calls me.

I used to call all of my sisters until they (Kay and Carole) decided that they did not need to reciprocate the phone calls, I still send them cards for Christmas, birthday etc. and I even tried to call Kay on her birthday but there was no answer. I called her in the morning for several days following her birthday but there was never an answer. Carole is never home and she has a lot more money than I have and could call me if she wanted to. It seems that the only time that Carole calls is when there is some catastrophic event going on, like last July.

Last July (around the 4th) Carole called me early in the morning saying that you had one foot in the grave, that you were very ill and dying and that Mom had to be put into a home because there was no one to take care of her. She said that she was flying up the next day and told me that I should get on a plane and fly to Lynchburg tomorrow also. Well, it is nearly impossible for me to pick up and fly 3000 miles the next day unless it was a dire emergency. So the next thing I did after hanging up with Carole was to call Betty and Laura and find out what the real TRUTH was. That is when I found out that you had been sick but were doing much better. As for Mom, there was basically no change from the previous months so I really wondered where Carole was coming from. Needless to say, it did not sound like you were almost in the grave and that Mom was so bad off that she would have to be put into a home and forgotten about.

I know that Carole and Kay insisted that Mom be put into a home to be taken care of. I back up your decision 100% and hope that you were not forced into the decision. I know that it must be easier for you as far as your daily living goes, but I also know that it had to be a very hard decision for you to make. Since I have not spoken to Mom while she is at the home, all I can go on as to how she is doing is by what you say and also what Betty and Laura say.

As you know, last July before you entered Mom into the Slagle home, there was to be a conference phone call (Carole was setting this up) between everyone EXCEPT me. Carole did not include me in this process at all. I don't know the reason other than I am sure Carole is influenced by Mary and Mary knows absolutely nothing about me. The reason the conference call did not take place was because Betty and Laura refused to be involved with this unless I was included also. You see, Carole and Kay have decided to leave me out of the family and do not care in the least whether I am informed about you or Mom or anyone else. That really ticks me off because I have never done anything to any of my sisters to be treated in this manner. I am fed up with it and will not go out of my way to speak to Carole or Kay. If Kay ever calls and apologizes for how she has treated me, then the apology will be accepted.

As for Carole, she thinks that Mary is a Saint and that everything Mary has ever done to me is OK. This is intolerable. Carole needs to learn to stick up for family instead of some one who is a cheater and a liar and a thief.

Now I will tell you why I say that Mary is a cheater, a liar and a thief. First of all, before we were even divorced she was running around with other men. I said to myself... She is going to do whatever she wants to do anyway. As far as a liar, she lied to the Judge in the divorce settlement about the money, stocks and bonds that you had sent for George's college education. Mary told the Judge that it was to be used for George for whatever was necessary, and I know that this is not true. My lawyer was incompetent and did not put up any objections as to the purpose of these funds nor did he tell me to get additional documentation from you to present to the Judge. As far as the thief part goes, when we moved from Portland to Atlanta, I borrowed $5000 from one of George's accounts to complete the closing costs. When the house in Portland sold (which was May of 1985), I replaced the $5000 back into George's account. It was never touched by me again after that. In fact, since we moved back to Portland, Mary has been the custodian of George's CD accounts. As of the court appearance for the divorce in August of 1991, Mary had spent more than $10,000.00 of George's college account. Now I am sure that Mary has told Carole who has told you that I spent the money. That is 100% incorrect. Mary has had control of the money despite my efforts at the divorce to regain control or at least have co-signing capabilities for the use of those funds.

I know that I have tried to explain this to you before and I don't know if you ever fully understood the full ramifications. That is why I wanted to sue my incompetent lawyer and I wanted to sue Mary for what she has done to my name plus the theft of George's college fund that you had established. Mary has refused to co-operate with the legal system here in Oregon concerning how she is receiving child support. Since she has not told the state of Oregon what she agreed on in the court room, my back child support liability is growing at the rate of $300 a month even though she is getting over $550.00 a month in child support through my federal disability, and she agreed in front of a Judge that that would take the place of the $300 child support so said in the divorce decree.

So Oregon thinks I am a deadbeat Dad who does not pay his child support and I could be arrested at any time. (I have talked with the District Attorney in my County and he said that he knows what is going on and that Mary will not cooperate and I should not be worried about being arrested.) But what happens when he is no longer in office? Also, the IRS thinks I owe some umpteen thousands of dollars in back child support, and the credit bureau reporting companies think that I owe back child support also. Until Mary signs the correct documents and files them with the state of Oregon, the IRS and the credit bureau reporting companies, I am screwed. There is no way I can get any credit for anything and if by chance I was able to go back to work, the state of Oregon and the IRS would take every penny I made to pay back child support that I don't even owe. What do you think of that?

That is why I wanted to sue Mary and the lawyer, but I did not have the money and I never got any support from you or anyone else. I don't know what I am going to do. There is no way I can clear my name without suing Mary and I don't have the funds to do it. What do you think I should do? The one lawyer that I presented my case to said that I had a valid case and probably would win. I would probably also be awarded damages that Mary has caused me. I would like to do this so that I could get my name cleared with the different parties.

I sure hope that you have not been sending money to Mary because she is getting over $550 per month to take care of George. The divorce decree only requires $300 per month. Did you know that she has been sending him to a private Catholic High School that costs a small fortune per year? Did you help him buy his 1967 Mustang or did Mary use more of his college education money to buy that? It would not surprise me if she has spent every penny of the college education fund that you had established for him.

As for George, I don't know what to think. It has been over 2 years since he has spoken to me or I have seen him. I know that his mother is tickled pink that he has nothing to do with me. It's probably her fault in the first place. I have tried to communicate with George by sending him cards and letters and even tried to call him. Mary answered the phone and said that he does not want to talk to me and hung up the phone very rudely. There is no way I am going to hang out around his house or continue to call because I know that Mary would get some type of injunction to make it impossible for me to even come into that neighborhood, and the Milhaus live in that same neighborhood. The last time I spoke to George was Feb 4, 1993 and he got mad at me because I would not buy him a certain Mustang that we had looked at over the weekend. We also argued that his Mom should pay for his drivers ed because of the $550 a month she was getting for child support. That's it ... and I have not heard from him or seen him since.

Also, Mary told this Catholic High School that I was not to see George nor are they supposed to send any information to me about George. I have called the school and that is what the principal told me. I told him that I will see him in court someday because what he was doing was against Oregon law. Well, I still never receive any information about George.

I am stuck with no place to turn because no one will give me any support as to what I need to do to get everything resolved.

As for me, I do the best I can from week to week. We are just starting up the bird toy business again since the Christmas holiday. That will give me something else to do and a way to earn a few dollars. I have been studying and working on my computer (learning new programming languages) quite a bit. I enjoy it and I am trying to keep up my skills so that if I can ever get back to doing consulting, I will be up to date on terms and technology. I had hoped that some day I would get back to work but with the way I get illnesses, I'll never be able to go back to work.

These are the illnesses I have:

Clinical depression
Gout
Chronic Fatigue Syndrome
Sleep apnea
Arthritis
Asthma
Psoriasis
and probably Diabetes (tests are still negative).

I don't know why God hates me so much that he has given me all these afflictions, but He does and He has. I have tried to live the correct life but apparently somewhere I went wrong. I keep trying but I am not really sure why I even attempt to. It seems that every year that passes by, some other illness takes over. It has gotten very difficult to make ends meet now that I don't do a lot of bird toys. My rent is $470 a month (very cheap actually). But my prescription medicines are over $400 per month. There is not much left in the budget for utilities, auto insurance, food and other necessities. Oh, well, I'll do the best I can until I can no longer survive. I will cross that bridge when I have to.

Take care of yourself and Mom. Let her know that I am thinking of her always.

Love,
[signed]
Larry

Appendix E
Larry's attempts to reconcile his sisters

Dear: Betty and King   804-xxx-xxxx   March 1, 1999
       Carole   954-xxx-xxxx
       Kay and Mac   540-xxx-xxxx
       Laura and Wayne 804-xxx-xxxx

All of you know that I have been talking to each of you concerning the "sibling situation" (the lack of harmony, love and respect for one another and the non-communication) over the past 6 weeks. Previously, I just stayed away from bringing this to the forefront, but that is over! It is a real tragedy that this situation has gone on for so long. When I visited last October, Dad expressed his concerns about it and said that things had better improve soon or he would be required to take actions that his children may not like. I know that he is serious and after talking to him this evening, he is going to change things such as Mom's funeral arrangements, his own funeral arrangements, his will etc. I should have done more about this last November but the holidays came and I was not really sure how to approach each of you about the situation.

The only one of you that I talked with about this in December was Kay. I asked Kay to try to open up communications with Betty by submitting a sincere letter of apology for whatever Kay had done or had said to her that broke that relationship. Kay did submit the letter to Betty and Betty responded with a letter that, to me, seemed very much out of place. Kay had asked Betty if they could rebuild their relationship and be loving sisters and valued family members again. Betty did not directly answer this question but in turn, brought up all sorts of incidences that had occurred in the past. This "remembering and reminding each of other of past" indiscretions is going backward instead of forward as Dad and I want. ** [**Author's note: See below for letters referenced.**]

I am sure that at some time or the other, we have each said something that we should not have or we did some action that we should not have and are sorry for them. But I find it so very hard to believe that "something" could be so hideous that we would cut off our family members. All of you know where I stand on this issue and I really think that all of

253

you know what Dad wants to happen. Why is it that you (plural) cannot approach each other, vent your anger, state what it is that the other party has done to cause this, sincerely apologize for whatever you have done or said or both in a civilized forum with Dad or me involved to keep the get together from getting into a shouting match or worse? I do not know exactly what it is that each of you have done to one another and I am not concerned about it... other than if you need to talk about it to each other in order to move forward, let's do it! NOW!!!

Rather than talk about past actions (verbal as well as physical), I propose to you that we get together with Dad and open up feelings so that we can heal each other and ourselves and get the family back together. It is long past time to do this. I realize that I have previously not talked to you *re* the non-communication, but that time has come to an end. I will no longer watch my "p's and q's" about this.

Dad is really distraught about this and it is extremely DISRESPECTFUL of us not to carry on his wishes. He has enough stress and concerns to handle with Mom etc., and with the death of Jimmy, brother and BEST friend, we do not need to place any of the petty differences we have with each other on him and we MUST re-establish the family unit. Each of us should be more supportive of him and with each other.

From my conversations with each of you, every one of you mentioned that you were tired of the other party making up lies, distorting truths, words and actions taken, undermining each other and "having some hidden agenda with Dad". But no one will tell me (or Dad) what it was that was so bad that it would break up the family. This is absolutely ridiculous and uncalled for. It may even be possible that what supposedly occurred never did happen, and we are holding on to it so hard for so long, that we actually believe it and have blown it out of proportion. The other common thread of my conversations with each of you was that you were "willing to accept apologies, bury the past and re-establish communications." I found that to be very encouraging and truly believed that significant progress could be made.

UNFORTUNATELY, only the words have been spoken to

me, and not to each of you directly. Words mean absolutely nothing if they are not sincere and you don't take actions that represent the meaning of the words. Each of you is old enough, wise enough and responsible enough to take the necessary steps to move forward in building your relationships with one another. Unless your TRUE agenda is not to forgive and move forward. I cannot control any of you. Dad cannot control any of you. You control your own attitudes and actions. I am tired of this and hope this letter will spark some type of family values that will get us all back together.

TIME IS RUNNING OUT! ... and we might not live long enough to "do the correct, responsible and loving actions" before it is too late! Can you not show the proper love and respect for Mom and Dad? None of us were raised to be like this!

As a side thought, don't think that members of the broad Fielder - Haley family don't know what's been going on... Let me assure you that they do know! Stop burying your head in the sand and think that no one "knows or sees" what we have done to Mom and Dad and to ourselves.

SO ... Grow up and stop the fighting, the lies, the innuendo and take responsibility for your words and your actions. If you need to discuss it openly, do it and then take the actions to get over it! You can use me as a sounding board if you need to. One thing you all could do is to write down all the awful things that have been said or acted upon by you and against you and place them in a small box. Then BURN the box and let that be the end of it. Release all of the anger and hostility that you may have.

Only you know what it takes to move forward with the healing process. Let each other know and then take the correct actions.

And show the love and respect that Mom and Dad so deserve, and tell Dad what you personally are going to do to mend the family situation. Let me know too! Do not wait until tomorrow!!! ...Tomorrow may be too late!

DO IT TODAY ... RIGHT NOW!!!!

I love all of you dearly and am going to try to be more responsive and communicate with you more often (probably via phone). PLEASE DO THE RIGHT THING!!! I know you can, but you must make a conscious effort to move forward. It may not be easy at first, but the end results will be well worth the pain.

Love,

Larry

My e-mail address: awk@cdsnet.net
Cc: Dad

**Author's note: Before Larry sent us the above letter in March, he had expressed to me by telephone his disappointment at Betty's apparent increased hatred towards Kay, *because* he had been trying to make peace between them, unknown to me. He asked me to look at the letters they had exchanged at the end of the year.

I looked at all three letters, applauded his efforts as peacemaker, and warned him that the letters indicated Kay's willingness to try almost anything conciliatory, but Betty's everlasting refusal to "bury the hatchet."

First, Kay wrote to Betty December 21, 1998, at Larry's urging, and expressed Daddy's concerns about the recent "scenes" at family events, especially funerals. (For a Southern gentleman, his own funeral was one of the most important social events of his "life.") I already knew from Daddy that he didn't want to permit any public funeral for himself for fear of what kind of scandalous scene his Virginia daughters would create. To him, public humiliation was taboo. Kay simply asked Betty to act cordially in public for the sake of our parents' declining years, and she offered an apology for any inadvertent insult or hurt she had inflicted on Betty. Kay had sent copies of her letter to Daddy, Larry, Daddy's brother in Lynchburg, and the cousin in whose home the "slugging incident" occurred between Laura and Kay.

Second was a note to Larry from Betty, who was apparently inflamed by Kay's letter and dashed off a hand-written note to Larry

December 26th, during a winter storm power outage. She feigned shock and ignorance about any hostility whatever. She proceeded to defend herself by accusing Daddy of living in "confusion" most of the time and not understanding anything. It was a typical twist of words, Virginia lingo style.

I already knew from many sources in the extended family that Betty drove Laura to the funeral of our Aunt Edith, whom Laura didn't even know, to the great surprise of our cousins. It was to that aunt and cousins that Kay and I had taken Mother the day before we persuaded Daddy to find an institution for her care. That family was very fond of Kay and my father, who visited there frequently with my mother, even after she was confined to assisted living. Everyone, especially Daddy, was aghast that Laura assaulted Kay. Many wondered who Laura was and why Betty brought her.

Betty wrote Larry that she realized that he had "not been involved with any of this—at least not from my mouth." It was as though she were trying to ingratiate herself to Larry and threaten him at the same time. She apparently did not like the fact that so many people were cognizant of the long-standing horrendous behavior of the sisters and its effect on our father.

The third letter which Betty typed January 2, 1999 to Kay would make angels weep. She pretended to be surprised and puzzled, but pleased that Kay would apologize. She was astonished that Kay had forgotten all "the hurtful things you have said and done to me. And yes, there are many things. I don't care to rehash things - I don't have the time or the desire. But certainly one incident that is prominent in my memory…." And she proceeded to rehash something or other. She then wrote Kay "If you are apologizing for that and for some other untrue things you have said, I accept the apology and I forgive you." Larry and I felt sorry that Kay had even attempted to make up with Betty.

Betty again accused Daddy of being in "confusion," and explained to Kay how she had "straightened him out" when he dared to express his concerns to her that his daughters would create a public scandal at his own impending funeral. She managed to twist everything to be Kay's fault, and wrote Kay, "I actually defended you and told Daddy that no matter what, for a funeral you would show up - that you would put aside your bitterness, jealousy, or whatever feelings you had towards others."

Larry and I had laughed together over the phone at Betty's twisted words, but we both were crying on the inside at the significant hatred manifested.

Betty chastised Kay for sending other family members a copy of her letter. She wrote that she and her husband never entered the fray, never chose "sides." To me, she seemed to be that little girl again in the car with me. After torturing me with her long reach until I yelled out, she proceeded to snicker quietly, acting totally innocent that she had manipulated Daddy to punish me for screaming in pain and anguish.

I pointed out to Larry that Kay had been in Betty's long reach for a long time, and I was grateful not to have been in it for most of my life, being gone so long and so far from Virginia. He still felt secure in his relationship with all his sisters, but was disappointed that his efforts to play peacemaker failed. He didn't want to give up trying. We laughed at Betty's final sentences to Kay. She wrote, "Again, I accept your apology. I hope we can get together soon. I told you years ago, my door is always open to you, you are welcome to visit at any time, and I look forward to seeing you in the very near future."

Larry commented, "Who is she kidding?"

He kept plugging at the problem, but when there was no apparent progress among his sisters by summertime, 1999, he wrote to each sister separately, and sent copies to Daddy and to me. They follow below.

June 22, 1999

Dear Dad,

I hope that this letter finds you doing well. I am still trying to put 2 good days together one after the other. It will happen soon, I hope. The main reason for this letter is to enclose copies of the letters that I have sent to all of my sisters. I wanted you to know what I said to each of them.

I am sorry that my attempts to get the family back together this spring failed. I hope that these letters will do something positive, but there are no guarantees. I really think that you ought to talk to Betty about getting the family back together and put the RESPONSIBILITY on her shoulders. She is the eldest and should do the most to move this process forward. I hope the letter that I sent Laura will help her to move forward as well. I am willing to do whatever I can.

I am not really sure when I will be able to travel to L'burg but I really want to come back and spend some time with you. It just seems that some health issue crops up every few weeks. I have to have the sinus surgery all over again and that should take place some time in July. That will mean 5 to 7 weeks of recuperating after that. I will let you know the specifics when I know.

I think that you should call Laura and find out when she will be back in town and see if you could take her to Madeline's or Virginia's house so that the truth about her birth and childhood can be brought out into the open. I know it won't be easy for you or for her. But I do believe that it is one of those painful growing things that must take place. Let me know what you think and if I can be of any assistance.

I must go now. I'll talk to you again very soon.

Love,

Larry

June 22, 1999

Dear Kay,

I hope that you and Mac and Kate are doing fine. I know that Mac is looking for new challenges in his work life and that will take shape the way it should. Dad told me that Kate was unable to get into the summer school class she wanted to take. I guess that changes all of your summer plans.

I was really hoping to be able to get to L'burg this summer but my health has turned so bad that I am now just trying to put 2 good days together one after the other. On the 11th, my back just seemed to give out and my vertigo got so bad that I could not get out of bed for 10 days except the day Barbra took me to the hospital emergency room to see what they could do. I was put on a couple of new drugs to help with the vertigo and was told to stay lying down as much as I possibly could. Needless to say, I got absolutely nothing done during that time.

This past Sunday was the first day I was able to get up and do anything and I do not want to overdo just in case something goes bad again. When my back was hurting so much and my vertigo was so bad, I could only stand to be up for about 8 minutes before having to go back to bed.

I also have to have the sinus surgery all over again and this time they want to put tubes in my head so that my sinuses drain. They also hope that that will take care of the vertigo problem. But if it does not, they will have to pursue other measures.

I am sorry I do not have better news this time. Hopefully next time things will be a lot better. I'll try to call you around the 4th or something to see how all of you are doing.

Take care.

Love,

Larry

June 22, 1999

Dear Betty,

Hi! I hope that you and King are fine and are getting ready to enjoy the summer. I hope that it is not too hot nor too dry this year. I have called you several times but have not been able to reach you. I do hope that King gave you the messages that I had called and asked him to ask you to give me a call when you had the chance. It has been quite some time that I have heard from you. I do hope that I have not done something to upset you or make you mad at me. I am sorry if such an event has occurred. I never intended anything that I have done or talked to you about to cause a rift between us.

All I ever wanted to accomplish this spring was to unite the family as it should be. It seems to me that that is not possible unless someone in a stronger more influential position takes the initiative. That means either you or Dad. I am not sure that Dad is able to take on this responsibility because of all the stresses that he is under right now. That means YOU have to be the one to unite our family. I now put this responsibility on your shoulders and extend to you whatever I can do to make this take place. Since you are the eldest and the one responsible for Mom and Dad and their affairs, you must take the initiative.

I am also very concerned about Laura's mental and physical health. Her actions (both physical and verbal) at the last two family funerals have not exactly been Emily Post. And I have heard this from several sources. Since you seem to be the closest to Laura, perhaps you can offer to help her with whatever stresses she is under. I know that she has numerous health issues that concern her, and I wish there was something I could do to help her. But being so far away, I do not know what to do. Do you have any suggestions?

I have heard that she takes Prozac, the antidepressant. I was put on that drug 7 years ago and after 3 days, I told the Dr. that I could not take it any more. It's effects on me were terrible, I was agitated, couldn't sleep and I would lash out at anyone that said something that I did not agree with. Anyway, the Dr. stopped the drug and after 2 weeks of drying out from it, she put me on Zoloft. This drug has been a godsend for me. I have been able to at least stay at what I call 0 - 0; not ever elated over anything but also not depressed into the negative part of the graph. Perhaps Laura should mention this to her doctor and see if she should change drugs (if she is taking any). I know that you must be concerned as well.

Again, I hope that you are doing fine. Please give me a call when you can and I will try to reach you again in the next week or so. Take care.

Love,

Larry

June 22, 1999

Dear Laura,

How are you and Wayne doing? I do hope that you are both doing fine. And I hope that your animal family are doing fine as well. I have been meaning to write to you for some time, but I just seem to put it off and then forget about it. What do you plan to do this summer?

There is something I need to speak to you about. And I hope that you do not take this the wrong way. I am really concerned about your health, both physical and mental. I know that you are taking some pretty potent drugs for your arthritis and I hope that you are doing what the doctor has instructed. For your knowledge, I take methatrexate (1 injection per week), Celebrex, Prednisone and Sulfasalazine for my arthritis. And for the pain, I take Darvastat (4 per day). I also have other things that you probably do not have so I don't think it is necessary to mention them. But for my Clinical Depression, I take Zoloft and Risperdal. They seem to work fairly well. I am never elated but I am also not depressed like I used to be. I have heard that you take Prozac. Is this true? 7 years ago, my doctor put me on Prozac and I couldn't stand it. Took it for 3 days and told the doc that I could not take it any more. It drove me crazy! I was agitated, irritated and was outspoken in ways that just weren't right.

I am really concerned about your physical and verbal actions at the last two family funerals. I realize that funerals can be a very stressful time and perhaps things at home and at work were also adding to your stress. Is there anything I can do to help you? I will do what I can if you let me. And as to the family situation, I wish there was a way that I could help you put the hate and distrust behind you so that you can make peace with the rest of us.

I think that you have heard some stories concerning your birth and childhood that may not be totally true. I only know some of this from what I have heard from others because I was only 8 when you were born. I know that Mom had a depressive episode after your birth but it was not due to you. It was other pressures and the normal depression that mothers go through after the child is born. You became Dad's darling because you had blonde hair and blue eyes like him. He took you everywhere he could. You even became the one that he took on walks down to the railroad yard to see the trains when you were old enough to keep up with his stride. I remember playing trucks with you because you had that truck-camper and trailer that carried horses. You also would make those neat bugs and stuff with that electric machine.

Betty was too old at the time to care one way or the other and she was dating and getting ready to attend Longwood College. Carole thought of you as her baby just like she did with Kay when she was born. Carole was also in her own little world as a 14 or 15 year old and you know how that can be.

I realize that how you FEEL about these things are REAL and perhaps you are carrying a lot of pain around with you. But if you could open up with Dad or Virginia or Madeline about your feelings, you may find that reality is a lot better than what may be in your mind today. And perhaps, you have received not so true info from someone who has a lot of influence over you in your life today. I really wish I could help you with this and I will do whatever I can. But YOU must make the first step and start seeking out detailed information about your birth and childhood.

I do not know what happened between you and Carole. But you two had a relationship all the way up until 1982... about the time you finished college. Carole is not married to Sam and he has stolen just about everything that she had accumulated. She lives in a small house in Pompano Beach, FL and has an old sailboat that is in dire need of an overhaul. Her house is not worth very much because it lies below the flood plain that she was not told about when she bought the house. Sam sold the house in CA and Carole did not receive any of the profit dollars. She has not owned the place in France in a long time. Remember I was there just last October. Believe me that what I have written above is true. And the last furniture that she got from Dad she paid for and had it shipped to her.

Both Carole and Kay would love to rekindle the relationships that they had before with you. But you also must give them the chance. Don't let miscommunication, untrue stories about your childhood or any feelings of being left out of the family create so much hate in you. I truly think that you would really like to rekindle these relationships too.

Please do not take this letter the wrong way. I love you and want things to go better in your life. I cannot say that I know how you feel because that would be a lie. But I do think there are some issues in your life that you should bring to the surface and seek out answers from whomever you can.

Take care and tell Wayne hello for me.

Love,

Larry

June 22, 1999

Dear Carole,

Hi! I thought I would write rather than just send an e-mail. How are you doing and how is your foot? You know it is going to take some time for your foot to heal so you will just have to learn to take it easier. I have written letters to everyone and am trying once again to try to get the family together. I do not know if it will do any good but this will probably be my last try. (Unless someone asks me otherwise.)

Have you done much in the stock market? I have not done anything for some time because I have been so sick it's unbelievable. On the 11th of this month, my back just gave out: and I could not even get out of bed except for the absolute necessary. My vertigo acted up again and on the 16th, Barbra took me to the emergency room because I was not getting any better. The best I could do as far as being up was about 8 minutes. Then I had to immediately lie back down or I would pass out. Just this past Sunday I was able to get up and do anything. I am really taking it easy because I do not know what to expect one day to the next. I am still trying to string 2 good days together. I hope that happens soon. I have more software to do and have not been able to work on it.

If you know of some sure bets in the market, let me know! I would like to make a few good deals in the options market before the July options expiration date. I could use the additional money.

I do not know when I will get to go to L'burg due to health and all. I also have to have the sinus surgery all over again. That will happen some time in July (I think) and then there will be an additional 5 to 7 weeks of recuperation. That pretty much takes up the entire summer. But maybe things will be better in the fall. I certainly hope so.

Give me a call or send me e-mail about how you are doing and what you are doing. By the way, how did your house guest work out? Did he get to do some of the things you were hoping he would around the house?

Hope to talk to you soon. Take care.

Love,
Larry

Appendix F
Eulogy for author's mother, 1999

[Read during service, taped and distributed by Tharp funeral home.]

Gladys Elizabeth Haley Fielder 1917-1999

My name is Carole Fielder, Gladys and Jack Fielder's 2nd child. Before I read excerpts from the poem my Mother requested be read at her funeral, I'd like to share three thoughts about her. Regrettably, as an adult woman I did not really know my mother, and saw her rarely after leaving Lynchburg in 1967. But this describes who she was to me, no longer just my mother, but my sister in Christ.

One. She loved being part of a large family, and was one of six children--three girls and three boys, and she had hoped to have six children herself. She was always close to her brothers and sisters, and is the last one of them. My thanks to my cousin and pastor, Robert Haley, for coming today. His father was my mother's only baby brother. I knew all of her siblings and spent summer times with them and my cousins, three of whom were girls, all of us born within twelve months of each other.

She loved being a mother; I remember how excited she was during her pregnancy with my sister Kay, whom I thought was my baby, created just for me to play with at age 4 ½. I remember how thrilled she was when my brother Larry was born, her only son. I was with her, and helped her the summer she had a miscarriage, thanks to the whooping cough that swept through our family. She was so disappointed because she had wanted two more children, and she wanted the last one born when she turned forty. She almost made her plan--her fifth child, my sister Laura, was born during her 41st year.

Mother shared with me in later life how terribly aggrieved she was that her own mother died so young, months after the birth of my sister Betty, her firstborn. I think her favorite poem may have been part of that experience. I think her resilience and longevity has been in part her plan not to leave her children too soon as she had been left.

Two. She loved Nature and Adventure. She took notice of all the delights of the changing seasons and scenery, of animals and plants, sky and water. She shared her enthusiasm and her observations with her children, and taught me the pleasures of the same. The last time I saw her, in 1995, she was fascinated with the clouds, and since that time I always think of her when I too enjoy gazing at them. Her favorite plant was the crepe myrtle tree. I planted nine of them in my yard this year, in honor of her.

Three. She loved God and lived her faith in making celebrations of life events for Jesus and for everyone around her--always a birthday cake, a covered dish for someone sick or grieving, Christmas presents, Easter baskets. I remember our young family's Christmas eve celebration of singing carols and reading--no, quoting from memory-- the Bible from Luke, chapter two. I knew how to say "swaddling clothes" and "manger" long before I knew what they were. Decorating the Christmas tree was a favorite family event that she cherished and permitted us children to indulge our childish tastes and ornaments. She liked to sing hymns of all kinds, and she was singing the words of her favorites when prompted by hearing a piano tape recording I made for her, long after her mental faculties failed in other ways. Her faith showed to the end through her sheer survival and by singing praises to God even under her suffering circumstances.

One of her favorite scriptures, and one I feel sums up her life is from Isaiah 6:8: "Then I heard the voice of the Lord saying, "Whom shall I send? Who will go for us?" "Here I am; send me." And so she came and lived among us these 82 ½ years.

In summary, my mother loved all her family, extended and immediate; she was first and foremost a mother; she loved nature, and she loved God. She taught me early the song "Jesus loves me this I know 'cause the Bible tells me so." She believed it, and so do I.

Finally, her requested funeral poem tells of her philosophy, adopted early in life. Excerpts from the favorite poem of Gladys Haley Fielder:

Thanatopsis by William Cullen Bryant (Published 1817)

When thoughts
Of the last bitter hour come like a blight
Over thy spirit, and sad images
Make thee to shudder, and grow sick at heart, --
Go forth under the open sky, and list
To Nature's teachings, while from all around --
Earth and her waters, and the depths of air --
Comes a still voice:--

Not to thine eternal resting place
Shalt thou retire alone--
All that breathe
Will share thy destiny.
As the long train
Of ages glides away,
All Shall one by one be gathered to thy side,
By those, who in their turn shall follow them.

So live that when thy summons comes to join
The innumerable caravan that moves
To that mysterious realm, where each shall take
His chamber in the silent halls of death,
Thou go not, like the quarry slave at night,
Scourged to his dungeon, but, sustained and soothed
By an unfaltering trust, approach thy grave
Like one who wraps the drapery of his couch
About him, and lies down to pleasant dreams.

And so she did.

Appendix G

Andrew Jackson Fielder   1911-2001

Jack Fielder: brother, pilot, artist-carpenter, teacher, father; who was that Lynchburg icon?

My name is Carole Anne Fielder, second of my father's five children. Although I have been physically unable to travel for many years, I want to personally share three gifts from my father, with all who will mourn his passing, the passing of an era, the passing of a Lynchburg icon. For many, my father represented THE TEACHER. I learned from him so much, but perhaps the three most important subjects are **1- Relationships**, **2- Self-reliance**, and **3- Change**.

1- Relationships
Over our lifetimes, we all have those very special relationships, and some seminal events, that move our lives. For his students, quite often, the teacher Jack Fielder was one of those. For my father, the first-born of five boys, it was the relationship with his brothers that remained forever the most important. There's a reason for that I believe, a seminal event in my father's life, which predates his relationships with his four brothers.

To explain, I go back two generations. I, like my father, learned my early history at the knees of his grandmother, the *grande dame* Keren English Saunders, who lived 103 years into the 1950's. (I was shocked upon learning in the fifth grade that the one described by my Daddy's Grandma Saunders, the man who ruined everything, was a President of the United States, a man named Lincoln who ran against the family-sponsored candidate Stephen Douglas.) My father, during ages three to six years, lived with his Saunders grandparents in remote and rural Franklin County, after his mother, Tabitha Saunders Fielder, their second-born child (of seven who survived as octogenarians), traveled long hours alone with him from Lynchburg by train and horse-and-buggy. He was sickly, she feared for his life, and she thought the country air would help him. (She had another young child and was pregnant with a third.) It also was a reconciliation for her, the first time she'd seen her parents since they wrote her off because of her rebellious, late-in-life marriage to my grandfather Fielder, whom they considered inappropriate for their daughter, as he was a mere hired hand in their general store, and worse, a German immigrant's son.

271

In recent years, my father frequently and repeatedly told the story of this seminal event: of being left in the country with his maternal grandparents that he'd never met before. He described how Grandma Saunders and some others offered him milk and chocolate cake, his favorite, and more cake, and more, until he looked around for his mother, realizing she was not in the room anymore. He ran to the front of the house to find his mama, who was just lifting her skirts to step up on the buggy that had been parked some distance from the house. He vividly remembered the curve of her calf, and the sound of the crack of the whip on the horse's back, as he screamed and cried in anguish for his departing mama.

There's a follow-up story he told, about returning to Lynchburg years later, with his father, by automobile, standing up the whole way looking down through the gear shift space, mesmerized by the undercarriage workings of the car. At the dinner meal with his un-known brothers, he looked up at his mother and asked "Are you my mama?"

We who had a relationship with my father today celebrate his long and productive life. We each now review our relationship with him. He was so talented, so straight-arrow, so uncompromising. Right was right, and wrong was wrong, and he often sacrificed popularity, and laid his career as a schoolteacher on the line, for that value. He refused to give special favors to certain students, inventing the multiple choice test for its precision in grading, long before it was generally used. When challenged, he'd point to his grade book. Simple arithmetic, simple percentages. No exceptions. Many thousands of his students are quick to say how much he af-fected their lives and careers.

Recently, when he repeated the story of being abandoned to his stranger grandparents as a child, I asked him what he thought of that incident. How did he feel about that today? (Feel was not a word one used with my father.) He answered, "Well, I'm a better person for it." After I recovered my breath, which I'd lost at his as-tonishing answer, I asked him why he felt that way, or how so? He said that he'd made up his mind right then and there that he'd never be hurt that way again. And that enabled him to get through his life accomplishing what he wanted to do. Knowing my father as an adult, I believe that his response to that seminal event, so pain-ful and traumatic to a young child, explains a lot about my father and his relationships, how I learned from him, and what motivated the achiever he was throughout his life. He learned self-reliance at a tender age, and he firmly believed in passing that value on.

My father bonded with his newly found brothers, and throughout his life they were the most important relationships he ever had. He told stories of babysitting; he laughed hardest about pushing his baby brother Jimmy's carriage back and forth on the front porch, suddenly losing his grip and sending baby and carriage falling down the steps, bouncing the baby out on his head. Then he had to hush him up and recover the carriage before Mama found out. He also told the story of his brother Tom's tragic death at age six, one of the earliest automobile fatalities. He was with his father at the store, across the street from the old high school. He described how the dead child looked in his father's arms, driving to the hospital, of his father's excruciating grief and incredulity at losing his son. I now can only imagine the pain and grief my father experienced on the loss of his only son, Larry, two weeks ago, at age 50.

After years of conversations with my father about family patterns, and how the life stories are repeated from one generation to the next whether or not the younger generations even know what went before, I asked him if he had been jealous (another word not in his vocabulary) of his younger, sportsman brother Frank, who got to play sports and court the girls while he, the oldest, had to work in his father's store. He eventually admitted to the jealousy, and that it might be a repeated family pattern, but added that he did what he was supposed to do.

His childhood dream was to become a pilot, and he early on rode his bicycle to the Preston Glynn airport, later planned to go to the school of aviation in St. Louis after high school. But his father told him that was a crazy, foolish idea, and absolutely forbade him. I asked why he didn't go anyway. He was shocked at my question, because he had no money, was never paid for his time spent working in the store. What his father ordered, my father did without question. Feelings of jealousy or rebellion were quickly denied. My father was much too busy with his own goals. That younger brother, Frank, who seemed to have it so much better than my father, died of lung cancer about age twenty-five. So my father remained with two brothers, Bill and Jimmy, during his adulthood.

My mother sometimes complained about the length of time my father spent with his brothers. For him, they came first. No one else could divert my father's attention and concentration from whatever labor with which he was involved. Before I left home, I remember the pool table my father installed in the basement, and the many joyful occasions spent around it. When Jimmy and Bill, and friend Buck Driscoll, dropped by to shoot pool with Daddy, the hoots and hollers and laughter resonated. Whatever Daddy was doing, he could be interrupted by them for a game or two. I saw him happiest then.

My last conversation with my father took place two days ago, Tuesday afternoon, January 16th, less than twelve hours before his death. He was obviously fading fast and could scarcely hold the phone, but he knew me when I asked. I assured him again, as I had in my longer, reluctant good-bye conversation with him Saturday night, that whatever he decided was ok with me, and that I was sure that Bill and Jimmy were in that hospital room with him, and would help him. He answered yes. He knew. Yesterday morning, in the double grief for my brother and my father that I was feeling, I heard again, in my mind's ear, the laughter and voices of those Fielder men, those good-looking guys with the beautiful blue eyes, breaking the pool balls, teasing each other. They're together again.

A wise man, writing about his own mixture of compulsive-obsessive behavior, perfectionism, prodigious productivity, accomplishments, and broken dreams and relationships, stated that in most of his life he failed to recognize his "total inability to form a true partnership with another human being." (Page 53 of Twelve Steps and Twelve Traditions.) He was a gifted leader. My father was a gifted man, a leader, the first-born, the teacher, the teacher of aviators that defended our nation during the second World War. I inherited many wonderful talents from my forbears, for which I am grateful. I am still learning, however slowly, that I must accept my bad traits along with the good, be aware of where they came from, and strive for change. I have not been successful in many relationships that I wanted, because the above statement applies to me. I see him in me, for good or bad. I agree with my father that "The apple does not fall far from the tree."

2- Self-reliance
My father was taught to stand on his own two feet, pick himself up by his bootstraps, and be self-reliant. If you want it done right, do it yourself. Neither a borrower nor a lender be. Be responsible. Birds of a feather flock together. Be sure you're right, then go ahead. Stand on your own two feet. Be self-reliant. Stick to the facts. I grew up hearing these things, and made them my own. I

grew up not hearing a vocabulary that included feelings and emotions, and have been learning for a long time the effects of those values and beliefs.

I lived with "Bamba," Daddy's mother, several years before her death, and know her versions of stories that my father told from his viewpoint. I recently learned how traumatized I was at age 16 by my failure to keep my promise to her that she could die at home. I was reminded of this in the past several months as I spoke to my father about specifying his final wishes. Not eight hours before his last fall, I spoke to him again about it, and he didn't think it was time to talk about those things, still. But he got very clear about his choices, two days later, in the hospital last Saturday and Sunday.

The lack of knowing how to grieve losses, affected me most of my life. I believe it was so with my father. I learned in my case, from the same wise man quoted above, "We could actually have earnest religious beliefs which remained barren because we were still trying to play God ourselves. As long as we placed self-reliance first, a genuine reliance upon a Higher Power was out of the question. That basic ingredient of all humility, a desire to seek and do God's will, was missing." (p. 72) I inherited a stubborn resistance to the idea that bad things happen to good people. Not talking about bad things was a solution my father, being self-reliant, used, as did I for much of my life. It was painful learning that self-reliance could be distorted, and not such a good value to hold. And bad things do happen to good people. It's hard to accept if self-reliance is over-emphasized. Where is God's will in tragic events?

My father never could talk about death. He, like me most of my life, didn't know how to label feelings, or share them. When his baby brother Bill died suddenly in his early fifties, my father marched into the hospital and shook his lifeless body telling him to cut it out, get up, get up. When his last brother Jimmy died two years ago, my father became more and more remote in his conversations with me. He couldn't talk about his feelings. Then two weeks ago, it broke my heart, and evidently his, when I had the task of telling him of my brother's death. His pain and mine are acute; he was alone, as I, in the horror and grief; I tried to share my feelings with him, as best as possible by telephone. He couldn't. He never had a vocabulary for deep feelings. But this final tragedy, that gave him so much pain, sharpened his vision and understanding of the reality he'd wanted to change, but could not.

3- Change

I grew up knowing for certain that "loan" was a four-letter word. But the same antipathy was radiated by my father for change. He hated change. It was always better the old way. Old was good. New was bad. Old habits are hard to change. I didn't realize for years how much I fell into paralysis as a result of my antipathy to change. Just like him. But in the end, he did change. It was gradual, but he changed in many of his closely-held ideas. It seemed to be an extraordinarily slow and painful process for him, and me, as most change is.

He did change. I watched my grandmother change in the same way. She, in her dotage came to understand things about people, especially racism and prejudice, that astonished her. I knew her struggle in breaking beliefs and values held by her parents. She was a rebel, even though she tried to prevent her sons from being the same. My father followed in her footsteps. He rebelliously married my mother, according to his parents, a foreigner from "up north." He dropped out of medical school and became a teacher. Horrible. And then he changed in his dotage. Seeing the suffering of my mother, he learned that self-reliance stopped working. Even his political views changed, and he even uttered the unutterable, that socialized medicine was a viable solution to this nation's most serious crisis. He changed. Even though my brother did not live to see it, my father finally understood my brother's pain and suffering. He changed.

His last communications with my sister Kay, and with me, and with his friend Charlie Loving, indicated his last great change, his comprehension, and acceptance of the truth of his life and relationships, self-reliance, and change. The truth set him free, and he has moved on. His suffering has ended. His accomplishments endure.

I want to personally thank all of you who supported my father during my mother's long illness and his last 14 months as widower. I could not be there in body, but I was in spirit, as I am today. I also have a final message to share with you, from him, and about him.

For all who knew my father recently, you know that he was aggrieved by his own fractured family. It was incomprehensible to him, who loved his brothers above all, how his children could be cut off from one another. He complained to me in every conversation about it; he spoke about it to almost everyone he knew in his later years, but during my last visit to Lynchburg in 1995, I learned from one sister that he had never even mentioned the subject to her. Then I learned the same from my brother. I asked Daddy why he had failed to communicate with all his children about this grievous issue, instead of only to me, and he answered that he assumed they all knew. There that word was: ASSUME. The way he started almost every science class was to admonish his students to never assume anything. He'd write it on the blackboard as he spoke, then strike a vertical line on either side of the "U", and conclude with the three new words. His assumption about his children was wrong.

My father, the consummate teacher, who inspired and taught so many young people chemistry, physics, aeronautics; the master wood craftsman, the prolific gardener, the sharp-minded investor, the entertaining and witty gentleman's gentleman, tried his best, with what he had received, to pass his values to his children. He was successful in so many ways, and so puzzled by this apparent failure; plus, his perfectionist mentality that the glass was always half empty, not half full, sadly persisted in his failure to see all his children together. Sixty percent was not good enough. He was grateful to my brother Larry for his last valiant efforts a year and a half ago. We who mourn the loss of my father, can share the crushing grief he felt his last days after the loss of his only son. I admired these two men in my life, I loved them, and I will grieve for them. Please share in my grief to lighten all our loads.

I want to end by sharing an e-mail received by my long-time friend and former classmate, Mary Sherman, now of Chicago. I believe she speaks for many:

> "Oh, Carole, I am so sorry. As you know, he affected my life in a huge way: I followed a career that he helped establish. And I am so glad that you and he were in touch so much at the end. Please accept my condolences."

[signed]
Carole A. Fielder
Pompano Beach, FL 33062
January 18, 2001

Appendix H

COUNTRY ROADS FARM
WELSH PONIES
Laura & Wayne Crews
xxxx Providence Rd.
Hayes, VA 23072
(804) xxx-xxxx/xxxx

Jan 29, 2001

Pompano Beach Police Dept.
Attn: Chief Danny D. Wright
100 SW 3d St
Pompano Beach, FL 33060

Chief Wright

I am contacting you reference a possible cult disappearance/suicide. I live in Virginia. I have a 50-year-old disabled brother in very poor physical and mental condition, living in Portland, Oregon, who is currently missing. I think he has been missing for a couple of months. I have a sister in Pompano Beach, Florida who has her own cult of which my brother is a member. I do not know how many persons my sister has under her mind control. She is 15 years older than me and left home and moved out of state when I was only four years old, so I have few memories of her. I have met her several times and have observed her mainly from an "outside" perspective. I recognized the "cult" aspect of her activities and control about 10 years ago. Other people are now recognizing it as well. She is aware that I recognize what she is and what she is doing. She (and her followers) are extremely afraid of me and literally physically run from my presence. This is not just a matter of family arguments. There is a very intense satanic aspect to this situation.

I am a civilian Military Police Dispatcher at Fort Eustis, Virginia, and I assure you that this is not a joke. I have openly told my co-workers that if another "Heaven's Gate" suicide/murder/whatever incident happens, don't be surprised if my sister is involved..... but she would never be included as one of the victims. I also have reason to believe that she may be preparing to fake her death.

At age 42, I am the youngest of five children. Only my oldest sister now communicates with me; as of this past summer, my elderly father was "not allowed" to communicate with me anymore, but my oldest sister was able to

279

forward occasional news. I shall include here some discussion we have had via e-mails within the past few weeks. My father died a couple of weeks ago and my Florida sister, who claims she is on her deathbed, faxed an essay which she ordered to be handed out and read at the funeral. It was not read, but I got a copy of it. In it she states four times that the brother is dead - not just missing. In my opinion this essay is rather incriminating. I am including it herewith.

My sister is extremely intelligent, vicious and cunning, and has amassed considerable wealth through her decades of deceit and manipulation of other people. She currently has a home and yacht in Florida; I am not sure of the status of her home and yacht in California, or of her home in France. I know that she has convinced a lot of people that she has been on chemotherapy for 38 years and is near death and cannot travel. I also know that that is a medical impossibility and that in fact she does indeed do quite a bit of traveling. I think she may have traveled to Portland and brought the brother to Florida so there would be no body to discover in Portland.

Do not underestimate the evil viciousness of this woman, and do not be deceived by her soft, "weak" voice and gentle persuasion. She has the charisma that has described Jim Jones, David Koresh and Marshall Applewhite. Via telephone, she has convinced a cemetery in Virginia to dig a hole on top of a relative and prepare a footstone for her. There is no death date in the stone yet, but it is in place, and the hole is ready to receive her cremains. Imagine the shock of my aunt when she discovered a hole dug on top of her late husband's grave. A few subsequent three-hour phone conversations had the aunt relieved and proud to share the grave with her.

2

I think she could very well send some cremains from Florida to fill the hole, but they will not be hers. She has too much to profit from other people's deaths for her to die anytime soon. She is enraged that she cannot control my mind; she has tried various attacks against me since 1974, but has had success only in the past few years, by commanding her followers to break off any relationship with me. She is desperately afraid of me and cannot afford to have her followers interact with me.

I expect the death of my brother is very highly probable, and I have no doubt that if she commanded him to go out and kill himself, he would readily do it "for her." At this point, the question of my brother's whereabouts and status is going to need to be resolved, as he stands to inherit 1/5 of my father's estate. My oldest sister does not want to get involved with any law enforcement aspect, and my husband wants me to not be involved in family matters of this type AT ALL. However, I cannot ignore what I strongly suspect may have happened. I truly think the situation has gone from "freedom of religion" to the criminal.

I certainly hope you will take me seriously on this. On the other hand, it would be a satisfaction, albeit perverse, for me to be able to say "I told you so" when some sort of bizarre incident hits the media. I am including below the addresses of me (Laura), my missing brother (Larry), my Florida sister (Carole), and my oldest sister (Betty). I am also including the e-mail conversations I have previously mentioned. My brother and my Florida sister do not know my e-mail address and I absolutely- want to keep it that way. I have also sent an e-mail to Portland police (police@teleport.com), but have not heard back from them yet.

Thank you. Feel free to contact me, preferably via e-mail but by voice if necessary. I will do whatever I can to help you investigate this matter.

Respectfully,
[signed]
Laura F. Crews
Laura F. Crews
Country Roads Farm Welsh Ponies
xxxx Providence Rd.
Hayes, VA 23072

(804)xxx-xxxx/xxxx
dob: 1958 xx xx
e-mail: juliaericblair@hotmail.com

Work:
Provost Marshal Office U.S. Army
Fort Eustis, VA (757) xxx-xxxx/xxxx

Missing brother:

Lawrence Jackson Fielder
xxxxx N.W. Cornell Rd. #xxx
Portland, OR 97229
(503)xxx-xxxx

dob: 1950 12 31
e-mail: awkessler@aol.com

3

Florida "cult" sister:
Carole Anne Fielder Cox Kahn Fielder / currently: Carole Anne Fielder
5555 NE 55 St
Pompano Beach, FL 33062
(954) 555-5555
dob: 1944 xx xx
e-mail: sailcarole@aol.com

Oldest sister who wishes not to be involved:

Elizabeth Lorraine F. Waddill
xxxxx Bollingbrook Dr
Richmond, VA 23236
(804) xxx-xxxx
dob: 1941 xx xx (I think!)
e-mail: lwaddill@aol.com

*[**Author's note: At the end of the typed third page,
she had handwritten**:]*

3 enclosures:
1 - Carole's essay
2 - summary e-mail I sent to my 2 cousins
3 - extended e-mail log with my sister Betty
& me

Appendix I
Sample Yahoo! Web Pages

SEX PARTNERS IN FLORIDA

Category: **Encounters**

Type: **Listed**

FLORIDA RESIDENTS FIND DISCREET SEX PARTNER

Yahoo! Clubs Page 1 of 1

Members

Listing members **341-360** of 787

Page **18** of 40. View page # [___] Go

Edit My Comments

Prev Page | Next Page

Yahoo! ID	Age	Gender	Location	Comment
HRSAC1	49	Male	Lake Park	
Hudsonvalleyinvestor		Male		
Huh777		Male		
Hungrylilwife		Female		
Hungsouthflm	30	Male	Fort Lauderdale	
Husky1 us	32	Male	Clearwater, FL	
Hydrojoe1		Male		
I lik clit 99	30	Male	Orlando	
Iam4fsu99	27	Male	Tallahassee	
Ibgr8lover	29	Male	Florida	
Iceman0	27	Male		
Idoher4u	50	Male	Hollywood, FL	
IHUNGWELL	N/A		If it's wet, LICK IT!	
imasophistmaster	57	Female		
			5555 NE 55th St.	
			Pompano Beach 33062	
				Anyone interested in sex-partying on my yacht? E-mail me.
Imhardagain		Male	Central Fla.	
Impellor	35	Male	Ft Myers, Fl	
Inca2002	29	Male	Clearwater, Fl.	I need love too.
Infra35	36	Male	Dunedin, FL	
Iogedengbe		Male		yea
Ironheadhd		Male		

283

imasophistmaster's profile

My E-mail

imasophistmaster@yahoo.com

My Interests

Lesbian, Gay and Bisexual
Furniture
New Age
Philosophy of Mind
Bisexual
Age Play
Relationships
Intellectuals
Relationships
Hypnosis
Disabled
Philosophy
Teens
Florida
Fisting

On Yahoo!

Add to friend list
Messenger

Basics

Yahoo! ID: **Imasophistmaster**

Real Name:	**Carole A. Fielder (954) 555-5555**
Location:	**5555 NE 55th ST Pompano Beach FL 33062**
Age:	**57**
Marital Status:	**Divorced**
Sex:	**Female**
Occupation:	**independently wealthy/retired**

More About Me

Hobbies: sailing, sunbathing on my yacht; investing; collecting Antiques; turning others' misfortunes into my profits
Latest News: Am about to acquire large inheritance (e-mail me privately for details)
Favorite Quote
"Your world is whatever you create it to be; you deserve the Power and profit that others owe you!"

Links

Home Page: *No home page specified*
Cool Link: *No cool link specified*
For quick access to this page, bookmark:
http://profiles.yahoo.com/imasophistmaster
Find more people like this on Yahoo! Member Directory

02/27/2001

Yahoo! Member Directory: Teens

Teens (1056 members)
Home>Religion & Beliefs

Related Interests:

.@**Atheism**
.@**Christianity**
.@**Judaism**
.@**Paganism**

What Is This List?

This page displays a list of
people who have added this
interest to their Yahoo! Profile.
Add this interest to your profile
now! Want to remove your profile from this list? Simply click
here.

Members: l (1 -9 of 9)

Join this list -Let others know you're interested in this topic.

Online Now l New l Women l Men l 13-18 l 18-25 l 25-35 l 35-50 l 50-70 l 70+

AlBlClDlElFlGlHllIJlKllLlMlNlOlPlQlRlSlTlUlVlWlXlYlZ

Online Yahoo ID	Gender	Age	Location	Contact
icantgonearsharpobjects	female			Msg
ifyaweremine	female	18	Thailand	E-mail
iluvboyz4eva14	female			
imasophismaster	female	57	5555 NE 55th St. Pompano Beach FL 33062	E-mail
imogen-stars	female	15	A place filled with magick and love.	Msg. E-mail
imperial god	male			Msg.
infinitytrini	female	18		Msg.
inyourdreams77772002	female	16	CALI	
irhackattack	male	16	Washington State	

Made in the USA
Columbia, SC
10 August 2018